The Charlatan

Robert Williams Buchanan

THE CHARLATAN

BY

ROBERT BUCHANAN

AND

HENRY MURRAY

> ' *Glendower.* I can call spirits from the vasty deep !
> *Hotspur.* Why, so can I, and so can any man,
> But will they come when you do call for them ?'
> SHAKESPEARE'S *Henry IV*. (Part II.)

> 'There are repentances more splendid than innocence itself.'
> BOSSUET

A NEW EDITION

WITH A FRONTISPIECE BY T. H. ROBINSON

LONDON
CHATTO & WINDUS, PICCADILLY
1896

In the clear light stood a white-robed figure. [p. 44

PREFATORY NOTE

THE following story, founded on the drama of the same name, has been written in collaboration with Mr. Henry Murray; but I was indebted for the original idea, and notably for the sleep-walking incident, to an unpublished sketch by Miss Harriett Jay, the authoress of 'The Queen of Connaught.' The drama was produced at the Haymarket Theatre in January last, and is still running in the provinces, while the story, after appearing serially in newspapers, is now for the first time republished in book form.

R. B.

December, 1894.

CONTENTS

CONTENTS

THE CHARLATAN

CHAPTER I.

AT WANBOROUGH CASTLE.

'But surely,' said the Dean, leaning back in his arm-chair, with the tips of his fingers delicately joined together, and his short-sighted brown eyes peering at his interlocutor under knitted brows of questioning surprise—'surely our modern religious thought has progressed far enough to reject such superstitions as these?'

'Thought, my dear Dean,' returned the Earl, 'should reject no kind of human evidence! You will pardon me, I am sure, if, as a layman, I venture upon a modest historical criticism of the Church to which you belong. Have not men of your stamp, Church-men who, still holding the more important tenets of revealed religion, are yet to a great degree open to the teachings of modern science—have you not, may I ask, too lightly and easily abandoned, at the bidding of

1

science, many minor beliefs which are sanctioned by
a great mass of reliable evidence, though their truth
is not to be proved by the scientific paraphernalia of
microscopes and solvent acids ?'

'That would be a very wide field of controversy,'
said the Dean, with a smile. ' Possibly we have, but
really, really, my dear Lord Wanborough, astrology
—the black art——'

'Were distinctly, in the hands of their noblest
followers, theosophic. We have proof — absolute
proof—that manifestations of the most extraordinary
nature have taken place. For instance, that remarkable man, Dr. Dee, in a *séance* at which Queen
Elizabeth was present, raised up the spirit of the first
Plantagenet.'

The Dean's brows went up, and he looked at his
companion with a wondering face, in which there was
a touch of pity.

'Do you actually believe *that* ?' he asked gravely.

'Why should I *not* believe it?' asked the Earl, in
return. 'It is a historical fact, like another. You
yourself accept miracles. The last sermon I had the
pleasure to hear you preach dealt with the raising of
the spirit of Samuel before Saul. What could be
done once can be done again.'

' Ah, but pardon me,' returned the Dean. ' In that
very sermon I was careful to guard myself by the
admission that the day of such special manifestations had long gone by, and such glimpses of the

Power which rules the world as are now vouchsafed to us come by other channels.'

'How can you say that the days of miracles are over?' said the Earl, now firmly seated in the saddle of his favourite hobby. 'All Nature is a miracle—a daily, hourly miracle.'

'Yes, but reduced to law—to a code of clear and immutable law, which admits of no deviation from settled order. Although a Churchman—and, I trust, a faithful and consistent one—I cannot blind myself to the wonderful discoveries of modern thought, to the inestimable blessings of modern science. I could, of course, wish—I *do* wish—that men of science would show more tolerance to the sacred mystery of our faith, and would not be so apt to treat it with contempt, and, as you say, regard acids and microscopes as the final court of appeal for beliefs which have been held, and are still held, by so many of the best and noblest of mankind. But even there I see gleams of light. Science is losing its cocksureness. These recent experiments in the Paris hospitals by Charcot and others, and the attention they have received from scientific men all over the world, show that faith in the Unseen—the occult—still survives, and is hard to kill.'

'Ah,' said his lordship, with a smile of triumph, 'so far you are with me! You believe in Hypnotism?'

'Most decidedly. The possession by many individuals of the hypnotic force is clearly a fact. One might as well doubt the power of steam. I myself possess the force in a certain degree. A year or two ago I hypnotized a servant-maiden, who revealed in a state of trance a number of petty thefts which had taken place in the kitchen. The power of one living will over another I can understand. It is one of the commonest phenomena of life. But I fail to comprehend the power of the living over the dead.'

'Well, well,' said the Earl, laying aside the paper-knife with which he had been absently toying during the conversation, 'that is a subject on which we shall never agree.'

'I fear not,' said the Dean gravely.

The Earl of Wanborough lay back in his chair and bent a sidelong glance on the emerald turf of the lawn beneath the window. He was a man in the early sixties, long, and a little loosely built. He had been one of the handsomest men in England in his day, and his face, though lined with years of thought and study, was beautifully venerable. His smile was singularly sweet, and his voice had the tender reson-ance of a musical instrument. Dignity and kindli-ness shone in his every word and gesture. He was carelessly—for a man of his rank and wealth almost shabbily—dressed in well-worn tweeds, and the elf locks of his silky gray hair fell about his face from under a skull cap of black velvet.

The Dean, a personable, jolly-looking divine, who

rode some fourteen stone, set his glasses astride his nose, and took advantage of his host's momentary abstraction to examine him closely. The Earl would have been vastly more surprised than pleased could he have guessed what was passing in his old friend's mind.

'He can't be *mad!*' thought the Dean. 'His father and grandfather were as healthy-minded men as ever breathed, and his life has been purity itself. And yet, how *can* a man of his brains and scholarship believe such rubbish as he has been talking?'

'You are expecting Lord Dewsbury down here, you were saying just now,' said the Dean, breaking silence after a rather lengthy pause.

'Yes,' said the Earl, rousing himself from his momentary abstraction. 'I had a letter from him this morning. He is in high feather.'

He selected the letter from a number of others in his jacket pocket.

'He wrote from the House of Commons. Let me see. Where is it? Ah, yes!

'"If the vote to-night goes against the Government —and I am all but certain it will—they must resign, and we are sure of a big reception and a thumping majority in the country. Salisbury regards our triumph as a *fait accompli*, and, although he made no absolute promise, he held out good hopes of a place for me in his Ministry."'

'Excellent!' cried the Dean. 'Why, the Government was defeated by twenty votes!'

'Yes,' said the Earl; 'and if Dewsbury is right in his calculations, the resignation will take place in a day or two, and we shall have him down here to stand for the borough again. I am afraid,' he continued, 'that his career in the Commons will soon be ended.'

'Is the Earl so ill?' asked the Dean.

'His condition is very serious. Dewsbury writes' —he again referred to the letter—

'"I grieve to say that my father's strength declines daily. He takes hardly any food, and has not left his bed for the last three days. Lawson, after taking the most hopeful view for weeks past, confessed to me this morning that he fears the end is inevitable, and near at hand. Poor old dad! Heaven knows, the prospect of the title is little consolation for his loss!"'

'Dear, dear!' said the Dean. 'Well, it is the common lot, and we can only be glad that he leaves such an excellent successor. Lord Dewsbury is a very fine fellow!'

'Yes,' said the Earl cordially; 'Frank is a very fine fellow indeed!'

'Do you know,' said the Dean—'pray don't think me impertinent for speaking of a family matter—I have fancied that Dewsbury may find his consolation *here.'*

'Isabel?' asked the Earl, with a smile. ' Well, yes; I have thought so myself. Setting aside money—and Dewsbury will have enough and to spare of that—I don't think he could do better. She is a most charming girl, and would make a wife for an emperor. I think she likes Frank, and I am sure he is greatly attached to her.'

'There is no formal engagement between them?' asked the Dean.

'None, so far; but I think they understand each other. I have noticed his letters by Miss Arlington's plate at breakfast every morning for the last two months at least, and she makes no secret of their correspondence.'

' There is still no news of her father?' continued the Dean.

As he spoke, he raised his eyes to a picture hanging on the wall above the Earl's head.

It was the portrait of a man in the prime of life, with prematurely gray hair and moustache, and clad in military undress. The face was handsome, but sad and stern, with a far-away, dreamy look in the eyes which somewhat contradicted the expression of the set brows and resolute mouth and chin. The Earl's eyes mechanically followed in the same direction.

'No,' he said, with a sigh. 'Nothing has been

heard of him since the last letter from Thalak, nearly two years ago, announcing his intention of crossing the centre of Thibet.'

' A wild scheme,' said the Dean.

' I don't like to think about it,' said the Earl. ' It is wonderful to me how Isabel keeps up her health and spirits.' He paused a moment. 'You and I, Dean, think differently on many subjects. Tell me what you think of what Isabel said this morning. She came down to breakfast radiant. I had never seen her look so beautiful or so happy. I questioned her, and her reply was, " My father is alive, and is coming home." " You have heard from him ?" I asked. " You have received a letter ?" " No," she replied ; " but I have seen him. He came to me in my sleep. He was haggard, and ill, and worn. His dress was all in rags, and there was a great scar upon his face. He spoke to me ; I heard his voice as distinctly as you can hear mine at this moment. He said, ' Have no fear, child, my task is accomplished, and I shall soon be with you again.' " '

' God grant it !' said the Dean fervently. ' We can ill afford to lose such men as Colonel Arlington.'

' But the dream,' said Lord Wanborough. ' What do you think of that ?'

' What can one think of it ?' asked the Dean. ' There are more things than are dreamed of in our philosophy. I have known dreams quite as extraordinary come true. It may have been a Divine message of comfort to the poor young lady. Let us hope so.'

'I spoke of it to Madame Obnoskin,' continued the Earl. 'She accepts it as an actual truth, and prophesies that we shall hear from Colonel Arlington very shortly.'

'God grant it!' said the Dean again. 'So Madame Obnoskin is still here?'

'Yes; and will stay for some time yet, I hope. A remarkable woman, my dear Dean—a *most* remarkable woman. You must meet her. If any arguments can lead you to consider the eternal mysteries from another point of view, hers will. I owe Madame Obnoskin a great debt, intellectually and morally. A woman of extraordinary attainments. She is in direct communication with the occult powers of Nature.'

'Indeed! And these communications — how do they come?'

'In many ways. Sometimes by direct intuition, sometimes by post.'

The Dean did his best to restrain an irrepressible chuckle.

'This is indeed remarkable.'

'What is remarkable?' asked the Earl.

'That spirits should use postage-stamps.'

'My dear Dean,' said his lordship a little testily, 'the matter is perfectly simple. Spirits can only work through material conditions.'

'Quite so—quite so!' said the Dean with recovered gravity. 'And this lady—Madame Obnoskin—what kind of person is she?—young?'

'Yes, comparatively. Not more, I should say, than thirty, at most.'

'Handsome?'

'Distinctly. A very charming woman. She would be an acquisition in any society.'

'A widow?' asked the Dean.

'Yes; a sad experience, I fear. Her husband was a Pole, like herself; a very able man, and an adept in the religion she teaches; but I gather from hints she has dropped that they were not happy together.'

'H'm!' said the Dean, with a slight pursing of the lips and another lift of the eyebrows.

'You must meet her, my dear Dean,' continued his lordship.

'I shall be delighted. Your description of the lady has quite fired my curiosity.'

'Since you are here,' said Lord Wanborough, 'why not stay to dinner?'

'Thank you exceedingly, but I fear it is impossible. I have a Church meeting in Wanborough at seven o'clock, and I promised faithfully to attend. But as Madame Obnoskin is staying on, I shall drop in some evening *sans cérémonie*, and ask for an introduction.'

The apartment in which they sat was a long gallery, traversing almost the entire length of Wanborough Castle, and lit at regular intervals by windows of the

height of the walls.   The autumn night was falling,
and the long perspective was gradually fading as the
shadows rose along the walls, adorned by family portraits and groups of statuary.

It was with a little shock of surprise that the Dean
suddenly perceived that he and the Earl were no
longer alone.   No sound of opening or closing door,
no footfall on the thick carpet, had announced the
presence of a lady, who stood within a few feet of him.

The red glow of the dying sunset fell full upon her,
and lit her face and form with a strange brightness,
which, taken in conjunction with the suddenness of
her appearance, had something weird in it.

She was taller than the average height of women,
and of a rather full but graceful figure.   Her features
were regular and beautiful, her eyes black, brilliant,
and inscrutable.

'Ah!' exclaimed his lordship, rising, 'this is fortunate.   My dear Madame Obnoskin, let me present
to you Dr. Darley, the Dean of Wanborough.   He is
burning to make your acquaintance.'

'Delighted to meet you, Dean,' said the lady in a
clear contralto voice, with a very faint and very
piquant foreign accent.

The Dean bowed, and murmured that he was
enchanted.

'I have heard so much of you from the Earl that I
can only regret that, owing to my annual holiday,
our meeting has been so long delayed.'

'You are very good,' said the lady, crossing to his lordship's side, and bending over his chair. 'You are well to-day, dear friend?'

'Perfectly, I thank you,' he answered.

'I have news for you.'

'Indeed?'

'Yes; good news—great news.

'You interest me profoundly. May I ask—— ?'

'I might have told you some days ago, but I delayed till I was certain. The intimations I have received to-day put the matter beyond doubt, and I can speak without the fear of raising false hopes. One of our most powerful personalities will soon be here; if I am not mistaken, an Adept.'

'An Adept?' queried the Dean. 'Pray, Madame Obnoskin, what is that?'

'An Apostle of our religion,' answered the lady; 'a person full of the effulgence of spiritual life, capable of communicating with spirits from beyond the grave.

The words were addressed to the Dean, but the lady's eyes were fixed upon the Earl.

'Dear me!' said the Dean a little fatuously.

Madame Obnoskin spoke with such a perfect calm, with so little recognition of the strangeness of her utterance in ordinary ears, that he was for the moment quite nonplussed.

'May I ask,' he continued, 'how you received this news? By letter?'

'No.'

'By wire, perhaps?' he slyly suggested.

'No,' she answered again, with a smiling shake of the head. 'By an intuition. I have had similar intimations before, and they have always announced the arrival of one of the Adepts. But this is the strangest I have ever felt. The impression has been overwhelming.'

'Dear me!' said the Dean again. 'And this person—is he a spirit or a ghost?'

'Neither; a man like yourself—a mere human being.'

'But, my dear lady——'

'He is a being who has discovered the secrets of the spiritual world. Still wearing the vestments of the flesh, he is, to all outward seeming, a corporeal projection like ourselves.'

'H'm!' said Dr. Darley, 'and you—are you also a corporeal projection?'

'My dear Dean!' exclaimed the Earl.

'Certainly,' said the lady, with a little laugh.

'A very charming one.'

The lady laughed again.

'And the charming dress you wear—is that also——'

'Of course! All that you behold, all material phenomena, is simply the Kama, adumbrating the ethereal or astral body!'

The Dean gave a sounding cough, and crossed his legs.

'My good friend Dr. Darley,' said the Earl, 'is a little sceptical.'

'Yes?' said Madame Obnoskin, with her little laugh, and the odd, pleasant accent in full play. 'Ah, well. perhaps we shall convert him!'

'I fear it is a little too late in the day for that,' said the Dean, rising, and glancing at his watch; 'though I should be delighted to receive instruction from so charming a tutress. I trust, madame, that we shall meet again.'

'I hope so, indeed,' she answered, frankly extending her hand. 'And I warn you to prepare your weapons of controversy; I shall convert you if I can.'

The Dean bowed and smiled, then turned to the Earl:

'I was going to ask your lordship, when I was so agreeably interrupted, if you had a copy of Burckhardt's great work on the "Apostolic Succession."'

'Yes; you will find it in the theological section of the library, on the third shelf from the ground, to the left of the oriel window.'

'Thank you. I wish to verify a quotation for to-morrow's sermon.'

He shook hands with the Earl, bowed again to Madame Obnoskin, and left the gallery.

'What a deplorable thing,' he murmured to himself, 'is human credulity!'

CHAPTER II.

IN THE DRAWING-ROOM.

AMONG the more frequent and favoured guests at Wanborough Castle was the Honourable Mr. Mervyn Darrell, a nephew of the Earl, a young gentleman blessed with a couple of thousands a year, perfect nerves and digestion, a more than moderate share of intelligence, and a colossal belief in himself. One of his few earthly troubles was that he had but very recently left his teens, and one of his secret joys sprang from the fact that he was prematurely bald.

There are a good many sorts of ambitions and aspirations in the world, and the Honourable Mervyn's chief aspiration was to be superior to everything and everybody: an ambition to which a too youthful appearance would have been a serious drawback.

He had acquired a habit of coming down to Wanborough at any odd moment when the idea might seize him, and he turned up there on the morning after Dr. Darley's introduction to Madame Obnoskin, sent his man upstairs with his traps to the room set aside for his accommodation, and strolled, with his usual air of tolerant boredom, into the drawing-room, where a young lady, a few years his junior, was playing softly to herself on the piano.

'Morning, Lottie,' he said, dropping into a seat. 'Uncle about?'

Lady Carlotta Deepdale, the only daughter of the Earl of Wanborough, was as complete a contrast to her father in temperament as could easily be found. His lordship was a naturally thoughtful man, given over wholly to the study of moral and religious problems, and, if fortune and indolence had not combined to make him avoid active labour, he would probably have made a great name as a writer on ethics and theology. He was dreamy, unambitious, and excessively unpractical. Lottie was a wide-awake young lady, who troubled her pretty head with no problem whatsoever, except that one—so easily solvable by a young and beautiful woman with a great name and plenty of money—of how to get the greatest amount of honest and harmless happiness out of everyday existence.

'Papa's somewhere about the grounds, walking with that awful woman, and talking theosophy, I suppose.'

'Whom do you mean?' asked Mervyn, taking up a book, and settling himself languidly in his seat.

'That Obnoskin creature,' said Lottie viciously. 'Why doesn't she go? She came here for a week, and she has stayed for over a month already.'

'I suppose,' said Mervyn, polishing his nails with a little apparatus in mother-o'-pearl and washleather, and admiring their sheen in the sunlight, 'that she stays because my uncle asks her to stay.'

'Of course; I know *that*,' said Lottie. 'And that's just where the aggravation comes in.'

'May I ask how?'

'Why, can't you see that papa has perfectly lost his head about her, and knows no more than a child what game she is playing with him?'

'And what game is she playing?' asked Mervyn, still admiringly examining his nails.

'Do you mean to say that *you* don't see it? It's as plain as the nose on your face. The woman wants to become Countess of Wanborough.'

Even Mervyn's affectation of indifference to everything on earth, an indifference he had feigned so long that it had well-nigh become real, vanished for the moment at these words. He concealed an unphilosophically violent start by a stretch and a half-yawn.

'My dear Lottie, what nonsense! Your father would never dream of such a thing!'

'Men at papa's time of life are foolish enough for anything, where a woman is concerned.'

'You are shockingly irreverent,' said Mervyn.

'It's true,' the girl continued. 'And you, with your usual absurdity, are encouraging him in his folly '

'I!' repeated Mervyn. '*I* encouraging him!'

'Of course you are, by pretending to believe in the rubbish she talks.'

'My dear Lottie, as a person philosophically interested in all human developments——'

2

'Oh, pray don't talk rubbish about philosophy and developments!' Lottie cut him short. 'I sometimes think you *do* believe in their tomfoolery, for if there *is* any moral complaint about, you're sure to catch it. At college you had the æsthetic scarlatina, and babbled about lilies, and sunflowers, and blue china. Then you became affected with Radicalism—went about disguised in corduroys, and lectured at Toynbee Hall. Then, after a few less serious ailments, you caught the last epidemic, from which you are still suffering.'

'And what may that be?' asked Mervyn, returning the nail-polisher to his waistcoat pocket.

'Individualism *you* call it, I believe; *I* call it the dumps.'

'Dumps!' murmured Mervyn, with a slight indrawing of the breath, as if the expression hurt him physically.

'A sort of moral influenza,' continued Lottie, 'which prevents you from enjoying anything bright and sunny. You are simply impossible!'

'I am consistent,' said Mervyn. 'I range through many varying moods. I am chameleonic in my outward symptoms, but I have never wavered from my faith in Nature, and what is to me its most interesting expression.'

'And what's that?' asked Lottie.

'Myself,' responded the youthful sage.

'That's true enough,' she answered, with a laugh. 'Self is your principal study, I think.'

'My only one,' said Mervyn. 'A great a little study. How to evolve—how to be.'

'Are you evolving at present?' asked Lottie, standing beside the sofa and looking down at him.

'I hope so.'

'It doesn't hurt you much, does it?' she asked with mock sympathy.

Mervyn merely closed his eyes for a moment, as if her flippancy were too much to bear, and, reopening them, bent them on his book.

'What's that you are reading?' Lottie inquired.

'"The Sublimation of Personality, or the Quintessence of the Ego."'

'Sounds like something funny,' said Lottie. 'Do you think I should like to read it?'

'If I may judge by your general literary studies, I should say not. It is necessary to have attained to a higher intellectual platform than, I fear, the one you stand on.'

'Really!' said Lottie. 'What's it all about?'

'It is an essay on the imperfections of human society. It shows, absolutely and conclusively, that everything is wrong except one's inner self—that Society, Morality, Duty, Respectability, and the other shibboleths, are only terms to express various phases of exploded bourgeois superstition.'

'Really!' said Lottie. 'So, you don't believe in Morality?'

'No.'

' Or Duty ?'

' No.'

' Or Respectability?   Whatever *do* you believe in?'

' In myself ; in my right to expand, to live, to evolve in my own way.'

And he threw out his chest, as if he were really expanding.

' H'm ! Isn't that a little selfish ?' said Lottie.

' Certainly,' responded Mervyn, with his own smile of superiority. ' Self is the only reality. *I* am; but, to *me*, everything else in the world is merely a phenomenon, a figment, which has no provable existence.'

' Oh ! Am I a phenomenon, and a figment, and the rest of it ?'

' Certainly,' replied Mervyn placidly. ' The object of Self is to realize phenomena, and in so far as Theosophy helps me to realize them, I accept it.'

' What a charming religion !' said Lottie, sitting at the piano.

She let her fingers wander aimlessly along the keys for a few seconds, and then broke into a rattling chorus from the last Savoy opera. Mervyn writhed upon the sofa like an eel impaled upon a trident, his countenance expressing extreme anguish.

' Don't !' he wailed, with his fingers in his ears. ' Please don't !'

' What's the matter now ?' asked Lottie, stopping short.

'That music!' said Mervyn, with a reminiscent shudder.

'Why, don't you like it?'

'Like it!' gasped the theosophic æsthete. 'Like it! It reminds me of—of—what shall I say? Plum pudding—or Dickens!'

'Poor Dickens!' said Lottie. 'And don't you like Dickens?'

'Vulgar optimist!'

'I don't believe you really like anything,' cried Lottie, laughing.

'You are wrong,' said Mervyn. 'I like myself.'

'Epicure!'

'And I enjoy the sharp, acute spasm of artistic agony, the aroma of social decay, for out of these comes Literature, which is Life.'

'I wish you would take something to do you good,' said his cousin. 'You're really in a bad way.'

Mervyn smiled with unmoved placidity.

'I'll tell you what it is, Mervyn.' You've adopted this last craze simply because you've failed in everything else.'

'Failed!' echoed Mervyn. 'My dear Lottie, the failures of life are its only successes!'

'Then, what a success you must be! But there, it's so easy to talk in paradoxes.'

'All nature is a paradox. The paradox of Life is Death.'

'Oh dear, oh dear!' cried Lottie, beating her little

feet on the ground, and clutching at her hair with a comic desperation. 'For goodness' sake, stop! My head's spinning round!'

'That's really not bad,' said Mervyn, pencilling his last utterance on his shirt-cuff, with his head admiringly on one side. ' " The paradox of Life is Death." Not bad at all.'

Lottie watched him for some moments with an amused smile, and was about to make another remark, not too complimentary to her companion, when a figure passed along the terrace beyond the open French windows of the drawing-room.

'Isabel, Isabel!' cried Lottie; and, in answer to the call, a beautiful young girl, carrying in her hand a bunch of newly-plucked white roses from the garden, entered the room. She paused on the threshold, glancing quietly from Lottie to Mervyn, and seemed about to retire, when Lottie ran up to her, and putting her arm about her waist, continued, with a merry laugh: 'Oh, do come in, Isabel! Mervyn is boring me to death!'

'Have you been quarrelling, as usual?' asked Isabel. 'Well, never mind, Mervyn. Lottie doesn't mean half she says.'

'But I do!' cried Lottie, still encircling Isabel's waist, and drawing her forward. 'Just look at him. Do you know what he's doing? He's—he's *evolving!*'

Mervyn made a deprecating gesture and shrugged his shoulders, glancing at Isabel with an expression

which plainly said, 'You see this little Philistine?
—she doesn't understand me in the least. I live in
regions far beyond her comprehension. But you, who
live in the ideal, doubtless comprehend me, and I
freely leave you to judge between us.'

Fortunately, just then Lottie's attention was diverted
from the contemplation of Mervyn's eccentricities to
the face of the new-comer.

'How pale you look!' she cried.

'I am a little tired, that's all,' replied Isabel gently,
seating herself on a couch near the window, and looking at the flowers which she held in her hand.

'We are all tired nowadays,' said Mervyn, glancing
up again. 'We are the inheritors of centuries of
decay.'

So saying, the Apostle of the New Culture rose
languidly to his feet, and sauntered to the window.

'I think I'll take a stroll,' he murmured. 'The
scent of those roses reminds me that relief from all
spiritual weariness is still to be found in Nature herself. Yes; I really think I'll take a stroll.'

Lottie tossed her head, and laughed.

'Yes, do,' she said; 'and leave me to talk to
Isabel; adding, as Mervyn was about to pass through
the window, 'Why don't you take to bicycling, Mervyn,
or something really energetic? I'm sure it would do
you good!'

The young man glanced at his cousin with a look
of profoundly supercilious pity, and murmured, as he

disappeared, 'Ride on a bicycle! Good heavens! I would rather *die !*'

Left alone together, the two young girls sat for some time in silence. A casual observer, seeing them seated side by side, could not fail to have been struck by the extraordinary contrast between them. Lottie, though 'the daughter of a hundred earls,' was as round, plump, and English as fresh air and a happy country life could make her. She was a blonde of the brightest type, fair-haired, fair-complexioned, and blue-eyed, with dimples in her cheeks, and a face all happiness and sunshine. One would have said, looking at her, that she had never known what trouble was; and one would have added, under the contagion of her good temper, a hearty wish that such knowledge might never come.

Isabel Arlington, on the contrary, with her dark, dreamy eyes, her dark hair, and her pale olive complexion, seemed the very incarnation of abiding melancholy. Beautiful as she was, her beauty seemed of the night rather than of the day, and her very voice, with its deep musical tones, increased the impression of settled sadness. She was tall and slightly built; in these respects also a contrast to her sunny companion.

'Well, Isabel,' said Lottie at last, with a little laugh, 'how should you like to have a lover like that?' And when Isabel smiled without replying, she continued, 'I'm really quite serious when I tell him that he bores my head off. He calls me a Philistine, whatever that means, but I'm sure I'd rather be a Philistine than a bore. But there! don't let us talk about him or about anything so absurd. What *shall* we talk of?— Frank?'

A faint blush flickered on Isabel's cheek, and she bent a still closer scrutiny on the flowers she held in her hand.

'He'll be here to-day, papa says, though I suppose you don't know anything about it? What an odd girl you are!' she continued, after a pause spent in roguish examination of Isabel's face. 'Aren't you glad he's coming?'

'Of course I'm glad,' replied her companion; but there was no great happiness in the tone in which she spoke, as Lottie's ear told her. 'I like Frank very much; he's—he's very kind.'

'He's very fond of you, Isabel. I don't know how you can take things so coolly. It must be lovely to have a sweetheart. If anyone loved me as Frank loves you, I should be jumping out of my shoes.'

'I'm afraid I'm not so enthusiastic as you, Lottie.'

'But just think of it! When you marry Frank, you'll be a queen of society. You'll have your portrait and pictures of your dresses in all the ladies' papers, and columns of description in the *Times* and the *Morning Post*. Lady Dewsbury! Doesn't it sound splendid? And Frank getting more and more famous every day! He's been in the *Punch* cartoons

thirteen times in the last twelve months. I've
counted, so I know. And then, when the Earl dies,
poor old man, you'll be the Countess of Loamshire; but
you mustn't let Frank go and bury himself in that
stupid old House of Lords. You must make him be
an ambassador, or something. Fancy! if he could
be ambassador at Paris!' She clasped her hands,
her cheeks flushing and her eyes sparkling, as if the
glories she dwelt upon were in store for herself rather
than for her companion. 'I could go over and live
with you, and you could chaperon me. Isabel, what
is the matter with you? I don't believe you're
listening to a word I say.'   ·

'Yes, I am, dear. And I was thinking how
much better you would fill such a position than I
could.'

'I?' cried Lottie, in genuine comic surprise. 'My
dear, I should never do for that sort of thing! I
haven't a bit of dignity—not an atom! I should be
doing something awful, and compromising my
husband's official position, before I had been married
a week. I know I should! But you're just cut out
for a statesman's wife.'

Isabel smiled faintly at her bright little companion's
frank and vivacious admiration of her.

'You love Frank, don't you, dear?' Lottie asked,
with sudden seriousness.

She was far too honest and loyal a girl, far too
unspoiled by the world of which she knew so little,

not to put love, where every true-hearted maiden is sure to put it, before all else that life can offer.

'I am very fond of Frank,' said Isabel.

She spoke quite steadfastly and candidly, but Lottie felt a reservation behind her words, and waited with a rather anxious face for her to speak again.

'Frank is very good and kind, and very clever; but—we are so different.'

'So much the better!' said Lottie gaily. 'It's the people who have differences of character who make the best couples. The people whose ways and tastes are alike, and who you'd think were just cut out for each other, are always unhappy together.'

'Then, what a splendid couple you and Mervyn would make!' said Isabel, with a little laugh, glad, perhaps, of a chance, however slight, of carrying the war into the enemy's country.

'Mervyn!' cried Lottie indignantly. '*I* marry Mervyn! What an idea! No; when I marry, I shall marry a *man*—a man who can do something—fight, or write, or paint, or—or anything! Mervyn can do nothing, except loll about and evolve, as he calls it.'

'Yes,' said Isabel, 'and that is just what I mean. There are women like that, women who are fitted to be the wives of the leaders of men, who can sympathize with their aims, and aid them in their struggles. I shall never be a woman of the world, Lottie. I shall never really care for politics, or be interested in Frank's pursuits, or be able to share his pleasures. All the splendid things you talk of, the social triumphs, the great positions, frighten me. I feel like the wife of the Lord of Burleigh, fading away beneath the burden of an honour unto which I was not born. The landscape-painter would suit me better than the great lord.'

She kept her eyes bent upon the flowers as she spoke, and Lottie watched her keenly, her dimpled face dimmed with a shadow of anxious wonder. Isabel, unwitting of the scrutiny, slowly picked the petals of a rose, and watched them as they flickered from her fingers to the carpet.

'Isabel!' she said suddenly, laying her hand on her companion's arm.

'Yes, dear,' Isabel answered, waking from her brown study with a nervous start.

'I have sometimes thought——' said Lottie, and then stopped short, with her eyes still fixed on Isabel's face.

Isabel, once roused from her abstraction, returned the gaze with eyes as clear and untroubled as Lottie's own.

'Yes, dear,' she prompted her. 'You have sometimes thought——'

'I have sometimes thought,' said Lottie, 'that there might be somebody else—somebody you had met, perhaps, when you were in India with your father, who——'

Isabel rose, and walked a step or two back into the drawing-room.

'My darling!' cried the impetuous Lottie, darting after her, and embracing her waist. 'I haven't offended you?'

Isabel looked down on her from her superior height with the air of affectionate but calm dignity which she could assume when she chose—an air which Lottie, who honestly admired and rather feared her, never dreamed of resenting.

'Don't talk nonsense, Lottie!' she said, softening the reproof with a kiss.

'But it isn't nonsense,' said Lottie, who, with all her practicality, had as keen a relish for a love-story, with a dash of mystery or romance to flavour it, as every pretty girl should have. 'You must have made hundreds of conquests, and among them all——'

'Hush!' said Isabel. 'What is that?'

A distant rumbling of wheels in the avenue, growing rapidly nearer and louder, drew them both to the balustrade of the broad terrace which encircled the entire castle. A carriage rounded the line of elms which had hitherto hid it from sight, and dashed up to the entrance. A face looked from the open window, and Lottie, clapping her hands with delight, cried, 'Bravo! It's Frank!' and danced down the steps to welcome Lord Dewsbury.

Isabel, after a momentary pause, followed at a slower pace.

CHAPTER III.

A MODERN LOVER.

LORD DEWSBURY will play a sufficiently prominent
part in the present narrative. to merit somewhat of a
formal introduction. The heir and hope of one of the
oldest and wealthiest families of England, he was a
man thoroughly fitted for the position to which he
had been born. He was proud, as was natural in a
man of such descent, and, as was natural to a true
gentleman of any degree, hid his pride for the most
part under a genial courtesy to all sorts and conditions of people with whom he came in contact. He
was brave, honourable, arbitrary and generous, as his
forebears had been before him, while he had a serene
conviction, which he had never paused to examine or
even to formulate, that he and men of his class were
the appointed rulers and leaders of the great mass of
mankind.

Since the most iron-bound aristocrat cannot escape
the influences of the environment of his day and
generation, he recognised, and was proud of the clear-
sightedness which enabled him to recognise, the right
of the great mass to just and kindly government.
The people's duty was to him and the class he represented; his duty was to his own instincts as an
English gentleman.

For the rest, he was acute, hard-headed, marvellously well-informed on every possible subject, a fluent and convincing speaker, rising sometimes to something like eloquence, keenly alert, obstinately logical, and he had never done five minutes' real thinking in his life. He was a man with no doubts about anything, a man who had inherited his opinions with his birth and his acres as part of the family property.

He was a Churchman just as he was a Tory, because his father and grandfather had been Churchmen and Tories before him. He believed in the superiority of England and Englishmen over all foreign countries and peoples as he believed in the superiority of his own class over all other classes. A Home Ruler or a Radical was to him a sort of political maniac, a clever and able maniac, it might be, but still a maniac, and he would cheerfully have given his life to save one acre of English territory from dismemberment.

Politically, in a word, he was a young Sir Leicester Dedlock, with more brains, and an up-to-date political education. Socially, he was a charming fellow, even-tempered, genial, and high-spirited. Physically, he was as fine a specimen as one could wish to see of the young English gentleman beginning to verge towards middle age; as hard as nails all over, a superb athlete, splendid shot, boxer, oarsman, rider, and golfer. Somehow, though one of the hardest-worked men of his party, he found time for all these varied pursuits, and for a good deal of innocent social dissipation besides.

A man of such gifts could hardly fail to be popular with women as with men, but a resolute ambition, and the hard work its fulfilment entailed on him, had kept him heart-whole to the verge of six-and-thirty. Since his college days he had never given more than a passing thought to any woman till, at Wanborough Castle, he had met the Earl's niece, the calm, pale, proud girl, who had recently returned from India, committed to her uncle's care by her father, a restless modern Ulysses, who, unable to cease from travel, had started on a desperate journey across the wilds of Thibet.

Isabel Arlington might have seemed the last woman in the world to attract such a man as Dewsbury. Perhaps her very indifference to everything he regarded as best worth having—wealth, social position, political battle and triumph—was the spell which drew her to him.

He had been the despair of mothers and chaperons any time for the last ten years. The prize beauties of successive seasons had surged about him like the waves of the sea against Ailsa Craig, only to retire defeated. He might have married any woman in England of less than royal rank, and his power of resistance had been tested a score of times with every weapon in the feminine armoury. Women with blood, women with brains, women with money, women with all three, had shot at him, and chased him, and angled for him in vain.

Yet here was a girl, beautiful, certainly, but not more beautiful than a dozen others he had known, not conspicuously clever, the daughter of a retired officer of moderate income, who did none of these things, who did not covet his prospective coronet, or flatter him about his prospective triumphs, but met him with calm friendship, and no more. He was as little of a coxcomb as any man living, but his first impression of Isabel Arlington had been that she was the most finished coquette he had yet encountered.

How else could the heir to seventy thousand per annum and a potential Prime Minister of England regard the penniless girl whose manner to him was as coldly friendly as it was to any country gentleman she met in her uncle's drawing-room? He had been tried with that bait before, and had not swallowed it, aware, like the shy fish he was, of the hook it covered. But he had soon learned that coquetry of any kind was foreign to this strange girl's nature.

Her calmness had first piqued his sense of humour, then interested, and finally captivated him. Here was the bride worthy of him, the ideal woman he had sought —no vulgar female fortune-hunter, no woman to be dazzled by wealth or the world's regard; but one calm, proud, queenly, and, above all, as he felt, beautifully womanly, full of the capacity of gentle and serene

3

affection for the man who could conquer her reticence
and win her love.

Dewsbury soon began to feel as much delight in
this quiet girl's lightest word of praise as in the
thunders of the crowded House, or the applausive
murmurs of London *salons*. Even the strong infusion
of mysticism he discovered in her character, which
would have bored and repelled him in another woman,
attracted him in her, though, as their friendship
thickened, he tried gently and genially to correct it by
administering sugared doses of his own hard-headed
common-sense.

'Family traits are wonderfully strong,' he had said
to her one day. 'You are very like your father.'

'Like my father!' Isabel had answered. 'How
can you know that? You have never met him.'

'I don't need to meet him to know that,' said
Dewsbury. 'You both have the love of the unknown.
He starts out to explore Thibet, the geographical
mystery. You try to pierce into the psychical *terra
incognita*. Allow for the difference of sex, and the
resemblance between you is striking.'

'Yes,' said Isabel thoughtfully; 'there may be
something in what you say.'

'And it seems to me,' continued Dewsbury, 'that
both expenditures of energy—if you will permit me to
say so, Miss Arlington—are equally, or almost equally,
mistaken.'

'Yes?' answered Isabel. 'And why so?'

'I can understand exploration when it has a useful
and definite end. The exploration which results in
the discovery of an America or an Australia, which is
useful in finding new outlets for capital and enterprise,
justifies itself. But what use can a dreary tract of
mountain, covered with snow, and populated by a
crowd of ignorant and brutal savages, be to anybody?
Such men as Colonel Arlington are rare, and I cannot
help thinking it a pity that he should risk his life for
such a very inadequate gain.   Then, as regards yourself——'

'I can gather your meaning,' said Isabel, 'without
your giving yourself the trouble to express it.'

'You are not offended?' asked Dewsbury.

'I am never offended by plain speech which is
honestly meant,' Isabel answered. 'If actual and
tangible results are all that are worth labouring and
suffering for, you are right. My father's life and my
life are wasted!'

'Pardon me,' said Dewsbury quickly; 'I did not
say that! I do not think it! But there is so much
tangible hard work to do in the world, that it always
seems to me a pity to see energy applied to negative
rather than positive results.'

He owned to himself later on that this particular
lesson on his favourite doctrine of 'common-sense'
had been rather a failure, though he knew that a
woman of Isabel's nature and intelligence was far
more likely to respect, and ultimately to love, a man

who discarded the ordinary methods of love-making, and gave her credit for the capacity—none too common among her sex—of dispassionate self-criticism. Isabel was not a woman to be caught by pretty speeches, and, for all her dreaminess and unpracticality, would rather listen to a home-truth than a conventional compliment.

And, indeed, so far as she was attracted by Dewsbury at all, she was attracted by his intellectual and moral honesty. His hard and fast ideas on all created things repelled her. But she liked and respected him for showing himself so clearly, although what he showed was not particularly lovable.

A great battle was going on in the girl's heart.

She knew that Dewsbury loved her. That he was wealthy, famous, and certain of a brilliant career did not affect her in the least. She left those figments aside. The only question in her mind was whether she could make him such a wife as such a man should have.

She liked him thoroughly, and respected him profoundly, but she did not love him, nor could she, after much conscientious effort, take a real interest in the world of which he was so brilliant a figure. As she had confessed to Lottie, his triumphs—or rather the prospect of her share in them—frightened her. And she held the grand old creed, less popular nowadays than it once was with her sex, that nothing but love can justify marriage. If she married Frank, her every thought, her very life, must be his.

Dewsbury sprang from the carriage, and returned Lottie's hearty greeting in kind, though he could not keep his eyes from wandering to the tall, lithe figure of Isabel, as she slowly descended the steps.

'And you, my dear Isabel?' he asked. 'You are well?'

'Quite, thank you, Frank!' she answered. 'I need not ask how you are. You look radiant. You bring good news?'

'The best. The Liberal Ministry has resigned. We are certain of a big majority.'

'I am glad, Frank—very glad, for your sake.'

'Ah,' said Frank, with a little sigh, 'you don't care much for politics, I'm afraid. Well, we must see what the election and a bit of canvassing will do for you, and you may blossom into a Primrose dame before I see the Clock Tower again. Hullo, Darrell, you here!'

'Yes,' said Mervyn, who had just lounged up to the little group. 'I came over from Oxford to interview the Obnoskin. Wonderful woman! You'll meet her at dinner, Frank.'

'I suppose so,' said Dewsbury resignedly. 'And Lord Wanborough? Still trying to solve the riddle of the universe, and running after the will-o'-the-wisp of Theosophy?'

'I am afraid so, Frank,' said Isabel, smiling.

'Has the Obnoskin converted *you* yet?' asked Dewsbury.

Isabel shook her head.

'No; I saw enough of Theosophy and Theosophists in India. I don't desire to know more of them.'

'Papa's gone simply crazy,' said Lottie. 'He's ready to swallow any amount of nonsense.'

'Dear, dear! the folly of it!' said Dewsbury. 'Seeking to know what never can be known! Opening his doors to every kind of humbug!'

'Ah,' said Mervyn, who had listened to the talk with his usual air of bored tolerance, 'talking of humbug, that reminds me.'

'Reminds you of what?' asked Lottie.

'Of an acquaintance of mine. A wonderful fellow! I was introduced to him the other day at The Travellers, just after his arrival from India. He's fresh from the headquarters of the occult faith, and an adept in all its mysteries. I told the Earl about him this morning, and he has asked me to invite him down here.'

'You'll do nothing of the kind, if you please, Mervyn,' said Lottie sharply.

'I've done it already, my dear Lottie,' answered Mervyn. 'I wrote to him this afternoon.'

'I'll stop the letter,' said Lottie, starting up the steps leading to the balcony.

'You can't. Simmons went off with the post-bag ten minutes ago.'

'It's shameful!' cried Lottie. 'As if the Obnoskin wasn't enough, without another importation!'

'Perhaps it's for the best, Lottie,' said Dewsbury.

'There's a good deal in what Dickens says—that "the harder an unsound hobby is ridden the better, because it is the sooner ridden to death."'

'This gentleman comes from India, you say, Mervyn?' asked Isabel.

'Yes; he's not a native, though—at least, not altogether—though I should say he had a touch of the tar-brush. Very gentlemanly person, and particularly well-read.'

'What is his name?'

'Woodville. Perhaps you've heard of him?'

'No,' said Isabel thoughtfully. 'I know nobody of that name.'

'I do, though,' said Frank; 'or, at least, I heard of him. He came over with an introduction to our chief. A Theosophist, you say?'

'The prince of Theosophists. What they call a Mahatma.'

'Oh, how I wish papa would give up all this rubbish and go in for something sensible,' said Lottie; 'billiards, or—or even politics!'

'Thank you,' said Frank, with a laugh. 'But you mustn't chaff *me*, Lottie; Mervyn will be jealous. Will you walk round the grounds, Isabel? You don't know how delicious it is to get away from the jar and clamour of politics to this quiet old place.'

They sauntered away together, leaving Lottie and Mervyn to continue the eternal squabble in which, during each of the latter's visits to the Castle, their lives were passed. The turf was soft beneath their feet, the encircling trees held the outer world at bay, the solemn voices of the rooks mingled with the chant of the birds singing good-night to the declining sun.

'You are sure you will win in the election?' asked Isabel.

'Certain!' said Dewsbury. 'The country is sick of Radical cheeseparing and muddling. We shall come back with a grand majority and a great programme. But I didn't ask you to walk with me to talk politics, Isabel.'

'I remember the time,' she said, 'when you scarcely cared to talk of anything else.'

'Times change,' said Dewsbury, 'and men with them.'

'Isn't that rather a Radical maxim for such a strong Conservative as you?' she asked, with a smile.

'Politics again! No, I am not to be drawn in that way. I want to forget them for a day or two, till the fight begins again.'

Isabel certainly had no great interest in the subject which Dewsbury tabooed for the moment, though she would have been glad of any topic which would keep him from speaking on the theme she feared was in his mind. But she could find no other, and so remained silent perforce till her companion spoke again.

They had reached a moss-grown stone bench at the

edge of a parterre of smooth turf, beneath which the park sloped precipitately to a line of immemorial beeches marking its confines. Through their thick clustered leaves the roofs and spire of the little town were visible against the fading glory of the sunset.

Isabel sat in obedience to Frank's silent gesture, and he stood beside her for another moment in silence.

'Isabel!' he said suddenly, and for him rather nervously, 'I have something to say to you.'

She shot a quick glance at him, and lowered her eyes.

'You can guess what it is. You know already that I love you. I ask you now if you will be my wife.' *proposal*

She sat silent, intertwisting her fingers, afraid to answer the question or to meet the eyes she felt were bent on her.

'If the proposal seems sudden, and I dare say it is, take what time you will to answer it. I am a busy man, and I have had little time for love-making, but I think you must know how much I care for you.'

He took her hand, and she made no resistance, but there was no answering warmth to his gentle pressure. He bent closer to her. She did not avoid him, but he felt her whole body shrinking.

'Have you no answer for me, Isabel?'

'I don't know what to say, Frank," she commenced at last. 'I—I am afraid.'

'Afraid!' he echoed tenderly. 'Afraid of what?'

'Of myself,' she said. 'Of my fitness to be your wife.'

'You are worthy of a far better man than I,' he said, 'worthy of any man alive. I love you, Isabel. I have watched and studied you. I have learned to know you, and every fresh knowledge I have gained has deepened my love. I have worked for you of late far more than for myself. Before I met you my ambition was cold and selfish, but now I feel that all that I could win would be valueless—mere dust and ashes, if you should refuse to share it with me. I feel as if, with you beside me, there was nothing I could not do; without you, there will be nothing I shall *care* to do.'

'Give me time, Frank,' she pleaded. 'Give me time to learn my heart and see my duty clearly. Don't think that I am insensible of the honour you do me. I know there is no woman in England who would not be proud to be your wife. I know you are brave and good and kind, and worthy of any woman's love, but I cannot answer you yet. Frank, I must tell you something. Don't call me childish and silly. I know beforehand what you will think, but we are not all made alike, and I cannot banish this thing from my mind.'

She then told him brokenly of the vision of her father, which, on the preceding day, she had told to the Earl of Wanborough.

'Frank, I am as certain as that you and I are here

together, as certain as I am of my own existence,
that my father lives and will return to me. Think if
he comes, how could I meet him if I had been false to
him ?'

'False to him!' repeated Frank in astonishment.

'I should feel so if I formed such a tie as
marriage at such a time as this. For two years
we have heard no word of him. He may be sick,
or a prisoner in that wild country, all alone, and
I, his daughter, whom he loved better than his
own life—don't you see how selfish, how horrible it
would be ?'

Dewsbury was in a cruel dilemma. It was hard
for a man of his shrewd, worldly common-sense to be
held back from the dearest of life's prizes by such
gossamer manacles as these, woven from the fabric of
a dream. Yet, what could he say? To ridicule the
hope to which she clung so tenaciously would have
been an unpardonable brutality. He had long ago
made up his mind as to Colonel Arlington's fate, and
had tried often, with the greatest tenderness and
gentleness, to instil into Isabel's mind his belief that
her father was dead, and to induce her to bow herself
to the unalterable decree of fate. And now the
foolish, impressionable child had received this
'intimation,' and clung to its message with a faith
which, during the recital of the dream, had almost
infected *him*. Revolted common-sense on the one
side, prudence and the desire, natural to a lover, not

to shock Isabel by a too open confession of his unbelief in the trustworthiness of her visions, made sad
havoc in his mind.

'Well,' he said at last, 'God grant it may be so!
But you will name some time, Isabel; some term
when you will feel conscience-free to act?'

'Do not press me now,' said Isabel. 'I know how
I am taxing your generosity, but at the earliest
possible moment you shall have my answer.'

And with that very doubtful consolation, Dewsbury
forced himself as best he could to be content.

The tranquil evening was succeeded by a night of
heavy rain and storm.

Lottie and Isabel, whose bedrooms communicated,
sat together till, in the early morning, the tempest
abated something of its fury. Lottie was ordinarily
a sound sleeper; but, as it seemed to her, she had
scarcely lost consciousness, when she was recalled
to it by an oppressive sense of a presence in her
room.

She started up in bed, and there, in the clear, cold
light of the early dawn, stood a white-robed figure,
looking towards her with wide-open, unseeing eyes.

Her first impulse was to scream aloud, but recog-
nising Isabel, she held back her cry for help.

Isabel walked slowly round the room, looking
sightlessly here and there, and turning her head from
side to side, as if listening to voices inaudible to her

companion. Presently she spoke, with the dead, level monotony of sleeping speech.

'Philip! Did you not call me, Philip? I am here. I hear your voice, but it is dark. Where are you, Philip?'

She stretched out her hands gropingly, and so stood for a moment, then, with a deep, quivering sigh, passed from Lottie's sight to her own room.

CHAPTER IV.

' THE ASRA.'

IT was a rather dull party which met next morning at the breakfast-table.

Frank and Isabel had their own reasons for being rather constrained in each other's presence, and Lottie, remembering the weird appearance of Isabel in her room only a few hours before, was too devoured with natural curiosity as to what her friend's dreaming utterance might have meant to be in full possession of her ordinary conversational fluency. A dozen times already it had been on the tip of her tongue to tell Isabel of her nocturnal adventure, but the ascendancy the latter so easily kept over her held her silent. Madame Obnoskin felt herself unpopular with all the inmates of the house save his lordship, who was busy with a pile of correspondence, and spoke but little. She held her own counsel, smiling, perfectly at ease, keenly and unobtrusively watchful of the others, and for the most part silent.

Mervyn did not appear till the others had nearly finished their meal. When he at last appeared, he walked up to his uncle, and, having exchanged greetings with him, gave him an open telegram.

'I have just received that, sir,' he said, 'from my friend Woodville. He will arrive here by the 6.15.'

The Earl glanced at the telegram, and returned it with a smile of contentment.

'He will be welcome,' he said; 'most welcome. My dear Mervyn, will you kindly see that a carriage is in waiting at the station to convey him here?'

'Woodville?' said Lord Dewsbury. 'Is that the fellow you were speaking of yesterday—that Mahatma fellow?'

'Yes,' said Mervyn. 'The Mahatma fellow will be here to-night.'

Dewsbury gave a scarcely-perceptible shrug, and, rising from the table, murmured something about having work to do that morning, and betook himself to his own quarters. Lottie and Isabel left the table a moment later, leaving the Earl, Madame Obnoskin, and Mervyn together.

'Isn't it rather a curious thing, Madame Obnoskin,' asked Mervyn, 'that you, who are so highly placed in the theosophical hierarchy, should not know so famous a man in your own line as my friend Woodville?'

'But I do not say that I do not know him,' replied madame. 'It is very possible that I do; it is almost certain that I know *of* him; but if so, it will be by another name—by his spirit name, perhaps. You will remember, dear friend '—she addressed the Earl —'that I warned you of the coming of an Adept, one of the elect.'

'You did, indeed, madame.'

'If this new-comer should be all that Mr. Darrell describes,' said madame, 'he may have been the person from whom I received the intimation. I felt it strongly last night; it is even stronger to-day. I feel that a great moment is coming; that we are on the verge of great events; that a grand triumph for our common religion may be near at hand.'

'A triumph, madame?' repeated the Earl. 'Of what kind?'

'How should I know?' asked madame, with her pleasant little laugh. 'I do not pretend to prophetic power. But something will happen — something remarkable—before long. Strange influences are about us, working upon us. The air is full of them. May they be benignant to this house, and to you, dear friend.'

The Earl inclined his head gravely. Mervyn, who was, in his own fashion, at least as much a philosopher as a Theosophist, made a pretty solid breakfast, undisturbed by the predictions of his fair neighbour, and strolled out with a cigarette on to the terrace. Lord Wanborough sat musing for a time.

'I have not your capacity, madame,' he said presently, ' of reading the subtler signs by which the approach of impending phenomena may be realized ; but I, too, feel that strange events are nearing us. Isabel's dream the other night, your prediction of the appearance of one of the Adept, Mervyn's chance meeting with this Mr. Woodville, for whom he claims such wonderful power; all these things combine to point to something—something of grave import.'

' Yes. At last, dear friend, you will be convinced.'

' For myself,' said the Earl, ' I need no convincing. Your inspired teaching, my own slight studies, have led me far towards complete belief. But there are others——'

' Your daughter, for instance,' suggested Madame Obnoskin.

' Carlotta, I fear,' said the Earl, ' is frivolous by nature. She will never take life seriously. I was thinking rather of my niece, Miss Arlington.'

' Yes,' said madame. ' Charming as Miss Arlington is, and profoundly capable by nature of becoming an adept in divine mysteries, she is an adverse in-fluence.'

' She has strong religious prejudices against Theosophy. She thinks it impious to attempt to pry behind the veil. I have tried to convince her that our attempts to pierce the mystery of living are absolutely compatible with full acceptance of the Christian doctrine, but hitherto I have failed. I do not think it likely that she will ever be converted. She will most probably marry Lord Dewsbury, and he——'

'Ah,' said madame. 'Another adverse influence, and a very strong one.'

'Yes,' said Lord Wanborough; 'I fear so. I like Dewsbury; he is a fine fellow, full of all kinds of good qualities, but a pure Materialist, though nominally, I believe, he belongs to the Church. We shall certainly not convince Dewsbury.'

'Yet I have known,' said madame, 'cases as hard to convince, people as full of prejudice as Lord Dewsbury himself, convinced of the truth. Natures such as his require actual, tangible, brutal proof. In other words, they must see and handle before they believe. Well, if this Mr. Woodville is worthy of his fame, he should be able to produce some sign, some manifestation of the powers whose secrets he has penetrated, to convince the most prejudiced.'

'May it be so,' said the Earl. 'It is my one prayer—"Lead us to the light."'

'Ah,' said madame, 'my life will not have been spent in vain, your charity to the poor widow will not have been thrown away, if any poor help I have given has been of real service. This atones for much, for the scorn of the incredulous and worldly, the contempt of the deaf and blind, who will not hear and see.

4

Dear friend, you will never let unkind tongues part us. I am alone in a world of unbelief—a weak and solitary woman.'

'An inspired one,' said the Earl.

'I have a favour to ask of you,' continued madame. 'A very little one. Will you grant it?'

'With more than pleasure, if I can.'

'Easily. Will you think of me sometimes by my spirit name—Evangeline?'

'Evangeline!' repeated the Earl. 'It is appropriate to our relation one to another.'

'Think of me by that name,' said madame softly. 'The name I bear is that of my husband, and reminds me daily of early sufferings, and an unhappy marriage. In the East, among believers, the spirit name is all-sufficient.'

'A small favour, indeed,' said the Earl. 'Far too small to recompense the services you have done me.'

'Ah,' broke in madame, with a vivid motion of deprecation, 'do not talk of recompense! I do not work for worldly gain. Your friendship, communion with a soul like yours, the knowledge that I have helped in some small degree to bring you to the light you craved—these things are recompense enough, and more than enough.'

She offered her hand with frank cordiality. The old gentleman took it, and raised it to his lips with a grace half courtly, half paternal.

'I must leave you now, Evangeline,' he said, smiling. 'We shall meet later in the day.'

He left the room, and madame, as she heard the door close behind him, dropped into a seat, with a quiet smile of triumph.

'I think I have him safe. All that I need now is Woodville's assistance.'

She took a folded letter from her bosom.

'I wonder what he means by this?

' " Keep your eyes open, and learn all you can for my information when we meet. There is a grand *coup* to be done at Wanborough Castle, something vastly more important than you can guess."

And what can that be, I wonder, my good Woodville? You are a clever man, Philip, and a bold one, but did you ever play a bolder game than mine? I think not.'

She sat silent for a moment, and then murmured to herself, so softly that her own ears barely caught the sound of the words, ' Countess of Wanborough !'

' Yes,' she continued voicelessly, ' I shall succeed. When did Woodville and I ever fail when we pursued one object faithfully together? And whatever his scheme may be, it cannot traverse mine. Countess of Wanborough ! Ah !'

A great mirror, which stretched from floor to ceiling of the breakfast-room, reflected her figure as she sat. She rose, and swept a bow to her image in the glass.

'Bon jour, Madame la Comtesse!'

Lottie's ringing laugh came up through the open window from the lawn below.

Madame's face changed as she heard it. She took a step or two forward to a place of vantage where, hidden by the lace curtains, she could see the two girls sitting together.

'I shall find an answer to your insolence, young ladies,' she murmured. 'You shall look on at my triumph and acknowledge my authority.'

Her eyes travelled over the rich verdure of the park, and rested slowly and caressingly on the priceless objects with which the room was crowded.

'What a triumph it would be! What a triumph it *shall* be—mad, delirious dream as it would have seemed but a month ago!'

'I wonder where Mervyn can have got to?' said Lottie that afternoon, as she presided over the tea-table. 'I never knew him miss tea-time before.'

'He has driven over to the station,' said Dewsbury, 'to meet Mr. Woodville. He ought to be back pretty soon now. How fast the evenings are drawing in! Mightn't we have the lamps lit, Lottie?'

'Not yet, Frank,' said Isabel from the window. 'I love the twilight. This is the best hour of the day.'

'I like it, too,' said Lottie. 'It's nice and creepy. Doesn't anybody know a ghost-story?'

'Perhaps Madame Obnoskin could oblige us?' suggested Frank.

'No; I am a very bad story-teller,' said madame. ('I wonder what you *can* do then, if you can't do that?' was Lottie's silent and uncharitable comment.) 'But would not Miss Arlington sing to us?'

'Yes, do, Isabel,' said Lottie. 'Something nice and twilighty, and I'll play for you.'

As she moved to the piano, Mervyn entered the room.

'You don't deserve any tea, Mervyn, for being late,' she continued; 'but I'll forgive you this once.'

'Thanks, very much,' said Mervyn; 'but I don't want it. I had a cup of tea at the station.'

'Oh, indeed! Then I suppose your wonderful friend has arrived?'

'Yes. He's *here!* I've just introduced him to my uncle, who has received him with open arms.'

Lottie struck a petulant chord on the piano.

'Come along, Isabel,' she said. 'What will you sing? Oh, I know. Sing "The Sultan's Daughter." That's romantic and twilighty.'

She played the brief and tender prelude of Rubinstein's beautiful ballad, and Isabel's clear voice, plaintive as the theme, rose on the darkened air—

> 'Day by day the Sultan's daughter,
> Wandered idly by the fountain;
> By the fountain in the garden,
> Near the splash of the white waters.

'Day by day the young slave watched her,
Standing lonely near the fountain;
Day by day his face grew paler
As he watched the Sultan's daughter.
'Then at last the Sultan's daughter
To the young slave ran, exclaiming,
"Tell me now thy name and kindred,
What thou art, and whence thou comest?"
'And the slave replied, "Mohammed
Is my name—I come from Yemen—
And my kindred are the Asra,
Who, whene'er they love, must *die!*"'

The listeners sat enthralled, too wholly given up to
the sweet influences of the hour and the delicate
charm of the voice to mark that their numbers had
been increased by two—the Earl and a second person
—who stood leaning against a console on the further
side of the room, his face in deep shadow.

Isabel's tones died slowly into a silence left unbroken for a second or two.

'Poor slave!' she said, with a sigh and a smile
together.

'Rather too sentimental for my taste,' said Dewsbury. 'What says Shakspere? "Men have died from
time to time, and worms have eaten them, but not
for love."'

'I don't suppose he died of love,' said Lottie. 'He
most likely had his head chopped off for daring to
love the Sultan's daughter.'

'No,' said Isabel. 'The Sultan gave him a kingdom, and he married the Princess.'

'And lived happy ever after,' added Lottie. 'Yes, that's the best ending to the story.'

'Yes,' said Isabel. 'I think the slave lived.'

A strange voice broke in from the darkness behind them: 'Yet Heine tells us that he died!'

Isabel started with a stifled cry, and all turned in the direction of the mysterious voice.

CHAPTER V.

PHILIP WOODVILLE.

THE butler and a footman entering at that moment with lamps filled the apartment with a sudden blaze of light.

The stranger, to whom all eyes were turned, had advanced to the middle of the room, and stood there, smiling deprecation of the alarm his unexpected utterance had given.

He was tall, and strongly though rather slightly built, swarthily pallid, with clear-cut, high-bred features, and rippling hair, worn rather longer than the fashion dictated, jetty black, save where it was touched above the temple with a few thin streaks of premature gray. Save for a slight black moustache, beneath which his teeth shone with ivory whiteness, he was clean-shaven.

'I fear I have startled your friends,' he said to the Earl. 'I hope they will pardon me.'

There was the faintest possible hint of a musical foreign accent in his voice, which was strikingly rich and full.

'Let me introduce my daughter, Lady Carlotta. Lord Dewsbury—Mr. Woodville.'

Dowsbury acknowledged the presentation with a curt nod. The eyes of the two men met, at first with no definite expression, but at the second glance they crossed like sword-blades. At Isabel's cry, Dewsbury had made an instinctive protective movement towards her, and his arm still lingered unconsciously round her waist as the Earl spoke.

A curious spasm, brief as a lightning flash, crossed Mr. Woodville's face as he noted their position; a second later his features had resumed the rather bored and languid calm which seemed to be their habitual expression. Dewsbury caught the flash of emotion, and his eyes answered it with a questioning challenge. The old Earl, noting nothing, went on with his introductions.

'My niece, Miss Arlington. Isabel, my dear, Mr. Woodville.'

Isabel had conquered the emotion which had for a moment overpowered her, and received the stranger with a quiet bow. Her face was deadly pale, and she was glad of the support of the piano, on which her hand was resting.

'Madame Obnoskin,' continued the Earl.

'I am profoundly happy,' said Mr. Woodville, with

a more marked deference than he had shown at any
previous introduction, 'to meet a lady so distinguished.'

Madame bowed low in answer to his words.

'It is strange, Mr. Woodville,' she said, 'that I
should never have heard your name. Your friend, Mr.
Darrell, speaks of you as one of our most remarkable
teachers.'

'The circumstance is easily explained,' said Mr.
Woodville lightly. 'I have borne my present name
only a little while. A relative of my father's, and a
devotee of the faith, died six months ago, and left me
his heir, attaching the condition that I should adopt
his name. Till then I bore the name of Carton.'

'Is it possible?' exclaimed Madame Obnoskin, in
a low voice, and with a look of almost awe-struck
reverence. 'My dear Lord Wanborough, you are
indeed fortunate. Mr. Carton—Mr. Woodville—is
perhaps the most remarkable man now professing our
religion. No wonder the intimation was so strong—
so overwhelming.'

'It is a very strange circumstance, Mr. Woodville,'
said the Earl—'a most remarkable circumstance, that
your appearance here was distinctly foretold by Madame
Obnoskin.'

'Indeed!' said Mr. Woodville a little languidly.
'I am glad to have been announced by so charming a
herald.'

'Such intimations,' said the Earl, a little puzzled

by the cool fashion in which his guest received his information, ' are, I suppose, matters of course among the adept ?'

' Yes,' said Mr. Woodville ; ' they are fairly common. I am afraid, Lady Carlotta,' he continued, ' that I was a little inconsiderate in startling you so. May I hope I am forgiven ?'

' Certainly. Though it *was* a little weird. Won't you have a cup of tea ? Ring the bell, Frank, please. The water is cold. I hope you had a pleasant journey from London, Mr. Woodville ?'

' More than pleasant,' he answered. ' This is one of the most memorable days of my life. I have had my first glimpse of real rural English scenery.'

' This is your first visit to England, then ?' asked the Earl.

' Yes, my first visit. I had read of its beauties, and tried to imagine them, but the reality goes far beyond any dream or description. To one who, like myself, has passed all his life in the East the effect is altogether indescribable.'

' Is it your intention to stay for long ?' asked the Earl.

' I really don't know. I have no definite intention in the matter. I shall stay as long as I am permitted, and go when I am sent.'

' When you are sent ?' repeated the Earl, puzzled anew by the phrase.

' Yes,' Mr. Woodville replied wearily ; ' when the

presences I serve require my services elsewhere. Pardon me, Miss Arlington. Your name is not a common one. Might I ask if you are in any way related to Colonel Arlington, the famous traveller?'

Isabel raised her eyes to his, and made as if she would speak, but no word issued from her lips.

'His only daughter,' said the Earl, speaking for her. 'Pray say no more on that topic, Mr. Woodville.'

Woodville gave him a quick sign of intelligence, and sipped his tea in silence.

'You know the East well, Mr. Woodville?' suddenly asked Lord Dewsbury.

'I was born there.'

'Then—pardon me—you are not an Englishman?'

'My father was English.'

'Your visit to England is not, if I may so express it, professional?'

'Professional?' repeated Mr. Woodville, bending forward in polite inquiry. 'I fear I hardly understand you.'

'I thought, perhaps,' continued Dewsbury, 'in view of your connection with Theosophy——'

'Do you call Theosophy a profession? In India we regard it as a religion.'

'And a noble one!' interrupted the Earl.

'I might,' continued Woodville, sinking back into his seat; 'I might describe any worldly pursuit— medicine, mechanics, or politics, for example—as a profession. I should hardly have thought of applying the term to Theosophy. If a disinterested inquiry into things spiritual is a profession, then Theosophy is my profession.' He added, with a seemingly casual glance in the direction of Isabel, ' In that case, I am here on a professional errand.'

' Candidly,' said Lord Dewsbury, ' I never associated disinterestedness with Theosophy.'

' Indeed! May I ask, my lord, if you have studied the subject ?'

' I have never taken the trouble,' answered Dewsbury. ' But I am sceptical.'

' Scepticism,' said Mr. Woodville, ' is often the offspring of uninstruction.'

' We are all sceptical,' said Lottie, who had been dividing a keen regard between Dewsbury and Mr. Woodville during their conversation, ' except papa.'

' And me,' put in Mervyn.

' Oh,' said Lottie to him, over her shoulder, ' *you* don't count !'

' And Miss Arlington ?' asked Mr. Woodville. ' Is she also among the sceptics ?'

' Yes,' Dewsbury answered curtly. ' My dear Isabel, are you going ?'

' Yes,' said Isabel.

She had risen from her seat as if to go; then, as if relenting in her purpose, remained standing.

' It is so close here ; I cannot breathe.'

' Shall I come with you ?' asked Lottie.

' No, no ; I shall be better alone.'

She passed through the open French window on to the balcony.

' Poor child !' said the Earl. ' You touched upon a tender chord when you spoke of her father. Poor Arlington! There is his picture, taken shortly before he left England for the last time. For more than two years we have had no news of him.'

' Well,' said Mr. Woodville, ' no news is often good news.'

' Do you think it possible——' began the Earl.

' That Colonel Arlington will return ? I think it more than possible. He and his daughter were much attached ?'

' Passionately ! Nothing will convince her that he is dead. Why should you think that he is living ?'

' In the first place, I know, as all the world knows, Colonel Arlington's record — his fearlessness, his wealth of resource, his indomitable courage and determination. They have saved him often before this, why should they fail him now? That is a purely human reason for hope, and a good one. Then—do not think me presumptuous for venturing on an opinion on so short an acquaintance—I should say that Miss Arlington is a young lady endowed with a large measure of psychic sympathy, what the spiritualists would call an undeveloped medium. The intuitions of such natures are often of enormous value, of far greater value than the common-sense, logical deductions of ordinary people. Since she is so convinced that her father survives, I think the chances are strongly in favour of her b ing right.'

The talk was abruptly ended at this point by the clang of the dressing-bell.

'Lottie, my dear,' said the Earl, reminded of his duties as host by the sound. 'I should have asked you before—where have you put Mr. Woodville ?'

'I told Brown to prepare the turret-chamber, papa. Mr. Woodville will find his things there.'

'The turret chamber ?' repeated the Earl a little dubiously.

'The turret chamber sounds interesting,' said Woodville ; 'nice, and antique, and ghostly.'

'Well,' said the Earl, with a smile, 'you have just hit upon the doubt in my mind. It is said—it is a legend connected with the place—that the room *is* haunted. It is occasionally used, but we make it a point to warn anybody who sleeps in it of its reputation.'

'Oh,' said Woodville, 'the turret chamber for me, by all means! I am profoundly obliged to Lady Carlotta. A well-accredited, authentic family ghost is rare. I shall be delighted to make his acquaintance.'

'*Her* acquaintance,' said the Earl. 'The ghost is —or shall I say was ?—a lady. If you will follow me, Mr. Woodville, I will conduct you to your quarters. By the terrace will be the shorter way.'

He led the way out on to the terrace, and along it to the foot of a steep flight of stone steps, flanked by a lofty wall pierced at regular intervals with cross-shaped *meurtrières*.

' This is the oldest part of the castle,' said the Earl, ' and dates from a century before the Conquest.'

He opened a ponderous door of oaken beams, clamped by huge stanchions of hammered iron, and pierced, like the wall, with slits, through which the besieged defenders of the castle had harassed their enemies with arrows and cross-bow bolts, and entered a gloomy corridor, paved and walled with huge slabs of granite.

' It is a little dark. Here are the steps.'

They mounted anew, and the Earl threw open a door, revealing a large, cosily-furnished apartment, lit by a large brass lamp depending from the ceiling and the flickering flames of a generous fire of coal and wood. The walls were hung with faded tapestry.

'This is the room,' said the Earl. ' I used, years ago, to make a study of it; but my legs and lungs are not what they were, and now I prefer a more accessible part of the house. Ghosts apart, I think you will be fairly comfortable here. You can be absolutely alone if you have need of quiet to write and study, and the view from the window is as fine as anything in the country.'

'A charming room, my dear Lord Wanborough !'

said Mr. Woodville. 'And you—did the apparition ever trouble you ?'

'No,' said the Earl; 'she never favoured me with a visit, or, if she did, she remained invisible.'

'May I ask the particulars of the legend? Ghost stories are always interesting.'

'Well, we are not fond of referring to the story in the family; but everybody knows it, and you would be certain to hear the details from somebody during your stay in the castle. A certain unhappy lady, the sister of an ancestress of mine, stabbed herself in this room two hundred years ago.'

legend

'Two hundred years ago !' echoed Woodville. 'A very venerable ghost by this time! Of course, she killed herself for love ?'

'Yes, a young fellow, a page in the service of the family, managed to entrap her affections, and used, it is said, to meet her at night on the battlements. The intrigue was discovered, and the lady's brothers lay in ambush in the room below, and killed him. There is a stain upon the stone floor, which is said to be caused by his blood.'

'Well,' said Woodville smilingly, 'if the White Ladye does me the honour of a visit, she shall be courteously received. Pray don't let me detain you longer, my lord. You have to dress as well as I.'

The old gentleman left him to himself, and Woodville, aided by a soft-footed, deft-handed man, who appeared from the curtained recess which formed his bedroom, performed his toilet, and descended to the dining-room.

The evening passed away uneventfully. The new-comer talked freely over the dinner-table with the easy and somewhat languid manner of a man of the world, but scarcely any allusion was made to what Dewsbury had called his profession or to the religion he was said to teach. Both Dewsbury and Isabel were very silent, and the talk was monopolized by Woodville, Madame Obnoskin, Mervyn, and the Earl.

At an early hour the party broke up, and Woodville returned to his new quarters.

CHAPTER VI.

IN THE TURRET-ROOM.

THE moment Woodville found himself alone, his manner underwent a sudden and extraordinary change. He was like a man who throws off an irksome dress and mask, used to cloak his true identity, and who appears altogether without disguise. The droop of the shoulders, the general lassitude of look and mien, the dreamy languor of the half-closed eyes, were altogether gone. He stood erect, expanding his chest, as if for air; his dark eyes flashed, his nostrils dilated, and he seemed to be drawing in a great breath of life.

Over the old-fashioned chimneypiece there was an

5

antique mirror in a panel of carved oak; the quick-silver had run, and the glass was misty and blurred; but thither his eyes turned, as if involuntarily, and he saw his own face, reflected as in a dim magician's glass.

He drew nearer, looked at the reflection, and then, with a quick gesture and a low laugh, ran his fingers through his hair, and looked again. The inspection seemed to satisfy him, for his eyes flashed brightly as he turned away.

The walls of the chamber were hung with old and faded tapestry, wrought with hunting groups, and other pictures of the chase. From the ceiling swung the large oil-lamp, burning very dimly, but the chimneypiece was lit with wax candles in quaint wooden candelabra.

Opposite the door by which Woodville had entered was a curtained recess containing a modern brass bedstead, and in front of the fireplace was a cosy modern settee; but the rest of the furniture was of old black oak—black oak chairs, an oaken writing-table, and an oaken wardrobe, dressing-table, and chest of drawers. The window, which faced the fireplace, was mullioned, and formed a recess, where there was an old seat, also of black oak.

Woodville had only had time to divest himself of his dress-coat, and throw on a dressing-jacket, when there was a knock at the door, and the old butler once more appeared, followed by two footmen carrying a tantalus-stand of spirits, glasses, a syphon of soda-water, and a box of cigars, all of which were set down on a small table near the fireplace. These preparations were scarcely complete, when the Earl himself appeared.

'Quite comfortable, I hope, Mr. Woodville?' he said, with his usual benignant smile. 'I think it advisable, on the principle of *similia similibus curantur*, to provide you with spirits of human manufacture, to neutralize the effect of those which are of superhuman origin, and are said to haunt the turret chamber.'

'Thank you,' replied Woodville, relapsing at once into his former subdued manner, and answering the Earl's smile with a look of gentle languor. 'I shall certainly try their efficacy; and since your lordship is here, perhaps you will join me.'

At a look from their master, the butler and servants withdrew, while the Earl sat down on the settee before the fire.

'The room has not been occupied lately,' he said, 'though my housekeeper sees that it is always kept habitable. I thought you would like a fire. Even in summer these old rooms are cheerless and comfortless without firelight.'

While the Earl was speaking, his guest had mixed two tumblers of whisky and soda-water, one of which he handed to the Earl, as he seated himself at his side.

'I am charmed with your haunted chamber,' he

said; 'and I prophesy that I shall sleep soundly. I do not think your White Ladye, or any other apparition, will disturb me to-night.'

'I hope not,' returned the Earl. 'It is my experience, indeed, that those who are most akin to spiritual influences fear them least. The wise man is too anxious to assure himself of the certainty of another world to feel daunted when assurance comes to him that that other world is a certainty.'

'I suppose so,' said Woodville, lighting a cigar. 'For my own part, however, I am not vain enough to include myself in the catalogue of wise men. With regard to spiritual influences, I am acclimatized, so to speak. They surrounded me from my cradle, and now they never surprise me in the least—on the contrary, if I may admit so much, I am often infinitely bored by them, and long to escape to the fresh air, the sunshine, and the daylight.'

The Earl looked at him in wonder, and not a little admiration. Woodville, conscious of the look, though he did not meet it, fixed his dark eyes on the curling rings of smoke, and round the edges of his finely-cut mouth there was just the ghost of a smile.

'You are very young, Mr. Woodville, to have seen and known so much,' said the old man gently, almost wistfully.

Woodville shrugged his shoulders.

'In the East, my lord, we do not measure time by years, but by episodes. I am thirty years old, and

often I feel as if I were a hundred. Let me compliment you on your cigars ; they are excellent. But
frankly, you spoil me. I should become a sybarite if
I remained long under your hospitable roof. I am
not accustomed, as I dare say you know, to such
consideration. In most houses which I visit, I am
looked upon either as something " uncannie " (as
the Scotch express it) or as a sort of vulgar conjurer,
who is expected to perform tricks for the public
amusement. Even here, I fear—though not, of
course, by yourself—I may be a little misunderstood.'

' The whims and prejudices of children ?'

' Lord Dewsbury is scarcely a child,' returned the
Theosophist, with a quiet smile.

' I must beg you to overlook Lord Dewsbury's
remarks ; they were certainly in bad taste. He is
strongly prejudiced against Theosophy.'

' Just so. He has never investigated the subject.'

The Earl shook his head, with a sigh.

' I do not think any form of religion attracts
Dewsbury very much, though, of course, as a politician
on the Tory side, he is a Churchman. His interests
are of this world only.'

Woodville did not reply, but, leaning back in the
settee, continued to watch the curling rings of smoke
that issued from his lips. He had the manner of one
watching and waiting to be cross-questioned.

' You have lived long in India ?' asked the Earl,
somewhat nervously, after a long pause.

'Nearly all my life,' answered Woodville. 'As I told you, this is my first visit to England.'

'May I ask what brought you so far from your birthplace?'

'Curiosity, I suppose. I myself am half English, for my father was an Englishman. I do not recollect him. He died when I was quite a child.'

'Your mother, Mr. Woodville?'

'She was a Persian, and, I believe, a sort of princess among her own people. She, too, died when I was very young. I was brought up by some of my father's kinsfolk, who were kind enough to give me a good education.'

'And where did you first study Theosophy?' asked the Earl eagerly.

'At its fountain-head—in Thibet itself. My uncle was a devout believer; in close communication with the Mahatmas.'

'The Mahatmas!' echoed the Earl. 'They exist, then? And their miracles?'

'Are performed daily, and extend over all animated creation,' answered Woodville, in a tone of extreme languor, as if the subject were too familiar to awaken in him the slightest thrill of excitement.

'Wonderful, wonderful!' murmured the Earl, his eyes fixed on the pale, impassive countenance of the young man.

'To you, no doubt, it seems so; to *me*, my lord, it seems the most ordinary thing in the world. I passed some time with one of these men, if men they can be called, and, frankly, I found him tiresome and not particularly clean. He was said to be several hundred years old, and, like many very old people, he seemed rather stupid. He spent his days and nights in a kind of trance, closely resembling catalepsy; but of one thing I am quite certain—that he had power to heal diseases, and that, so far as the ordinary necessities of the flesh are concerned, he was practically unconditioned.'

As Woodville talked on, with the *blasé* indifference of one talking on the most ordinary matters, the Earl seemed more and more surprised and puzzled. Possibly, indeed, this was just the impression which his visitor intended to produce, and, if so, he succeeded to admiration. In speaking of the phenomena of his strange religion, he seemed to take the position of a somewhat sceptical outsider rather than that of one with any living belief. This made his testimony towards the truth of Theosophy carry unusual weight, since it was impossible to believe him swept away beyond reason by any fanaticism or enthusiasm.

'You are not in the least like what I should have expected,' remarked the Earl thoughtfully.

'Indeed! May I ask in what respect?'

'Certainly. If you have not deceived yourself, you have been favoured far beyond ordinary men, in so far as you have been permitted to see into the secrets of the superhuman. You have had proof, absolute proof, you tell me, that what we call death is merely phenomenal, and that the spirit is—as our own religion teaches us—endowed with immortal life. You have witnessed miracles, yet, if you will pardon me for saying so, you seem little impressed by the solemnity, the awful import, of what you have seen.'

'Does it strike you in that way?' asked the young man, smiling. 'Well, I am honest; at any rate, honest enough to admit that the certainty of another world does not help me to explain the inconsistencies of this one, and that infinite life may only, after all, mean infinite *ennui*.'

'Surely,' cried the Earl, 'you cannot think *that!* Surely the assurance that personality is permanent explains everything, justifies everything! What is evil here will be set right. What is unexplainable in this life will be explained fully in another. The Divine Fatherhood will be justified to its children!'

As he spoke the old man rose to his feet in great agitation and stood looking down at Woodville, whose impassive demeanour underwent no change whatever.

'You are aware, no doubt,' said Woodville, 'that some of our Theosophists deny the existence of God altogether—that is to say, deny that God possesses any attributes of personality? I myself hold that opinion, since the Infinite is absolutely inconceivable and unthinkable.'

'Call it what you please—Infinite God or Infinite

Goodness, Infinite Law or Infinite Love—it amounts
to the same thing.'

'Just so,' returned the Theosophist, with a shrug
of the shoulders. 'To the Mystery which will never
be solved, here or yonder.'

'You yourself, in accepting miracles, admit the
solution?'

'Far from it. All that I admit, all that I know, is
that life is not merely corporeal, and that the universe
is full of intelligence which controls matter in a way
no known science can explain. How does that answer
my question? It does not answer it at all. If all
the said intelligences were beneficent, if all their
influence was for good, it would be another matter.
But the merest tyro in spirit-rapping is aware that
our ghostly friends are subject to the same infirmities
of character as ourselves; and no man who contem-
plates the universe can fail to see that it has no
consideration for human sentiment. Evil things, evil
acts, evil influences, are at work on every side—
disease, earthquake, pestilence attest their existence;
and really, there is no argument whatever in support
of the thesis that the operations of nature point to a
beneficent First Cause!'

Curious language, indeed, for the apostle of a new
religion! The Earl wondered more and more as he
listened, but at the same time he was impressed more
and more—as, doubtless, Woodville intended him to
be—by the absolute honesty of the speaker.

' After all,' continued Woodville, ' the whole question
is one of evidence. While speculation as to the
Absolute is mere waste of time, verification of
actual phenomena is at once interesting and scientific. If I can prove to you, as I hope to do, that
the soul survives the body, and is independent of
it——'

' If you can do that,' cried the Earl warmly, ' I
shall ask no more. I have faith in the Infinite
Goodness ! All I seek is some assurance to strengthen
that faith ; and the proof of personal immortality
would be, to *me*, at least, the crowning proof of the
beneficence of God.'

So saying, he held out his hand to Woodville, and
prepared to leave him for the night. The young man
rose to see him to the door.

' Good-night, my lord,' he said. ' Forgive my plain
speaking. I did not wish to impose upon your good
nature with any profession of an optimism I do not
feel. Although I am thoroughly convinced of the
mysterious influences surrounding us, although I am
personally conscious of them every moment that I
live, I have seen too much misery to be very sanguine
about the future, and my own experience, moreover,
has not been a very happy one.'

' I am sorry for that, Mr. Woodville,' returned the
Earl, pressing his hand. ' One so gifted, so favoured
as yourself, should certainly be happy.'

He was leaving the room, when a thought seemed

to occur to him, and he turned back, pointing to the door underneath the tapestry.

'I forgot to tell you, Mr. Woodville, that the room you are occupying has another exit, long disused. Under the tapestry here'—as he spoke he lifted the heavy hangings on the wall facing the fireplace—'is an old door. It opens right out on the battlement, but it is many a long year since anyone has turned the rusty old key.'

Holding up the tapestry with one hand, he touched the door with the other, and, reaching forward, attempted feebly to turn the key, which remained immovable in the lock.

'The tradition is,' he continued, 'that the unfortunate lady, of whom you have heard, used to meet her lover out yonder, passing out to the rendezvous by this door, and the tradition goes that her spirit still does so nightly. So strong is the belief in this tradition, that no member of my household cares to visit the battlement after nightfall.' He dropped the tapestry again, adding: 'You may sleep securely, knowing that no one can open that door from without. As for the mysterious lady——'

'I don't think she will trouble me,' said Woodville, smiling. 'If she does, I will receive her with all the respect due to a ghost of her years and experience.'

The Earl smiled also a little sadly, and then, with another gentle 'Good-night,' left the room, closing the door softly behind him.

Left once more alone, Woodville sat down before the fire, and remained for some time in deep thought, still smoking his cigar. Presently he rose again, threw the remains of the cigar into the fire, and began slowly walking up and down the chamber.

His manner was restless now, his look troubled. From time to time he paused as if listening, and then, with a deep-drawn breath, resumed his walk.

It was now past midnight, and not a sound disturbed the silence of the night.

Once more he approached the mirror and looked at himself; but there was no touch of pride or vanity in the gaze which he fixed upon the face in the glass—a pale, thoughtful face, with bright, wistful eyes, and sinister lines about the delicately-cut and mobile mouth. The black hair clustering round the high forehead was just threaded with gray, and it was the threads of gray hair, so unusual in a man of his years, that seemed to fascinate his regard.

'What does she think of me, I wonder?' he muttered to himself. 'Does she find me changed? Why should time spare *her* and play such tricks with *me?* I look ten years older, at the least.'

Again he resumed his monotonous march up and down the room, angrily now, with a dark frown upon his handsome face. Late as was the hour, he seemed to have no intention of retiring to rest.

Presently he approached the window and stood still,

as if listening. Then he drew the curtain back and looked out.

Just beyond the window was the battlemented roof, communicating by the flight of old stone steps with the terrace below, and far away over this roof was a distant prospect of park, greensward, and woodland glimmering faintly in the moonlight. Low down in the west hung the crescent moon, glimmering like a silver sickle in a field of misty blue.

Save the long-disused door underneath the tapestry, the only entrance to the room was by the door by which he had entered. It opened on the granite corridor, at the end of which was another door, leading on to the battlement.

For reasons of his own, Woodville was curious enough to leave the chamber, cross the corridor, and open the further door, emerging from which he stood on the battlement itself.

There he paused for some moments, looking down upon the shadowy vistas far below him ; then, quietly and stealthily, he descended the stone steps, and did not pause again until he reached the terrace.

All was very still, and the air was full of the heavy scent of flowers growing in the great stone urns and clustering on the walls. In two of the great modern windows opening on the terrace a light was burning, but scarcely had Woodville appeared when one of them was extinguished, as if some occupant of a chamber had retired to rest.

Very quietly, making little or no sound with his stealthy footfalls, he stole along the terrace until he reached the spot where it widened out from the drawing-rooms and led to the broad flight of marble steps descending to the open lawn in front of the modern mansion.

Following these steps, he gained the lawn, and, pausing in the shadow of a large lilac tree, he surveyed the façade, gleaming white in the moonlight.

His eyes glanced from window to window, resting at last on the one blind where the light was still burning.

An owl flitted past him, winging silently towards the dark turret tower, which rose like a black shadow to the left of the modern mansion, and the only sound in the air was the thin z-like cry of the bats, which flew high in the air between the lawn and the turret.

Minutes passed, and he still gazed, as if fascinated, on the lighted blind.

At last a shadow appeared behind the blind, the shadow of a woman, and he knew, by some subtle instinct, that the woman was Isabel Arlington.

He drew back under the darkness of the tree, and as he did so, the blind was drawn, the window opened, and Isabel leaned out, looking towards him.

The moon's rays fell upon her face, and upon a wrapper of some white material which she had thrown loosely around her.

Woodville did not stir, but stood, well concealed in

the shadow, with his eyes fixed upon her. He was too far away to distinguish her features, or to see exactly what she was doing, but she seemed to be gazing forth intently, spellbound, and listening, and, as she did so, Woodville also seemed under the influence of a similar attraction. His heart throbbed tumultuously through all his pulses, and a great wave of yearning filled his heart and flooded his dilated eyes.

He seemed to be drawing her towards him, and also to be drawn towards her, by some mysterious and irresistible force.

The spell was broken by another figure, which appeared behind Isabel in the lighted chamber, and, stealing forward, embraced her, and seemed persuading her to leave the window.

Woodville heard the faint sound of voices, but was too far away to distinguish what was said, or rather whispered. Almost immediately, however, the window was closed, the blinds drawn, and directly afterwards the light also disappeared.

For nearly a quarter of an hour Woodville remained in the same spot without stirring; then, quietly and stealthily as before, he reascended the steps, reached the terrace, and made his way back in the direction of the turret chamber.

As he passed the window where he had seen Isabel, he paused for a moment to listen, but all was quite still,

A few minutes later he climbed to the old battle-ment, and regained his solitary quarters.

CHAPTER VII.

ISABEL.

EARLY the next morning Woodville was astir, and long before the early breakfast hour he was out wandering in the park.

The sun was shining brightly, the morning air was alive with light and sound, and even amid the shadows of the great trees, where the dews were still sparkling like drops of gold, the warmth of the summer day was already felt. Here and there, where the groups of deer gathered,

'Twinkled the innumerable ear and tail.'

A drowsy murmur of life was heard everywhere, and, loud over all, from the interwoven branches came the clear, brooding cry of the stockdove, like a call from the glades of Sleep or Fairyland.

Accustomed to scenes so different, born and bred in a land where Nature is profuse even to luxuriance, Woodville could not fail to be charmed and attracted by the placid and gentle beauty of the scene around him.

Again and again he paused to look and listen.

Far as eye could see stretched the park, with its clusters of woodland, its shady colonnades, its open glades, and from almost every point of vantage a view could be had of the white mansion, with its long façade and stately terrace, and, beyond these, the dark outlines of the old castle and the turret tower.

About a quarter of a mile from the house was a large sheet of ornamental water, in the centre of which was an old group of stone statuary representing Tritons and Nereids, and surmounted by a semi-naked figure of Amphitrite. Around the margin were flowering shrubs of all kinds, and here and there was a garden-seat.

Tired of wandering to and fro, Woodville at last sat down, and amused himself by watching the swans and waterfowl which swam hither and thither on the lake.

He was seated thus, enjoying the beauty of the morning, when he suddenly became conscious that he was not alone. Unseen and unheard, like some creature of another world, Miss Arlington crossed the greensward, and stood before him, clad in a light morning dress, and carrying a bunch of white roses which she had just gathered. Although the sun was burning brightly, her head was uncovered, and the full rays of light fell upon her dark, luxuriant hair and beautiful face, which was pale with mingled pride and anger.

The moment he saw her, Woodville rose politely, raising his hat. She took no notice of his greeting,

6

but, fixing her eyes on his, demanded, in a voice which trembled with agitation :

'Why did you come here?'

For a moment he seemed surprised, and was at a loss how to reply. Still more emphatically and angrily, though without raising her voice, she repeated the question :

'Why did you come here?'

This time he was master of himself, and smiled quietly.

'I do not quite understand you,' he said gently.

At a glance he saw that she was greatly agitated, and could with difficulty calm herself sufficiently to meet his gaze.

'You understand me perfectly,' she answered, drooping her eyes and looking on the ground, only stealing quick, nervous glances at him from time to time. 'I insist upon an answer to my question.'

'Since you insist, Miss Arlington, I must obey,' said Woodville, still smiling. 'I came here to meet *you*.'

The answer seemed to surprise her. She had expected, no doubt, that he would prevaricate.

She drew a quick, startled breath, and seemed trying to speak again, but no words came.

'You see, I am quite frank with you,' he continued. 'If you will sit down and listen, I will explain my motives fully, such as they are. You will not? Then I will explain them all the same. Being

in England, and hearing that you were here, I could
not resist the temptation to see you again. Let me
take the opportunity of expressing my gratification at
finding you well and happy, and, if I may say so, as
beautiful as ever.'

There was no concealment now in the look of
admiration he cast upon her. But the look was not
merely one of admiration; it partook to some extent
of triumph and command. Conscious of this, her face
flushed angrily, and she was about to turn away, when
her strength seemed to fail her, and for a moment
she seemed on the point of bursting into tears.

But when he made a movement as if to support her,
she drew herself up proudly, and waved him back.

'You will go as you came, and at once,' she said,
adding, as he bent his head in apparent assent: 'No
one here knows that we have met before, and there is
no reason that they should know it. You can readily,
no doubt, invent an excuse for departing so suddenly.
If you decline to go, I shall have to tell my uncle that
I cannot remain.'

Woodville watched her intently, but it would have
been very difficult to divine his thoughts. His expression was one of surprise, mingled with a certain pain,
but he seemed, at the same time, to be quite confident
of his power over her, and of the strength of his own
position in regard to hers.

'Pray sit down in the shade,' he said softly,
motioning her to the garden-seat. 'Your head is

uncovered, I see, and the sun is very hot. Afterwards
I will do exactly as you wish. You have only to
command, and I promise to obey.'

Almost involuntarily she obeyed him, and sank into
the seat, trembling nervously, and averting her face.

The bunch of roses fell from her hand. He stooped
and offered them to her, but she did not take any
notice.

He retained the flowers, and held them to his face,
inhaling their scent as he continued :

'I see that I have blundered, and I am sorry.
Candidly, I did not expect to find you so bitter against
me. I am not conscious of having ever done you any
wrong; I have preserved since we parted in India the
memory of the one deep friendship of my life ; and I
thought that perhaps—forgive me for saying so much
—that you, too, might remember.'

He paused as if waiting for her to speak, but she
remained silent.

He placed the flowers by her side, and sat down ;
then, after a pause, he proceeded in his deep, musical
voice, with just an inflection, a half-tone, of foreign
accent.

' Had I guessed for a moment that my presence
would give you pain, I would have returned to India
without seeing you at all. All I can do now is to
express my regret, and ask your forgiveness. Be
assured also that I fully sympathize with your feelings
on this subject. I have no claim whatever upon your

friendship — none even upon your sympathy. I
possibly deserve neither, and since you deny me the
one, I shall never ask for the other.'

The tone in which he spoke, even more than the
words he used, was so gentle and respectful, that it
obviously made an impression on the hearer. She
glanced at him nervously, and then said, 'I understand now why you came. Why did you come under
an assumed name?'

'Did you not hear me explain?' asked Woodville
quickly. 'Since I last saw you, I have inherited a
small fortune from one of my father's relations, and
a condition attached to my taking it was that I should
take the donor's name as well. I did so willingly
enough, as you may believe, for you possibly remember that I was very poor. Henceforward, Miss
Arlington, I can live my own life, without any danger
of being mistaken for either a pauper or a fortune-
hunter.'

As he spoke, he watched her keenly, waiting for
the effect of his words, but she made no sign.

A long pause ensued; it was broken by Isabel, who
rose quietly, and walked slowly away.

Woodville remained seated, and watched her go.
She went about twenty yards along the water's edge,
and then paused nervously, and looked back and met
his eyes.

He sprang up with a cry, and approached with
outstretched hand.

'Why can we not be friends?' he cried. 'Why are you so cruel to me? Why do you drive me away from you as if my very presence was an insult—a contamination?'

'I do not wish to drive you away,' she answered, looking down at the water. 'All I know is that it is better we should not meet.'

'Why?'

'For the reasons that I gave you long ago; I do not trust you, and I have no faith in the things you profess to do.'

Woodville shrugged his shoulders and laughed.

'You share the opinion of your friends in Bombay —that I am a trickster, a charlatan?'

'I did not say that.'

'That is what you mean. Once, I believe, you judged me differently.'

'That is all over,' she replied, trembling nervously.

He was close to her now, his dark, wistful eyes fixed upon her face, which flushed beneath his gaze, as he said, in a low voice, which seemed to vibrate through her whole living frame: 'For me it will never be over, Isabel!'

'I forbid you to call me by that name!' she cried.

'As you will; but by whatever name I call you, I cannot forbear telling you that I am still unchanged. You resemble the Sultan's daughter, of whom you sang so sweetly yesterday. I am only the poor slave in the garden, whose sole happiness was to watch her

come and go. He was silent, and *I* can be silent—
but never forget that I love you; never forget that
mine is a love which can never pass away.'

' For Heaven's sake, leave me !' she cried, shrinking
from him. 'You don't know what you are saying—
you—— Go away, I implore you! If they should
see us here together——'

' I understand,' answered Woodville, 'and I will
go; but perhaps, before I leave this place, we shall
meet again ?'

' Perhaps ; but go now !' she said, in a low voice.

He gazed at her for a moment, and then walked
rapidly away. Quitting the shrubberies surrounding
the lake, he crossed the lawn leading to the terrace
of the mansion.

Only once glancing back, he saw the girl standing
where he had left her, looking after him. His face
brightened to a curious smile of triumph and exultation as he wandered on.

As he ascended the terrace steps, he came face to
face with Lord Dewsbury, who greeted him with a
stony British nod.

' Have you seen Miss Arlington ?' asked the young
lord.

' I think I caught a glimpse of her over yonder by
the lake,' replied Woodville carelessly, and passed on,
unconscious of, or indifferent to, the frown which his
answer called up on Dewsbury's face.

Reaching the terrace, he was passing by one of the

open French windows, when a voice called him by name; and, looking into the room, he saw the Apostle of the New Culture seated alone at breakfast. It was a large but cosy chamber, containing a number of small tables, and a large, well-provided centre table, at which the butler was presiding.

'Have you breakfasted?' asked Mervyn, holding out his hand. 'They've been wondering where you were. They've all had breakfast, I believe, except us two.'

Woodville sat down, and was soon discussing a substantial meal of coffee, dry toast, and new-laid eggs.

Mervyn, whose breakfast consisted of some very thin dry toast, and some weak claret and water, watched him with critical interest.

'I envy you your appetite, Mr. Woodville, and yet I *don't*. Eating is a disagreeable reminder that we are still mere animals. Why can't we exist on air and dew like the roses, if we must exist, which I take leave to question.'

The contrast between the speaker's airy affectation of manner, and the chubby, solid, clean-shaven face, amused Woodville, and he laughed gaily.

'I've an excellent appetite,' he said. 'Besides, I've been up and about for several hours.'

'And you can drink English coffee?' exclaimed Mervyn.

Woodville nodded, and called to the footman for another cup.

'My uncle is curious to know if you slept well last
night. I think he would be rather pleased than sorry
if he heard that you had been visited by the White
Ladye.'

'She left me severely alone,' replied Woodville,
'and I slept quite soundly. I generally do.'

CHAPTER VIII.

A TÊTE-À-TÊTE.

LATE that night, Lord Dewsbury received a wire
summoning him to Downing Street, for a private
interview with the chief of his party; so he rose
early and breakfasted, preparatory to driving to the
station and catching the morning train. The only
member of the family down to meet him was Lady
Carlotta. To his great annoyance, Isabel did not
appear.

'Tell her that I shall return this evening,' he said.
'I am sorry that I cannot see her before I go,' he
added irritably. 'How long does that fellow remain?'

'Mr. Woodville?' inquired Lottie. 'I am sure I
can't say, Frank; but I wish with all my heart that
he would go. But don't worry yourself about Isabel,
Frank. *She's* all right!'

'But why is she so changed? Since this man
came here, she has not been like the same girl. I am
perfectly certain that they have met before.'

'I dare say,' said Lottie; 'but, in any case, I am sure she dislikes him quite as much as you do.'

The young man looked rather dubious; but at that moment the carriage was announced, and there was only just time to catch the train. As he left the house, and was about to enter the carriage, he saw the man of whom he had spoken quietly regarding him from the terrace.

Their eyes met, and Woodville waved his hand in careless salutation.

'Curse the fellow!' muttered Dewsbury, as he drove away. 'I'm sure he is a scoundrel, and I don't like to leave him here with Isabel. Never mind; I'll demand a full explanation from her when I return.'

Meantime Woodville had turned into the breakfast-room, where he found Lady Carlotta in a brown study. She looked up as he entered, and greeted him quite sweetly.

'You'll have papa to yourself to-day, Mr. Woodville,' she said. 'Lord Dewsbury has gone to town, Miss Arlington has a nervous headache, and Mervyn and I are going to lunch at the Deanery, and go a round of parochial calls.'

'I shall be sorry to lose your society, Lady Carlotta,' returned Woodville; 'but even if I were quite solitary in this house, I could find plenty of occupation. The place is so peaceful, so beautiful, and among the books in the library alone one could pass many days without weariness.'

' Have you many friends in England?' asked Lottie,
after a pause.

'Very few. Why do you ask?'

'Nothing; only I was wondering.'

' Shall I tell you what you were wondering about?'
said Woodville, with a smile, sitting down and signal-
ling to the butler to bring him some coffee. 'You
were wondering, Lady Carlotta, how soon you would
be rid of a tiresome visitor.'

Lottie looked astonished, and Woodville quietly
proceeded :

'You may make your mind easy. I am going
almost immediately. If I remain at all, it is in
deference to your father's wishes.'

' Papa is so absurd !' cried the young lady im-
patiently.

' Thank you, Lady Carlotta,' said Woodville, laughing outright. ' You are frankness itself, and I am
not in the least annoyed. You may be still more
frank if you like without fear of giving me offence.
Why are you so anxious that I should go ?'

' Because——' Lottie hesitated, and bit her lip.

' Because,' said Woodville, ' you regard me as a
dangerous person ? Or because you are quite sceptical
as to the religion in which I am supposed to be an
adept? In the last case, be reassured ; I am almost
as sceptical as yourself. I have said as much to the
Earl. I have assured him that such supernatural
manifestations as I have myself seen interest me

very little, and leave me very doubtful as to their value.'

' What is it you are supposed to do ?' asked Lottie sharply. ' Turn tables, or something? It always seems to me that spirits, if they are spirits, behave very absurdly, and, at any rate, ever since papa has gone in for Theosophy, his conduct has been ridiculous. Then there is Isabel. She used to be as sceptical as I am, but, for some reason or other, she has got it into her head that there may be something in Theosophy after all, and that you could tell her something about her father.'

The butler had left the room, and Woodville was quietly sipping his coffee. He made no reply, but looked very mysterious.

' Suppose I could ?' he said, with the same quiet smile. ' I am perfectly convinced that Colonel Arlington, whether he is alive or dead, desires to communicate with his daughter, and that I shall be the fortunate medium of communication.'

' What !' cried Lottie. ' And yet you can talk about it so coolly! That is what frightens me in you, Mr. Woodville—you are so awfully cold-blooded !'

' I exist in two worlds, you see,' returned the Theosophist; ' while you, fortunately for yourself, exist only in one. Spiritual existences are so real to me, so ever present, as to have lost their power of surprising me. Even your White Ladye, if she condescended to visit me up yonder, would find me severely cool, and possibly critical about her looks and her wardrobe.'

They talked for a little longer in the same strain, and then Lottie left the room, with her dread and suspicion of Woodville increased tenfold.

For secret reasons of his own, or possibly out of sheer bravado, he seemed perfectly indifferent to the impression he created. Possibly this was one of the secrets of his influence. Had he taken himself more seriously, and assumed the airs of omniscience common to professional charlatans, he might have awakened a very different impression.

During the forenoon, Woodville had a long talk with Lord Wanborough in his study, after which the old man ordered his hack, and prepared to take his daily ride.

'I would ask you to accompany me,' he said, ' but I have to see my steward this afternoon on some matters of business, and you will find better entertainment at home. No doubt, Madame Obnoskin will join you at lunch, and you will find her society far more interesting than mine.'

Thus it happened that the two Theosophists found themselves alone together, almost for the first time. The Earl had ridden away, Mervyn and Lady Carlotta had gone to the village, and Isabel kept her room. This was exactly what Woodville wanted. During luncheon, of course, in the presence of the servants, there was no opportunity for private conversation,

and the two addressed each other with the formality
of comparative strangers ; but, luncheon over, they
walked out together, and found a quiet seat by the
lake, where they could converse undisturbed.

'At last!' said Madame Obnoskin, with a little
laugh, holding out her ringed hand with the manner
of an old comrade ; then, drawing from her pocket a
cigarette-case anu a match-box, both wrought in gold,
and adorned with the letter 'E' in rubies and diamonds, she selected a cigarette for herself, and invited
him to select another.

'I see,' observed Woodville, 'that you still preserve
the little *cadeau* of the Maharajah ?'

The Obnoskin nodded, and showed her white teeth,
while Woodville struck a match, lighted her cigarette,
and then his own.

'Well?' said the Obnoskin, blowing a wreath of
smoke, and looking through it with sparkling eyes.

'Well?' repeated Woodville, doing the same.

Both smiled, and then there was a long pause.

'How droll that we should meet here!' said the
Pole, at last. 'How still more droll that they should
think we have met for the first time! Ah, *mon ami*,
you have used me very cruelly! There was a time,
not so long ago, when you would not have cared for
so long a separation ; but since then——'

'Since then, my dear Eva, you have found company more attractive. Well, I do not blame you, nor
shall I blame you when the day comes that I have to·

say to you, "Accept my homage and my congratula-
tions, Madame la Comtesse." '

Madame Obnoskin smiled, and shrugged her pretty
shoulders.

'Perhaps that day will· never arrive. But, at any
rate, he is very good to me, is he not? My dear
Woodville, there is nothing in the world to compare
with a perfect English gentleman ! He treats me like
a princess, and he is shocked at nothing I say or do—
not even at my constant cigarettes !'

'It is unfortunate, however, is it not, that the
Earl's enthusiasm does not extend to the other
members of his household ?' said Woodville, with
a sarcastic smile.

The Obnoskin changed in a moment, and her calm,
almost 'purring' satisfaction gave place to malicious
anger.

'I hate them all !' she exclaimed ; ' the pert English
miss, his daughter, the proud, cold Miss Arlington,
the dull, imaginative fool who is her *fiancé*. Yes ; I
hate them all as cordially as they hate me ! But I
will prove to them who is the strongest. I will prove
to them who is mistress ! It is not I, but they, who
will be shown the door.'

'You think that Miss Arlington is cold ?' asked
Woodville quietly, without seeming to notice her
anger. 'My own impression of her is somewhat
different. She is certainly proud, as you say, but
cold, no !—except, of course, superficially.'

Something in his tone and manner arrested the attention of his companion, and checked her indignation.

'You are interested in Miss Arlington?' she asked.

'Exceedingly, since it was on *her* account that I came here.'

'Then it is as I suspected—you have met before?'

'Oh yes; in India, some time ago.'

The Obnoskin regarded him for some moments attentively, then, laughing lightly, touched him on the arm.

'What a fool I was not to understand!   You met in India, and there, where the climate is more favourable, the lady was more complaisant, and now—well, it is inconvenient when one has a *fiancé* to encounter an old lover.'

climate

'Your guess is not very clever,' said Woodville, without any sign of annoyance; 'for so experienced a woman as yourself, it is commonplace.   You are entirely wrong.   Miss Arlington is a young lady beyond reproach, and I have never been her lover.'

'*Vraiment!*' cried madame, smiling sceptically. 'Possibly, however, you hope to be?'

'Say I mean to be, and you will have hit the mark.'

'I think you will waste your time.   Miss Arlington is wise enough to appreciate her own good fortune. She is engaged to marry one of the richest men in England, and in due time she will be Lady Dewsbury.'

She was about to say more in the same strain, when, struck by a sudden change of manner in her companion, she cried : ' *Mon Dieu*, Woodville, what is the matter ?'

The man's face looked as black as night, his eyes flashed, his mouth was set fiercely, and with a savage gesture he had thrown his cigarette away. The storm lasted for a moment, but during that moment it was terrible.

Commanding himself with a violent effort, and forcing back his former supercilious smile, Woodville said :

' Once again, my dear Eva, your talk is not clever. Miss Arlington will never marry Lord Dewsbury !'

' And why not ?'

' Because it is my intention to prevent it.'

' And why, again ?'

' I will tell you—I will, in fact, be quite frank with you, since I stand in need of your assistance. We are rowing in one boat, my dear Eva. If Miss Arlington married Lord Dewsbury, *you* would never marry Lord Wanborough.'

' I am to infer, then, that you wish to marry her yourself ?'

' You may infer what you please; but still, again, you are not clever. I may have other designs, which are less conventional.'

' I don't understand you in the least,' cried Madame Obnoskin, ' unless—unless '—here she looked at him

7

nervously and anxiously—'you mean something really diabolical.'

'I see, you are qualifying in English morality,' said Woodville. 'Once upon a time you were not so particular. Forgive me for reminding you of the fact, which you seem to have forgotten.'

The Obnoskin shrugged her shoulders.

'The reminder is not very chivalric,' she returned; 'but let it pass. In what way do you wish me to assist you?'

'Oh, in the simplest way possible! You are anxious to convince the Earl of the truth of our religion. I am equally anxious to convince Miss Arlington. In carrying out what I may call our professional arrangements, we shall both be forwarding our private wishes.'

'You are simply impossible!' exclaimed madame. 'You constantly infer, in very bad taste, that our religion is one of imposture—the marvels which I myself have seen, the spiritual influence which has guided my whole life——'

'May I remind you,' said Woodville dryly, 'that you are not talking to the Earl of Wanborough? Between you and me, my dear Eva, there need be no concealments. Well, cards on the table, if you please. Miss Arlington already almost believes that her father, the missing traveller, still lives. I intend to convince her, with your assistance, that the belief is a certainty.'

'As before?' asked Madame Obnoskin nervously.

'As before.   In the only way possible.'

'Suppose we fail?'

'We shall not fail.'

'Let me implore you not to risk anything of the kind,' cried the lady, now greatly agitated.   'You know what took place at Petersburg; it may occur again, and ruin and disgrace would follow.   Besides, it is so horrible, so wicked !   You may despise me for my weakness, but I swear to you that I never think of these things without a shudder.   It seems tampering with holy mysteries, inviting the punishment of Heaven.   Besides, the very articles of our religion forbid us to resort to means so abominable, save in cases of extreme necessity.'

'This is one of them,' said Woodville firmly. 'Now, listen.   I myself know already, by a supernatural communication, that Colonel Arlington is alive.'

'A supernatural communication, my dear Woodville ?'

'Such scepticism is shocking in one of our faith ! Well, say a communication which is not supernatural. I *know* that Colonel Arlington is alive.'

'You know it !   How ?'

'From a correspondent in Thibet; one of our people.   Some months ago, before I left for England, I wrote to him, bidding him to keep watch, and should he ever receive news of the missing traveller, to give him what aid he could, and to inform me at once that he survived. Well, three days ago I received this.'

He drew from his breast-pocket a square sheet of flimsy paper. Unfolding it, he read aloud to his companion :

'The sahib you wrote about is lying in this house, struck down by fever. We have watched over him so far, as you commanded, and when he recovers we will help him to the frontier.'

'No,' he continued, as madame stretched out her hand for the despatch ; 'not that I doubt you, my dear Eva, but I run no risks.'

He drew out his matchbox, struck a match, and set fire to the paper, which fell in a little rain of gray ashes to the turf.

'If this is true——' began madame.

'It is certain !' said Woodville.

'Then you will tell Miss Arlington that her father lives ?'

'In my own time and way. You see, my dear Eva, how the celestial ones are working on our behalf. With this knowledge at our command even a miracle is possible. But time is precious, and we must not fritter it away. We must hasten, or Colonel Arlington may anticipate us by writing to his daughter !'

'I understand,' said the lady.

'I am sure you do,' said Woodville, with his own inscrutable smile.

'But,' she continued, 'I still fail to comprehend your object with regard to this girl.'

'It is not necessary that you should comprehend it,' returned Woodville, in a tone of quiet mastery. 'But you will work for me and aid me, for all that.'

'If money is your object, I may tell you at once that she is almost penniless.'

'My dear Obnoskin,' returned Woodville, with the same inscrutable smile, which lent no more cheering warmth to his dusky features than the play of sunshine lends to an icicle, 'I know it. I do not work for sordid gain.'

'I understand.'

Madame went pale, and, after a half-frightened glance around her, to assure herself that they were quite alone, continued in a lower tone:

'You love her?'

Woodville slightly shrugged his shoulders and elevated his eyebrows.

'Well, if love is too fine a name, you have a passion for her, which you would gratify at any cost.'

'Well?' asked Woodville, placidly turning his eyes upon her.

'It is madness—sheer raving madness! I beg you to abandon the idea!'

'Mad or sane,' said Woodville, still speaking tranquilly, 'it is the errand which has brought me here. Yes, I love her! Once I thought I had won her heart. Had I, indeed, done so, I would have been her servant, her slave, till life was done. Then, through the calumny of evil tongues, she learned to despise me. She drove me from her with insult. I pursued her; I accepted humiliation upon humiliation. Her door was closed in my face. My letters were returned unopened. At last, to avoid me, she came to England. I followed her; and I am here!'

'And now you are here?' asked his companion.

Woodville placidly puffed a circle of smoke into the air, and watched it melt.

'Now I am here,' he said, 'you will help me to bring Miss Arlington to her senses.'

'Is that really and truly the object with which you came all the way from India? The girl must have fascinated you indeed. Did you ever take so much trouble for a woman before?'

'Never,' he answered quietly. 'But I might have done so had I ever met one who was worth it!'

'You are not very polite to present company,' said madame.

'You asked a question,' responded Woodville, 'and I answered it. When I want a thing, I take enough trouble to get it. No more, because more is not needed; no less, because I never accept or recognise defeat in any project I have really made up my mind to carry through. Let me give you an illustration. Last year I went antelope-hunting in the Himalayas. I heard from the hill-tribes of a certain White Gazelle, so scarce, that it had hardly been seen within the

memory of living man. Snow-white, observe. It
was to be found only among the most inaccessible
peaks. My curiosity was excited. I resolved to kill
or capture this mysterious creature, even if I lost my
life in the attempt. I lived for months high up
among the snows, watching day and night. Nothing
to eat but the roots of plants, nothing to drink but
melted snow. I was worn to skin and bone, but I did
not despair.'

'All this for a wretched antelope?' exclaimed
madame.

'My dear Eva, the White Gazelle! On one occasion, at dead of night, I saw something white flash by
me. I fired, but it was gone. At last, when I had
almost abandoned hope, fortune favoured me. One
morning, at sunrise, I saw among the whiteness of
the snow something almost as white, nearly indis-
tinguishable against the shining background. There,
not a hundred yards away, was the creature I had
sought so long. As if spellbound, it came slowly
towards me, regarding me quite fearlessly, with soft,
still, almost human eyes, so beautiful that I felt
almost afraid. I hesitated. I watched it approach
till it was within a score of yards, then, quietly, steadfastly, I raised my rifle to my shoulder, took aim,
and——'

'You killed it?' cried the Obnoskin, with a little
scream.

'No; I let it go!'

'What a strange mixture you are!' she said, after a pause.

'Am I? Well, you see, I never resign pursuit. In the same spirit, I came here. Miss Arlington is my White Gazelle. Chance has favoured me again in the accidental meeting with that booby Darrell, in the interest Lord Wanborough takes in our religion. Your help is all I need now.'

'I have more than half a mind to refuse it,' said Madame Obnoskin. 'Philip, I *will* refuse it, unless you assure me——'

'Assure you of what?' asked Woodville, rising and looking down on her.

'That you mean no absolute harm to Miss Arlington.'

'You have developed a wonderful interest in Miss Arlington very suddenly,' he said, with a scarcely perceptible sneer.

'I do not like her,' said madame; 'I do not pretend to like her; but we are both women, and——'

'And you will help me, my dear Eva,' said Woodville. 'Do I mean her harm? I really don't know myself. I mean to make her love me. I mean to hold her pride, her heart, her life, in the hollow of my hand. What I shall do with them when I have won them is another question. Hark! what is that?'

A sound of carriage-wheels crunching the stones and gravel of the drive a quarter of a mile away reached their ears.

'Lady Carlotta is returning,' said Woodville. 'We had better go back to the house.'

CHAPTER IX.

INTUITIONS.

THE Earl of Wanborough saw very little company, and passed the greater part of every day in his library, which was rich in the literature of Theosophy and the occult sciences, only issuing thence to wander musingly in the gardens, or to ride on his hack about the park. After lunch that day, however, he invited Woodville to join him in a carriage drive, in company with Madame Obnoskin; and they had a pleasant excursion of several hours, during which the old man talked volubly on his favourite subject.

It was soon very clear which way the wind was blowing, so far as Madame Obnoskin was concerned. The handsome Pole, with her voluptuous and almost feline beauty, her gentle manners, her air of perfect sympathy allied to tender omniscience, had completely fascinated the old Earl, and the intellectual *rapprochement* between them was closely allied, on one side, at least, to a tenderer feeling. Her manner was that of a frank companion, as well as that of a thoughtful attendant. She watched every look, studied every word, without for a moment seeming obtrusive or over-zealous. And yet, with all this, she seemed to do exactly as she pleased, and preserved the ease and freedom of a thorough woman of the world.

When they had returned home, and Madame

Obnoskin had retired to her room, the Earl walked with Woodville on the terrace.

' A truly remarkable woman !' he said. ' I have seldom met a person of greater natural gifts or more perfect discernment. I cannot forget, Mr. Woodville, that she actually predicted your visit.'

' Yes ; it was singular,' returned Woodville, smiling to himself.

' It was revealed to her in a dream; that is to say, she had a warning, an intuition, that one of the Adept would shortly come to Wanborough, and at that time neither she nor I had ever heard your name, or had any suspicion that a stranger was coming here.'

' I understand such intuitions. I have often felt them myself, and they have generally been realized.'

' Just so—just so ! Evangeline—humph ! that is to say, Madame Obnoskin. Her spirit name is Evangeline,' explained the Earl rather anxiously.

' Quite so,' said Woodville, smiling. ' In the East, among people of our religion, such names are frequently employed in preference to the baptismal names. I was not in the least surprised when I heard you so address Madame Obnoskin.'

The Earl looked somewhat relieved, and Woodville continued :

' Madame has resided with your family for some time ?'

' Yes ; for several weeks, as a visitor—merely as a

visitor. At my request, she has from time to time prolonged her stay. But she is sensitive, very sensitive, and though she is strongly attached to my daughter, I regret to say that the feeling is not reciprocated. Lady Carlotta, in fact, has conceived a strong dislike to Madame Obnoskin.'

'You surprise me! For what possible reason?'

'Chiefly, I believe, because Evangeline—hem!— Madame Obnoskin is a Theosophist. These young people are so sceptical, they believe in nothing, care for nothing, save what is purely conventional.'

'Miss Arlington—is she of the same way of thinking?'

'On this one subject, yes,' replied the Earl. 'She also is strongly prejudiced against Theosophists and Theosophy. Then again, there is Lord Dewsbury. On more than one occasion he has almost told me to my face that I am *non compos mentis*.'

'The way of the world,' said Woodville, shrugging his shoulders. 'Politics, my lord, is no school for either religion or philosophy. Every great and living faith has been thus despised, every discovery, of even science itself, has had to survive the contempt of the great majority. I am not at all surprised that Lord Dewsbury should deny what he does not understand; but with Miss Arlington the case is very different. She has a strangely spiritual face, and she must, I am sure, be subject to the subtlest spiritual influences.'

'She is a noble girl,' cried the Earl warmly; 'and

spiritual, as you say, in the extreme. But one thing alone absorbs her whole nature—the dream, the hopeless dream, that her father will return.'

'Is there no possibility that he survives ?'

'It is possible, of course, but most improbable. Two years have now passed since he disappeared, and though every inquiry has been made, both privately and at the instance of the Royal Geographical Society, it has been quite useless. I have no doubt myself that he has perished.'

Woodville remained silent for a time, as if plunged in deep thought; then he said, in a tone more serious than was common to him :

'Surely the religion which Miss Arlington despises might help to set her mind at rest ? It is in cases like these that Theosophy has worked its great wonders.'

'Do you really mean that ?' cried the Earl, looking at Woodville in agitated surprise. 'Do you really think it possible that——'

'I think that the affair is simple enough,' replied Woodville. 'Whether Colonel Arlington is alive or dead, whether his Upadana is still allied to mortality, or free of its functions, he still exists as a spiritual being, and it is in the power of Theosophy to ascertain the truth concerning him by actual communication.'

The old man looked startled, almost stupefied, and could find no words to express his surprise. Sinking upon one of the terrace seats, he passed his thin hand nervously over his forehead, and then gazed wistfully at the calm, impassive countenance of his companion.

At that very moment, Woodville himself started, and made a gesture as if enjoining silence.

Standing just within the open window of the drawing-room, aware of every word that Woodville had said concerning her father, was Isabel herself.

Her face was pale as death, her eyes dilated, and she was gazing at Woodville in mingled wonder and terror.

'Isabel, my child,' cried the Earl, rising and moving towards her, 'you were listening? You heard what Mr. Woodville said ?'

Without answering, Isabel continued to look at Woodville, and her expression was now almost imploring; then, with a low cry, she turned away, and sinking into a large settee within the embrasure of the window, seemed about to lose consciousness.

Trembling like a leaf, the Earl bent over her, and took her hand, while Woodville, now greatly agitated himself, watched her with keen solicitude.

'She is fainting!' cried the Earl. 'Isabel, my child !'

At this moment another person appeared upon the scene—Lord Dewsbury, who ran from the further end of the long drawing-room, where he had been reading a newspaper, and, kneeling by Isabel, supported her in his arms.

'What is the matter?' he asked anxiously. 'She was all right only a few minutes ago. She strolled over to the window, and then——'

As he spoke, Isabel revived, and, releasing herself from Dewsbury's embrace, rose nervously to her feet.

'It is nothing, Frank,' she said. 'I felt a little faint, that is all. I'm quite well now,' she added, forcing a faint smile.

'Shall I get you a glass of wine?' asked Dewsbury,

'No, thank you. A glass of water.'

And as the young man turned away to procure it, she clung to the Earl's arm, and whispered, 'Please say nothing of this to Frank.'

CHAPTER X.

PREMONITIONS.

THE next morning, Woodville did not appear at the breakfast-table, but sent a polite message to the Earl that he had slept very badly, and was indisposed.

Not until the afternoon did he descend from his room. He found his host alone in the drawing-room, seated near the window, and wistfully gazing out on a dreary prospect of flying vapour and falling rain.

'I was about to send up to you, Mr. Woodville,' said the Earl, 'to inquire if you were better. I should have come myself, but I feared to disturb you.'

As he spoke, he was arrested by the expression of

the young man's face, which was very pale, worn and troubled.

'There is not much the matter,' replied Woodville. 'I am absurdly sensitive to atmospheric changes, and your climate, when it is at its worst, depresses me. I am usually a sound sleeper, but last night——'

climate

He paused, with a slight shiver; then, sinking into a chair, inquired in a low voice, 'You observed nothing unusual during the night?'

'Nothing,' answered the Earl. 'The rain fell heavily, that was all; but I was not disturbed in any way.'

'That is singular,' said Woodville, and seemed plunged in thought.

The Earl watched him anxiously for some moments, and then inquired, 'What do you think is singular, Mr. Woodville?'

Woodville did not immediately reply, but remained in deep abstraction.

'I think I had better return to London,' he said, at last, passing his hand nervously across his forehead.

'Return to London? So soon; and before'——

'Before my visit leads to any more mischief,' cried Woodville, rising and pacing up and down the room. 'I know now, I am certain, that something strange is about to happen—what, I cannot tell. I am a perfect child in these matters, though I am, unfortunately, a powerful medium for spiritual influences. It is better, far better, that the thing should go no further; and so, with your permission, I will leave your house this evening.'

'Pray do not think of it!' said the Earl. 'Remember your promise! If, as you imply, some extraordinary communication has come to you, that is all the more reason that you should remain, and permit us, possibly, to share your knowledge.'

'Long experience has taught me,' answered Woodville bitterly, 'to have little or no faith in these premonitions. They may mean nothing, or they may mean everything. I will tell you frankly what has occurred. I had just fallen asleep, when I was awakened by something like a cold human hand being passed over my face. I opened my eyes, and saw nothing. The rain was beating on the windows, and the wind was moaning loudly. As I lay listening, I became conscious of feet moving up and down the corridor, then of a low sobbing, as of some human creature. I sprang up, opened the door, and entered the corridor. I may tell you that I was not in the least nervous, though I thought of your ancestral ghost, the White Lady. I closed the door, and returned into the room. The air seemed full of voices. Then I heard, as clearly as I hear my own voice now, a voice cry, "Isabel! Isabel!" I should know that voice if I heard it anywhere; it was the deep, low voice of a man.'

Trembling like a leaf, and lost in deepest amaze, the Earl listened.

'Good Heaven!' he murmured. 'And then—and then——'

'Then the usual saturnalia, which so often renders these manifestations contemptible, began, and disturbed me for hours. The voices continued, crying sometimes, sometimes laughing, as if the turret were peopled with demons; but from time to time I heard the voice of which I have spoken repeating the same word, "Isabel." I was naturally excited, of course, but I exerted all my will-power to discover the source of the voice. For a moment I succeeded. Suddenly, for a moment only, I saw, or thought I saw, a face in the darkness—the face of a man, gray-haired, gray-bearded, and clad in some filmy raiment.'

'Arlington!' cried the Earl, panting, as if for breath.

'Heaven knows! I should warn you that these apparitions are often utterly delusive. It is in the power of disembodied spirits, good or evil, to assume corporeal likenesses, in order to influence and amaze the human mind. The whole business is ugly, and as unsatisfactory as it is ugly, and that is why I suggest that it should go no further.'

'What you tell me is amazing,' said the Earl. 'You are sure, quite sure, that you were under no delusion?'

Woodville gave a curious laugh.

'In such matters as these I am not likely to be

8

deluded,' he replied. 'I saw and heard exactly what I have described.'

'And how do you explain it? What, I mean, do you think that it portends?'

'I would rather not answer that question,' returned Woodville.

'Let me beg you to do so!'

'My explanation, I have no doubt, would only provoke the ridicule of most people,' said Woodville, hesitating. 'You, I know, are different; but ever since I came here, I have been conscious, as you know, of very strong prejudice and antipathy. That is another reason why I would rather take my departure.'

'Mr. Woodville,' said the Earl solemnly, 'you may be perfectly sure of my faith in you personally, and of my deep interest in the subtle and mysterious truths in which you are an adept. I must beg of you as a gentleman, as a man of honour, as a friend, not to withhold from me any knowledge which may affect my happiness, or the happiness of anyone dear to me. Tell me, I beg you, what is in your mind.'

'Since you put it in that way, my lord,' answered Woodville, 'I will answer you. I think that this house is surrounded by disembodied spirits, and that, through their agency, it may be possible to ascertain, once and for ever, the fate of Colonel Arlington.'

'If the vision you saw was that of my kinsman himself, would it not portend the worst?'

'By no means,' replied the Theosophist. 'These apparitions are not necessarily those of the dead. The astral body can separate itself from the corporeal body—in sleep, for example—and yet project the image of the latter while it is still living. But it is because I am uncertain of the truth in this instance that I dread proceeding further. I should never forgive myself if I were the means of communicating news of more sorrow and disaster.'

'Whatever the truth may be,' said the Earl resolutely, 'it is well that we should know it, and, in any case, why should we flinch if the very messenger of Death brought proof of the soul's immortality? Think what a victory it would be to convince the most blind, the most sceptical, of this Divine truth; and do not, I entreat you, leave us in uncertainty or despair!'

After much apparent hesitation, Woodville at last consented to postpone his departure until he had endeavoured to procure, in the presence of the Earl and his immediate friends, some kind of manifestation. It was agreed that the experiment should be made that very evening; but before anything was finally decided, Woodville insisted on an interview with Miss Arlington.

'I wish to ascertain,' he said, 'if she has received any intimation, however slight, from the mysterious presences now surrounding her, and I may tell you frankly that I rely far more upon her power than on

my own to bring our inquiry to a satisfactory conclusion.'

'I will send her to you at once,' returned the Earl
eagerly. 'Fortunately, Dewsbury has ridden over
to the village with my nephew; and as for Isabel, I
have no doubt that she will grant you the interview
you seek.'

Left alone, Woodville walked up and down the
drawing-room in no little agitation.

His look was that of a man undergoing some
terrible mental struggle. From time to time he
paused, listening eagerly, and when at last the door
opened, he turned with an exclamation.

To his disappointment, however, the new-comer was
only Madame Obnoskin.

She entered the room quickly and stealthily, closing
the door behind her.

'What has happened?' she asked, sinking her voice
to a whisper. 'I have just met the Earl, and he
seemed terribly agitated. All I could gather from him
was that you had made some remarkable communication.'

'Do not question me now,' answered Woodville,
frowning. 'Go away. I am waiting here for Miss
Arlington.'

'But what is it?' she persisted. 'You yourself
look pale and agitated. My dear Woodville——'

At that moment the door opened again, and Isabel
herself appeared.

She paused a moment on seeing that Woodville was not alone; then, with the proud and haughty bearing peculiar to her in his presence, she advanced into the room, and said quietly, 'You sent for me? What is it you wish to say to me?'

Never had she appeared so cold, so antipathetic. There was something almost contemptuous in her very tone, and her face was pale with anger.

'Will you leave us, madame?' said Woodville. And, without a word, Madame Obnoskin left the room.

There was a pause, during which the young girl kept her eyes fixed on Woodville, holding her head erect, and compressing her lips with cold determination. He offered her a chair; she declined it with an impatient gesture, and waited haughtily for him to break the silence.

'Possibly,' he said, 'the Earl has explained to you why I wished to see you?'

'He has explained nothing,' was her reply. 'He has merely hinted that you desired a private meeting, because you had some important communication to make to me.'

'In that case, I am at a disadvantage. I fear also from your manner that I am still labouring under your displeasure.'

'Kindly leave me out of the question,' answered Isabel.

'Pardon me,' said Woodville; 'that is impossible. What I have to say concerns you only. Am I right or wrong in assuming that you were anxious, until a few hours ago, to be assured as to the fate of one who is very dear to you, and that you fancied, rightly or wrongly, that I could give you that assurance ?'

Isabel trembled, her face grew very pale; but she answered with the same coldness and hauteur : 'Whatever I may have thought, I have changed my mind. I have no faith whatever in your power to help me. I feel for such pretensions as yours only contempt, and I decline to countenance your deceptions in any way.'

Their eyes met, and Woodville, now quite master of himself, smiled quietly.

'In that case I had better say no more. I have made a mistake. I did not think that you were quite so bitter against me.'

'I am neither bitter nor angry,' returned the girl proudly.

'You despise me too completely!'

'At any rate, I despise the impostures by which you live. I desired you to leave this place; you have remained. I have avoided you ; you have presumed, again and again, to remind me of your presence. It is cowardly of you to presume upon your influence in this house in order to put me to humiliation.'

'I quite understand,' said Woodville, still with his dark eyes fixed upon her. 'It is the voice of Miss Arlington which speaks, but the spirit is that of Lord Dewsbury.'

Isabel's eyes flushed angrily, and she made a movement as if to leave the room, but, turning quickly,
she replied : 'You should have understood that my
whole nature revolted against everything you say
and do. You would not have remained if you had
been—a gentleman. You would have known that
either you or I must go.'

'Pray do not distress yourself,' said Woodville, as if
deeply wounded. 'After what you have said, I shall
certainly not remain. I had already arranged to go,
when I yielded to Lord Wanborough's entreaties, and
delayed.'

'Lord Wanborough does not know you; he believes
in your impostures, which I think blasphemous. Is
that all you wish to say to me?' she added.

'I think so,' said Woodville. 'Only, before we part,
I should like to ask you one question.'

Isabel waited, and he continued : 'Last night,
between midnight and one o'clock, were you awake or
sleeping? And if awake, did you observe anything
unusual?'

Woodville himself was surprised at the effect of the
question. Isabel uttered a low cry, and pressed her
hand upon her bosom, while her eyes filled with tears.

'Let me go!' she cried faintly, turning to the door.

Before she could resist, Woodville had stepped
forward, taken both her hands in his, and was gazing
intently into her face.

'For God's sake,' he whispered, 'answer me!'

She scarcely seemed to hear; all her thought seemed concentrated on something terrible. Her lips quivered; she shivered from head to foot.

'Look at me, and answer.'

As if involuntarily, her eyes looked into his, while she struggled to release herself from his hold. All her strength and pride seemed to have fled. She had changed from a proud, determined woman into a weak, hysterical girl.

'Father—father!' she moaned, sinking on a settee, and covering her face with her hands.

CHAPTER XI.

WEAVING THE WEB.

WOODVILLE watched her for some moments with an expression of mingled triumph and pity; then he bent over her, and stretched out his arms as if to embrace her, and so calm her sorrow.

She sprang up as if stung, and, with the tears streaming down her beautiful face, confronted him angrily.

'Do not presume upon my weakness!' she cried. 'If you knew how all my nature revolts against you, you would understand why I wish never to see your face again.'

'How have I offended you?' asked Woodville gently.

'I believe you to be utterly false and cruel. I am certain that what took place last night was your doing —a falsehood, a trick, like all the rest.'

Woodville shrugged his shoulders.

'You have not yet told me what *did* take place. Whatever it was, I am sorry, since it has caused you so much distress. But since my very solicitude on your account seems an offence to you, since my very anxiety to serve you is so misconstrued, I have really no more to say, except this—if we must part, let it be in friendship, not in anger.'

And he held out his hand, as if inviting her to say farewell. She did not take the hand, but, turning her head away, said in a low voice :

'Can you swear to me, on your honour, that you know nothing of what took place last night—that you had no part in it—that it was not a device to terrify and deceive me ?'

'Certainly,' he replied. 'I can go further than that, and swear that I am entirely ignorant of what occurred.'

'Then why did you ask me whether, between midnight and one o'clock, I observed anything unusual ?'

'Because I had a strange experience of my own, and was curious to ascertain how far the same phenomena had presented themselves to *you*. That is why I asked for this interview ; not, believe me, because I wished to run the risk of your displeasure.'

He then rapidly described to her, in much the same language as he had used to the Earl, what he had heard and seen in the turret chamber.

She listened breathlessly, and when he described the voice which had called her name, and the apparition which had followed, she uttered a low cry, and wrung her hands.

'It was my father!' she cried. 'He came to *me* also. I did not see his face, but I heard his voice crying, "Isabel, Isabel!" You have told my guardian of this?' she added.

'I have told the Earl everything,' replied Woodville. 'I have told him also that I have no faith in these manifestations, that they are, and have ever been, hateful to me. See,' he continued more passionately, 'what they have done for me already! They have made you shrink from and despise me; they have made you think me infamous! Even now there is a doubt rankling in your mind—a doubt whether or not I am the meanest of mankind, capable of playing upon your holiest feelings, and of inventing these manifestations in order to terrify you.'

He paused, watching her eagerly.

She was now comparatively calm, but she avoided his gaze, and made no answer.

'Let it end here!' he cried. 'Good-bye!'

And he made a movement as if to quit the room.

Simultaneously she rose, and walked slowly to the window, making no attempt to detain him.

He paused irresolutely, looked at her, and then, mastered by a sudden impulse, approached her again.

'Forgive me, Miss Arlington!' he cried. 'I have been like an evil shadow on your young life. I should never have come here. I should never have tried to revive in your heart a feeling which was long dead. I was a fool for my pains, but I have been punished—cruelly punished!'

Still not looking at him, but gazing sadly out on the dreary landscape of mist and rain, she said, quietly, as if speaking to herself, 'When you leave this place, what will you do?'

'God knows!' he answered. 'But set your mind at rest; you will never be troubled with me again!'

She turned, and looked him in the face with an expression so sad, and yet so penetrating, that his eyes fell.

'I wish I could believe in you, but I cannot,' she said. 'Even if things which have happened to me are real, I am sure that they are evil. I have prayed God to deliver me from them, and from *you*.'

'Since you hate me so much——'

'I do not hate you, Mr. Woodville. I pity you too much for that. If you have deceived me, as I instinctively believe——'

He interrupted her with an angry exclamation.

'Judge me as you please! Why should I defend myself, since I am already condemned? It is the old story, Miss Arlington! Why should you trouble to

wear a mask ?   I stand in the way of your good fortune,
and you wish to get rid of me, in deference to the
scruples of Lord Dewsbury.'

Her face flushed angrily, and she motioned him to
silence ; but he paid no attention.   His passion
seemed now thoroughly aroused, and he was now
no longer master of himself.

'You have been cruelly frank with me ; let me be
equally frank with you.   When we first met, out
yonder in India, you were less fortunate, and I was
less despised.   You showed no anger *then*, when I
told you of my devotion.   You taught me to care for
you.   Afterwards, through the calumnies of your
friends, you turned away from me.   You came to
England, you forgot that I existed, you found another
lover, rich and powerful.   The old story, as I have
said !   But there is a new side to the story, after all.
We met once again, and I tell you now that we have
met never to part again, save by my wish and will.'

ominous/ threatening

'What do you mean ?' cried Isabel.   'You and I
are nothing to each other.'

'We are nothing or everything to each other, just
as I choose,' answered Woodville sternly.   'It will be
well for you, perhaps, if my *choice* is to leave you.   I
am as proud as you are, but my pride, unlike yours,
is the pride of power.   You say you know me.   You
never were more grievously mistaken.   If you *did*
know me, you would think twice before treating me
like a dog !'

Surprised and indignant at this unexpected tirade, Isabel once or twice attempted to speak; but before she could find words, Woodville had turned away. Crossing the room to the fireplace, he threw himself into a chair, and covered his face with his right hand.

Several minutes passed, and neither of the two stirred or spoke. At last the silence was broken by Isabel.

' Mr. Woodville !'

He did not seem to hear.

' Mr. Woodville !' she repeated, approaching him quietly.

He drew his hand from his face, and looked at her.

' We are both to blame,' she continued. ' I should not have spoken as I did; and you—you should not have reproached me unjustly. I hope you will not go away—at least, not yet.'

So saying, she left the room.

No sooner had the door closed upon her, than Woodville rose to his feet, his features breaking into a sardonic smile.

A short time afterwards, when the Earl returned to question him as to the result of the interview, Woodville said quietly:

' I shall not leave you to-night. Miss Arlington has asked me to remain.'

CHAPTER XII.

THE APPARITION.

'DR. DARLEY, Mrs. Darley, and Miss Olive Darley,' chanted the footman.

Lottie rose from her seat in the white gallery, and welcomed the new-comers.

'Good-evening, Dean.'

'Good-evening, Lady Carlotta. Permit me to introduce my daughter, Olive, whom I have taken the liberty to bring with me to-night, as she is profoundly interested in Theosophy. The Earl told me in his letter that he was in hopes that your visitor, Mr. Woodville, would perhaps produce some sort of a manifestation to-night.'

'I believe there is going to be some sort of rubbish of that kind,' said Lottie, 'if the spirits, or the shining presences, or whatever they call them, are propitious.'

'You are not a believer, Lady Carlotta?' asked Miss Darley.

She was a distinctly pretty girl, with a rather priggish manner, and was newly emancipated from Girton. As she spoke, she fixed a pair of *pince-nez* on her supercilious little nose.

'In Theosophy? No, I certainly am not.'

'I have not yet arrived at a satisfactory solution of the mystery,' said Miss Darley, rather with the air of

addressing a numerous audience from a platform. 'It
is a wide subject, and one requiring considerable time
and thought.'

Lottie shrugged her shoulders. Problems requiring
time and thought were not in her line.

'I will let papa and Miss Arlington know you are
here, Dean, if you will excuse me for a moment.'

She left the room, and the Dean turned to his wife,
a large and severe-looking lady, who had taken a seat
near the window.

'My dear,' he remarked, 'you look nervous !'

'I have misgivings,' said Mrs. Darley, in a deep
bass voice, which accorded with her physical propor-
tions. 'I doubt the propriety of our being present on
such an occasion.'

'It is out of the merest curiosity, my dear !'

'We are warned,' proceeded the lady, 'to have
nothing to do with profane and pagan mysteries !'

'Really, my dear,' said the Dean mildly, 'you
exaggerate the importance of the matter. We are
here to witness a sort of conjuring entertainment, that
is all. My child,' he continued to Olive, who had
gone to a table and taken up a book, 'what are you
reading ?'

'The life of Paracelsus, papa.'

'Para—who ?' inquired Mrs. Darley.

'Paracelsus, mamma.'

'And who was *he* ?'

'Paracelsus ? A mediæval physician, mamma,

who professed to have discovered the philosopher's stone.'

'He was not, I presume, a Churchman?'

'Well, no,' said Olive, with a smile of gently pitying superiority; 'hardly. The Church, as we understand it, hardly existed then. Here he is, seated on a stool, surrounded by a lot of little devils with tails.'

'Olive,' exclaimed the elder lady, in tones about an octave lower than usual, 'close that book!'

'Professor Marrables!' said the footman, appearing again at the door.

Mrs. Darley started and glared.

'Dean, do you hear? Professor Marrables?'

'Yes, yes, my dear,' said the Dean hastily and soothingly.

'The writer of those dreadful books! Are you aware of what he is?—a materialist, an Atheist!'

'Nothing of the kind, mamma,' said Olive, in a sharp undertone. 'Professor Marrables is an agnostic!'

'And what is the difference, pray?'

'A materialist is one who says that he knows everything; an agnostic is one who says he knows nothing. Do speak to him, papa. We heard so much about him at Girton.'

The subject of debate, a very tall, lank, angular old gentleman, with a shining bald head and a quizzically benevolent aspect, dressed in an evening suit, which might have been fashionable somewhere about the forties, had ambled into the drawing-room, and collided with a group of statuary, to which he had addressed a polite apology, delivered in a high-pitched, piping whisper, before he had readjusted his spectacles and determined the real nature of the obstacle.

'Good-evening, my dear sir,' said the Dean, approaching him. 'I presume you have come on the same errand as myself.'

'What is your errand?' piped the scientist, blinking vacantly.

'To meet the eminent Theosophist, Mr. Woodville. A very remarkable man, I am told.'

'Just so,' said Mr. Marrables. 'Living in the near neighbourhood, and being an old college friend of his lordship's, I have come for that purpose, on his invitation.'

'May I ask if Theosophy interests you?'

'It professes,' said the Professor, 'to have a scientific basis, and, as a humble student of nature, I am always ready to learn.'

'Quite so,' said the Dean—'quite so, though I suppose your own conclusions——'

'I am too old to have arrived at any conclusions,' said the scientist, with a faint little chirp of laughter. 'That is a privilege reserved for very young people.'

'Very true, sir,' said the Dean, with an approving smile. 'We have,' he added, with sudden gravity, 'but one light to help us.'

'Precisely,' said the Professor. 'The light of truth.'

9

'Exactly,' said the Dean.   'The light of truth.'

'In other words,' piped the Professor, crossing his long, ungainly legs—'the light of Science.'   The Dean started and stared.   'For many centuries the Spirit of Humanity has wasted its energies upon the search of the Unknown, the Unknowable.   Beguiled by various forms of anthropomorphism, misled by a blind and ignorant clergy——'

'A blind and ignorant clergy!' echoed Mrs. Darley.

'Sir!' cried the Dean, with as near an approach to fierceness of tone and manner as the good old gentleman could accomplish.

The Professor rose, peered at him from head to foot, and back again, and then piped apologetically:

'If I am addressing a member of the Church, let me apologize.'

'My name is Darley, sir,' said the Dean, rather with the air of delivering a challenge to mortal combat; 'Dr. Darley, Dean of Wanborough.'

'The Dean of Wanborough!   Dear me!' said the Professor in evident distress.   'Bless my soul!   I beg your pardon, sir.   I am very short-sighted, and I did not at first perceive——'

The Dean waved him away.

'Say no more, sir—say no more, I beg.'

And he strode across the room, and joined his wife and daughter.

'After this, I presume you will return home at once?' said Mrs. Darley.

'What nonsense, mamma!' said Olive. 'It was merely a mistake.'

'A blind and ignorant clergy!' intoned Mrs. Darley.

'A mere figure of speech, my dear,' said the Dean. 'In these days we must be tolerant. One meets these people everywhere, even at the table of the Bishop. . . . My dear Miss Arlington, you are well, I trust? Professor Marrables, I believe?' he added severely, noticing the direction of Isabel's glance.

'The *great* Professor Marrables!' said Madame Obnoskin, who had entered the room with Isabel and Lottie, speaking in an awe-struck whisper, carefully calculated to reach the old gentleman's ears, and sailing forward with extended hand.

'My dear madam,' he said, with his peculiar little chuckle, 'the epithet is misapplied.'

'Indéed, no,' said the lady. 'May I introduce myself? Madame Obnoskin. Perhaps you have heard of me?'

'I think so,' said Marrables, tapping his forehead! 'in connection with—— Dear me!'

'Theosophy,' said madame. 'It has much in connection with natural science, in which you are so distinguished.'

'True. But our humble labours are merely experimental, while yours embrace enormous generalizations.'

At this moment Woodville entered the drawing-room. His face betrayed nothing, but it was with almost much surprise as pleasure that he beheld Isabel.

Dressed in a robe of white silk, with no ornament
but a few white and red roses, she had never seemed
more beautiful, and, strangely enough, all traces of
pain and agitation had disappeared from her face, and
she was talking quite cheerfully with Olive Darley.

The Dean was sitting apart with Mrs. Darley,
casting severe glances from time to time at Professor
Marrables, who was in animated conversation with
Madame Obnoskin and the master of the house.

'But, of course, my dear professor,' Madame Obnoskin was saying, 'you believe that the Soul exists?'

The Professor smiled—the secret, self-satisfied,
sceptical smile of science; then, hesitating for a
moment, and blinking at the fair Pole like a benignant
owl, he said, in his thin piping voice, with his little
deprecating cough, 'Hem! I have been told so. I
have never,' he added, with a quiet chuckle, 'verified
the fact. You see, my dear lady, my investigations
are chiefly confined to such phenomena as are revealed
by the microscope.'

Not at all shocked, the Obnoskin tapped him playfully with her fan, and then beckoned Woodville to
join them.

'These dreadful men of science!' she cried, as
Woodville approached the group, 'they believe actually
nothing!'

'Pardon me again,' chirped the Professor. 'To
believe anything may be difficult, but to believe *nothing*
is impossible. But, after all, what do our beliefs

matter? How should mere ants on an ant-heap presume to criticise the great mystery of the universe?'

'Is it not equally presumptuous,' said Woodville,
with a smile, 'to insist too strenuously, as some of us
do, on our own insignificance? We may resemble
ants on an ant-heap, but surely we are not complimentary to the Power which created us when we
assume that we are nothing more.'

'Is it necessary that we should be complimentary?'
laughed Marrables.

'Alter the word, my dear sir, and say respectful.
It is better, with the theologians, to assume that we
are undeveloped angels than to argue with the
materialists that we are mere automata. There is
nothing so demoralizing or so paralyzing to all
human effort as to assume that we are of little or no
importance in the scheme of Nature.'

'That is true enough, Mr. Woodville,' returned the
Professor; 'but no one doubts the importance of
humanity as a link in the chain.'

'As the highest and most wonderful of phenomena!'
broke in the Earl, who had joined the group. 'You
are quite right, Mr. Woodville. The higher we
estimate our own humanity, the nearer we come to
God.'

During this conversation, Woodville had been
quietly observing Isabel. She had not looked up at
his entrance, but a slight flush had come upon her
face, and he knew that she was conscious of his

presence. Without a shadow of annoyance, or even constraint, she continued her conversation with Miss Darley.

The dinner passed off very quietly; but never, since his arrival at the Castle, had Woodville talked so much, or seemed in such excellent spirits. He was the more voluble because he noticed that his gaiety seemed greatly to annoy Lord Dewsbury, who scarcely spoke a word, but regarded him with a stony stare.

The talk turned on many themes, and on all the Theosophist was more or less eloquent. He seemed to have been everywhere, to have known all sorts and conditions of men, and to have had all sorts of adventures, afloat and ashore. He told of his own wanderings in far-off Thibet, and as he did so, he was aware that Isabel listened intently. Once or twice, when he addressed his remarks to her, her colour came and went, and once, when their eyes met, hers seemed full of a sweet understanding.

When the ladies had left the table, Woodville relapsed into silence, leaving the chief conversation to Mervyn and the Professor, who got along together admirably, the Earl and Dr. Darley talking in whispers, now and then glancing towards Woodville, while Dewsbury leant back in his chair, moodily smoking his cigar.

Presently Woodville rose, and asked the Earl's permission to join the ladies.

'Won't you have a cigar?' asked the Earl.

'Not to-night; at any rate, not now.'

'A glass of wine? During dinner, I observed, you drank only water.'

Woodville shook his head with a smile, and, bowing politely to the company, left the room. The moment he had gone, Dewsbury rose, threw his cigar away, and prepared to follow.

'Going too, Frank?' said the Earl. 'Isabel has told you, I suppose, about to-night's experiment? I have persuaded Mr. Woodville to endeavour, if he can, to procure some kind of a manifestation.'

'I have no doubt he will oblige you,' returned Dewsbury, with a sneer. 'From what I have seen of him, I should say that he is an expert in deception.'

'That remark is unworthy of you,' said the Earl warmly. 'Kindly remember that Mr. Woodville is my guest.'

'If I had *not* remembered it,' replied the young man, 'I should have adopted a very different tone towards him, I assure you.' And so saying, he left the room.

'I think we had better follow him,' said the Earl nervously. 'He and Mr. Woodville are best kept apart.'

'You surely don't think Lord Dewsbury would be guilty of the bad taste——'

'Upon my life, I don't know,' said the Earl. 'The mere sight or mention of Mr. Woodville acts on him

as a red rag acts on a bull. I live in constant dread
of an explosion.'

He rose, and, followed by the Dean, Mervyn, and
the Professor, led the way into the drawing-room,
glad to find no signs of coming conflict there as yet.
Woodville was chatting with Lottie, Madame Obnoskin
with Mrs. Darley, and Olive and Dewsbury were in
earnest conversation with Isabel.

'Ah, here you are, Mr. Woodville!' said the Dean.
'Well, is the oracle prepared to speak to-night?'

'Who knows?' answered Woodville, with a smile.
'In deference to Lord Wanborough's wishes, I shall
endeavour to present some sort of a manifestation;
but, to be candid, I am not over-sanguine.'

'We are all in Mr. Woodville's hands,' said the
Earl.

'Really,' said Woodville, with a little laugh, 'you
put me rather at a disadvantage. We Theosophists
make no pretence to supernatural power. All we con-
tend is, that everywhere around us there are forces
which are unexplained, and possibly unexplainable.'

'My dear sir,' piped the Professor from an arm-
chair, 'if you go no further than that——'

'Just one step further. We believe that the forces
I have named are obedient to the will of inspired
individuals.'

'Inspired!' repeated the Professor. 'Yes; but
how inspired?'

'Yes,' echoed Dewsbury dryly; 'that is what I want to know. How inspired?'

'By temperament,' answered Woodville easily. 'Just as the magnetized needle is sensitive to the polarity of the magnet, so certain natures are sensitive to the spiritual world about them. Of course,' he continued, with a smiling glance at Lord Dewsbury, 'this only applies to persons of imagination.'

'No doubt,' said the Professor, 'science admits that extraordinary manifestations are obtained, but how and wherefore?'

'Precisely,' said Mervyn, 'the influence of the Kama over the Upadana——'

'Do be quiet, Mervyn,' said Lottie. 'Let us begin and get it over, Mr. Woodville.'

'By all means,' said Woodville. 'Kindly close those curtains,' he continued to a footman, who was moving about the room. 'It is necessary that we should be entirely secluded and undisturbed.'

The heavy curtains which divided the long room were lowered.

'I must explain to you that each individual present has the result in his or her hands. The only condition necessary is complete mental concentration— obedience to impressions from within.'

'Understand, Davidson,' said his lordship to the footman, 'that we are on no account to be disturbed!'

The footman bowed silently, and left the room.

'And now,' continued Woodville, 'for our arrangement. Will you take this seat, Lady Carlotta? Madame Obnoskin, you might remain where you are.'

'I should suggest,' said Dewsbury, 'that Madame Obnoskin, since she shares your wonderful sensitiveness, should sit elsewhere.'

'Certainly. Madame Obnoskin, will you sit by his lordship? Does that satisfy you? But I must ask your lordship, whatever you see or hear, not to interfere, otherwise our efforts will be useless.'

Dewsbury nodded curtly.

'Isabel,' he said, 'will you sit here?'

'Excuse me,' said Woodville; 'it is now my turn to object. I desire that you and Miss Arlington will sit apart.'

'Why?' asked Frank.

'Because you are an adverse influence, while Miss Arlington is distinctly a sympathetic one.'

'Absurd!' muttered Dewsbury.

'Pray be fair to Mr. Woodville,' said the Earl mildly. 'Let him conduct his experiment in his own way.'

'As you please,' replied Dewsbury, leaning back in his chair.

'The next step,' continued Woodville, 'is to darken the room.'

'The usual preliminary!' said Frank, with a short laugh.

'The usual preliminary, as you say,' said Woodville, with calm good-temper. 'I do not make the conditions; I only apply them.'

'Quite so!' said the Professor.

'Professor Marrables will tell you,' continued Woodville, turning towards the scientist, 'if you are unaware of the fact, that brain sensitiveness is largely disturbed by light.'

'Quite so, quite so!' chirped the Professor.

'I place you in darkness,' Woodville went on, 'just as the artist treats the sensitive plate which is to receive a photographic impression.'

'That is not unreasonable,' said the Professor. 'It is well known, moreover, that certain psychic impressions are closely dependent on obscuration of the optic nerve. In the case of a monkey, for example, on which I once experimented——'

'I beg your lordship's pardon,' said the footman, re-entering. 'Telegram, my lord.'

Madame Obnoskin half rose from her seat with a sudden gasp. Woodville, as if he had not heard the servant's voice, pressed the electric button, and plunged the room into almost complete darkness.

'Did I not tell you,' said the Earl testily, 'that we are not to be interrupted?'

'It has come by special messenger, my lord,' said the man.

'Very well; go away! Pray proceed, Mr. Woodville; the telegram shall wait.'

Woodville crossed over to the window, through
which a broad band of faint moonlight was streaming,
and drew the heavy plush curtain, thus totally darken-
ing the room.

'I must ask you,' he said, 'for perfect silence. In
the event, however, of a manifestation to any person,
that person may speak.'

His voice, which sounded strange and cavernous
in the deep darkness, ceased, and perfect silence
reigned for what, to the tense nerves of every person
present, seemed a long time.

'It is useless,' said Lord Dewsbury, moving in his
chair with an impatient gesture.

'Patience, if you please,' Woodville's calm and
level voice answered. 'Someone in the room,' he
continued, 'may desire to communicate with one who
is far away, dead or living. If so, let that person will
with all his or her might, to be assured of the beloved
presence. Fix your minds on those with whom you
desire to communicate. Will that they shall appear.
Help them ! Summon them ! Perhaps they will
obey !'

'May they do so !' said the Earl fervently. 'It is
the will of all here !'

'I do not pretend to know how or wherefore,' continued Woodville; 'but I know that every person
present must have felt at one time or other, in supreme
moments of joy, of sorrow, or of insight, that there
are forces in life which are beyond us, above us, yet

ever surrounding us, as they surround us possibly to-night!'

He was interrupted by a sudden exclamation from Madame Obnoskin.

'Ah!'

'What is it?' asked Woodville.

'A form appears before me!'

'Speak to it!'

'I cannot!' madame panted. 'I am terrified!'

'I see nothing,' said the Earl.

'Hush!' said Woodville. 'The presences are here! They are growing!'

'I see a form in a white dress!' said madame. 'It is moving to and fro!'

'Near whom does it stand?'

'Near Miss Arlington.'

'It is false!' cried Dewsbury. 'We see nothing!'

'Silence, Lord Dewsbury!' said Woodville commandingly. 'Describe what you see,' he continued to Madame Obnoskin.

'It is too vague! It changes shape! Ah, it grows! I see the face—sad-eyed and stern, with hair and moustache white as snow! His lips move! He is trying to speak!'

'To whom?'

'To Miss Arlington.'

'And does Miss Arlington see nothing?' asked Woodville.

'Nothing!' panted Isabel. 'Ah,' she cried, 'something touched me! Something bent over me!'

'If your thought is of anyone near and dear to you, will with all your might that he may appear.'

'I do! I do! If he lives, let him appear to me!'

A strange sound, a universal sob of superstitious awe, broke from the throat of every person in the room. Something white, mystically luminous, began to grow in the darkness. It grew slowly almost to completed human form, then wavered half-way back to nothingness, grew and strengthened again, and finally amid the awe-struck silence of all present, seemed to solidify into the shape and face of Colonel Arlington. Isabel rose with a hysteric scream.

'Father, father, you live!'

Her groping arms encountered nothing but the empty air.

'A vile imposture!' cried Dewsbury. 'It shall go no further!'

He sprang to the electric button, and the figure vanished in a blaze of light.

'Father, father!' cried Isabel again, and sank back quivering into her seat.

'Look up, dear,' said Dewsbury. 'It is nothing! Draw back those curtains! Give her air!'

Woodville, pale and calm amid the universal excitement, spoke in measured tones of certainty:

'Of one thing Miss Arlington can rest assured—her father lives.'

'It is false!' cried Dewsbury. 'Colonel Arlington is dead!'

Woodville smiled quietly, as at the petulance of a spoiled child, and crossed to where the Earl was standing like a man dazed.

'Will you not open your telegram, my lord?'

The Earl started, and passed his hand across his forehead.

'The telegram? Yes; certainly!'

He opened it with tremulous fingers.

'Good God!' he exclaimed. 'What is this? Read it!'

He thrust the missive into Woodville's hands.

'Read it aloud!'

Woodville glanced at the telegram, and then at the ring of white faces about him. He read calmly:

'I am safe and well, and on my way to England. Break the news to Isabel!'

CHAPTER XIII.

IN THE TURRET-ROOM AGAIN.

ISABEL slipped from Dewsbury's supporting arm, and fell on a sofa near at hand. Lottie ran and bent over her, and the rest of the people stared from her to each other with faces of wonder and amazement.

Woodville was the only one among them who

showed no emotion. There was neither triumph nor surprise in his face as he walked quickly to a console, where a decanter of water was standing, and, pouring out a glass, offered it to Isabel. Lottie took it from his hand, and held it to her friend's lips.

'No,' said Isabel, feebly waving it away. 'Help me, Lottie—help me to my room.'

The two girls passed out together, and the same astonished silence reigned till broken by Woodville's voice.

'Miss Arlington is very naturally moved by what has happened,' he said. 'The manifestation was unusually distinct, and Colonel Arlington's telegram, coming so directly after it—— Well, joy does not kill. The shock will pass. The happiness of knowing that her father is alive will remain.'

The Earl, to whom these remarks were more directly addressed, made no reply. He was as a man who has been stunned by an unexpected blow. Dewsbury, angry and incredulous as ever, certain in his own mind that the whole affair was trickery, had left the room.

'I am a little tired,' continued Woodville. 'This kind of thing,' he explained, with an air of casual affability, to the Dean, 'is a little exhausting. If your lordship and your friends will excuse me, I will retire.'

The Earl offered his hand, and seemed for a moment inclined to speak, but said nothing, and

Woodville, bowing to the rest of the company, passed
out upon the terrace, giving a barely perceptible sign
to Madame Obnoskin—a sign she answered with a
quick movement of the eyes. He lit a cigarette, and
strolled along the terrace in the moonlight, walking
up and down for an hour or so before he was disturbed,
when the butler, making his rounds with a lighted
lantern, accosted him.

'Lord Dewsbury has been asking for you, sir.'

'Indeed,' said Woodville carelessly. 'I shall be in
my room presently, and shall be glad to see his
lordship.'

The man passed on and Woodville continued his
stroll back and forward along the terrace.

The clicking of bolts and the rattling of chains told
him that the household were retiring to rest, and
presently lights began to twinkle in the upper
windows. The castle clock struck twelve, and as the
last strokes died out on the air, Woodville heard
the French window of the drawing-room cautiously
unclosed, and Madame Obnoskin stepped out upon
the terrace.

'Well?' he asked calmly, flicking the ash from
the tip of his cigarette.

'What an escape!' she said, with an involuntary
shudder. 'If that telegram had come but one minute
earlier!'

'We should have had to invent some other form of
manifestation,' said Woodville coolly. 'As it was, it

10

came delightfully *apropos*, and put the finishing touch
to our little drama.'

' I have not your nerves, Woodville ; I am trembling
yet.'

' Rather a waste of emotional force,' said Woodville, ' to tremble over dangers we have passed and
defeated.'

' You are a wonderful man,' said Madame, with
genuine admiration. ' After all, it has been a great
triumph !'

' You think so ?' said Woodville. ' Well, we shall
see to-morrow.'

' But can you doubt it ?' cried madame. ' The
manifestation alone might have been questioned, but
borne out, as it was, by the arrival of the telegram,
the Earl, I am sure, is finally convinced. He never
spoke a word after you left the room, and he has gone
to bed dumfounded, like a man walking in his sleep.'

' And Miss Arlington ?' asked Woodville.

' I have not seen her ; but Lady Lottie told us
that, after a brief hysteric fit, she fell asleep, and is
now sleeping soundly. But I must not stay here. It
might ruin all if we were seen together like this.
Why did you signal me to follow you ?'

' Merely to warn you,' said Woodville, ' that the
battle may not be won yet. You are a little excited,
my good Evangeline—a little disposed to take victory
for granted. Keep your ears and eyes open, and
follow my lead.'

'You surely cannot complain of me so far,' she said.

'No; you have backed me admirably. But don't let your amiable optimism betray you now that we are on the eve of triumph. *Festina lente* is a good proverb. Don't make too much of to-night's success, and don't run the Earl too hard. He is the only person in the house who is ignorant of your ambition to become Countess of Wanborough; and if you play your cards too openly, you will ruin both your game and mine. We have convinced nobody but the Earl, and perhaps, Miss Arlington.'

'I shall be careful,' said madame. 'Good-night.'

'Good-night,' he answered, and she slipped back into the drawing-room and noiselessly re-fastened the shutters behind her.

Woodville finished his cigarette, and, mounting to his room, drew a chair to the fire, and sat moodily gazing at the glowing coals.

He was sitting thus when the door opened, and Lord Dewsbury entered the room. He was followed by Mervyn Darrell, who carried a lighted bedroom candle.

'I wish to speak to you,' said Dewsbury, looking pale and determined. 'I may not have another opportunity, and, in any case, I could not let the night pass without seeing you and saying what I have to say.'

'I am at your service,' answered Woodville coldly. 'Will you sit down?'

Lord Dewsbury paid no attention to the invitation,
but remained standing with his eyes fixed sternly on
Woodville, who continued quietly, addressing Mervyn,
who seemed rather anxious as to the result of the
interview, 'Won't you sit down, Mr. Darrell?'

'I—I think I will,' replied Mervyn, suiting the
action to the word, and taking a seat near the
window, still holding the lighted candle in his
hand.

'I have come, Mr. Woodville,' said Dewsbury, after
a pause, 'to tell you what I think of you.'

'Indeed!' returned Woodville, with a smile and a
shrug of the shoulders. 'And you have brought Mr.
Darrell with you that he may hear you express your
sentiments? Pray proceed. Mr. Darrell, will you
have a cigar?'

'I—I really think I will,' said Mervyn, rising and
helping himself from the box which the other held
carelessly towards him. 'Thank you very much.'

Woodville had assumed his old manner, but it was
clear that he was uneasy under the young lord's
steadfast and contemptuous gaze. He lighted a cigar
himself, and waited for the diatribe which he knew
was coming.

'Do not imagine for a moment,' said Dewsbury,
'that to-night's performance has in the least degree
altered my opinion concerning you ; on the contrary,
it has simply confirmed my belief that you are a rogue
and a charlatan.'

Woodville started, but, controlling himself, knocked the ash from his cigar, and smiled contemptuously.

'I was unwillingly, as you know, a party to your performance; but I watched you throughout, and formed my own conclusions as to the trick you were playing. It was clumsy enough, after all; fit to impose upon children, not upon grown men and women.'

He paused, while Woodville looked at him with the same quiet smile, saying, 'If this is all you have to say to me, my lord, it is surely superfluous. I did not imagine for a moment that *you* were converted.'

'Under other circumstances, I might treat such a piece of vulgar folly with the contempt which it deserves, or might laugh at it, as at any other impudent piece of conjuring. But you have exceeded your functions, even as a privileged professor of legerdemain. You have played, in a cowardly way, on the feelings of a lady who——'

'Do you mean Miss Arlington?'

'It is of Miss Arlington I am speaking. Her private grief was known to you, and her sorrow for one who is lost to her should have been sacred; but in spite of this, and in defiance of all decency, you have tried to persuade her into a belief that your powers are superhuman, and that you have placed her in communication with her dead father. Such cruelty removes your conduct from the category of ordinary imposition, and renders it basely criminal. So convinced am I

of this, that I should take your punishment into my
own hands, if I did not fear by doing so to provoke a
public scandal.'

Woodville rose, stood upon the hearthrug, and faced
his accuser. He still forced a smile, but it was cold
and mechanical, and he could not altogether conceal
the dark and malignant passion awakened by the
young man's words.

'You are not polite, Lord Dewsbury,' he said, between his set teeth. 'Politeness, I fear, is not your
forte. Let me warn you that there is a limit to my
patience, and, *au reste*, that your personal opinions,
of which you are so lavish, do not interest me in
the least.'

For a moment Dewsbury seemed about to lose
self-control. He made a movement towards Woodville as if to strike him in the face, but Mervyn sprang
up and caught him by the arm.

'My dear Frank, be calm! Mr. Woodville, I am
sure, will explain everything to your satisfaction.'

'Oh, then, there is something to explain, of which
his lordship has not yet spoken?' said Woodville,
raising his eyebrows.

'Only this!' cried Dewsbury. 'I wish to hear
from your own lips—and I *will* hear—under what
circumstances you met Miss Arlington in India.'

'Pardon me,' returned Woodville, 'but these
suspicions are unworthy of you. You are putting
a question which reflects on the character of a lady

whose name is spotless, or should be so in your estimation.'

'Answer my question!'

'Kindly speak lower. You will disturb the house, where, I must remind you, you and I are only guests.'

'My dear Dewsbury!—My dear Mr. Woodville!' cried Mervyn, looking from one to the other.

'I ask you again,' said Dewsbury, 'what is the secret of your influence over Miss Arlington? It is to be referred back in some way to your former acquaintanceship in India. I demand to know the true nature of your relations there.'

'The true nature of our relations?' repeated Woodville, with a significant smile.

'Yes.'

'If you desire any information, why not consult Miss Arlington herself? *I* shall tell you nothing.'

'You cur!' cried Dewsbury, turning livid.

'Dewsbury—Dewsbury!' implored Mervyn.

'Since you are Lord Dewsbury's friend,' said Woodville quietly, 'advise him not to go too far. I might imitate his charming example, and lose my temper.'

'But, my dear Woodville,' murmured Mervyn, 'you cast a slur upon Miss Arlington's reputation.'

'It is not I who cast a slur upon the lady; it is the man who introduced her name into this discussion. I regret that Miss Arlington has such a champion.

Lord Dewsbury, you have been frank with me, and I
shall return the compliment. If I am a trickster,
what are *you*? A coward, who, mad with his mean
suspicions, gratuitously insults the woman he is
supposed to love. A man who loves a woman has
faith in her honour. You have none!'

In spite of his anger, Dewsbury winced under this
home-thrust.

'I do not accuse *her*, but *you*!' he cried.

'You couple our names together. You imply that
there is a secret understanding between us.'

'I am convinced of it. Do you deny it? Answer
me, or——'

'I think, if you ask me, that you are unreasonably
jealous,' said Woodville, with a contemptuous shrug
of the shoulders. 'But you may make your mind
easy. *I* respect Miss Arlington, if *you* do not, and I
leave this house to-morrow, never to return.'

'Is that the truth?'

'Yes.'

'You leave this house to-morrow?'

Woodville nodded.

'You will not seek out Miss Arlington, on any
pretext, before you go?'

Woodville hesitated, then replied very quietly:

'I will not seek out Miss Arlington, on any pretext,
before I go.'

'That you promise?'

'Oh! My promise surely is worth nothing?'

returned Woodville. 'But such as it is, I give it.'

'Very well.   See that you keep your word.'

'Now, my dear Dewsbury,' said Mervyn, 'let me entreat you to go to bed.   You've been exciting yourself unnecessarily.'

Dewsbury walked to the door, and, turning on the threshold, gazed sternly at Woodville, who listened to him with well-assumed indifference.

'I warn you,' he said, 'that if we ever meet again, I shall feel it my duty to denounce you as a cheat and a rogue.   You will be wise, I think, to quit England, and to return to your old haunts, where roguery is more in fashion.   Remember, I have warned you!' And so saying, he left the room.

For a moment Woodville, losing his self-command, seemed about to spring after him or to call him back, but, controlling himself with a fierce laugh, he simply shrugged his shoulders, and continued to smoke his cigar.   Then his eye fell on Mervyn, who stood looking at him with a most forlorn expression, and he motioned him to the door.

'Good-night, Mr. Darrell.   You had better follow your friend.'

But the apostle of culture, still holding his bedroom-candle, lingered apologetically.

'I am so sorry, my dear Woodville, that this has occurred.   Let me beg you to dismiss it from your mind.   Dewsbury is upset, and doesn't mean half he

says. For myself, I wish to assure you of my pro-
found respect.'

Again Woodville motioned to the door, but Mervyn
had not finished.

'Between beings of advanced intelligence there
should always be confidence. You know I am at
heart a Theosophist, but am I right in assuming that
there was in to-night's manifestation just a spice of
what the vulgar call Humbug?'

Angry as he was, Woodville could not repress a
smile.

'What the vulgar call Humbug! My dear sir,
there is humbug everywhere—even in Nature.'

'True,' said Mervyn. 'Nature is, of all things, the
most unnatural. You admit, then——'

'Wise men never make admissions.'

'Ah, well, I have no right to ask you,' said Mervyn,
walking slowly to the door; then, pausing for a
moment, he added, 'I have always had the greatest
respect for impostors. They are the men of genius,
who perceive by instinct the utter absurdity of human
existence. They only do on a small scale what the
spirit of the Universe does on a large scale—conceal
the sublimely hideous reality with the amusing mask
of Idealism. Hem! Good-night!'

He smiled fatuously, nodded, and left the room,
closing the door softly after him.

Left alone, Woodville threw himself on the settee
before the fire, and remained for a long time in

gloomy meditation. At last he rose, and began walking slowly up and down the chamber.

'So I am a rogue, a charlatan!' he muttered to
himself, with a low bitter laugh. 'Yes. He is right.
I *am* a rogue and a charlatan, but he shall see which
hand is the stronger, his or mine. I have done with
all scruples now! My will against her will, my
strength against his strength. She shall never be
his wife!'

He drew back the curtains with an angry gesture,
and a brilliant flood of moonlight poured into the
chamber, suffusing him from head to foot, and casting
his black shadow on the floor of the room. Outside
on the battlement it was almost as light as dawn.
High in the cloudless sky above the moon swung
like a great electric lamp, surrounded on every side
with palpitating stars.

'She is sleeping!' he murmured, gazing out. 'If
my will has conquered, she dreams of me! I have
bent her pride like a reed, answered her innermost
yearning, sown in her consciousness the one thought
paramount—that our lives are eternally blent together.
They are—they *must* be! If there is any of the old
power left within me, she must feel it now!'

Leaning against the window, and watching the
silent skies, he was thinking it all over. His mind
wandered back to the hour of their first meeting,
when they had been drawn together as if by some
magnetic spell, and when all that was good and noble

in his nature had seemed to awaken suddenly, under
the divining rod of her sweet sympathy. She had
loved him then, he was sure of that; but afterwards?
Scandal and calumny had done their work, and she
had begun to fear him and shrink away from him,
and at last, to his despair, she had told him that she
was coming to England, and that they must never
meet again. All his passionate nature had revolted
against a change that looked like treachery. He had
thought her an ideal woman, but he had found her of
the world, worldly, like all the rest. Nevertheless,
he had been drawn after her, haunted as he came by
her loveliness, and at last he had found her again, to
discover—as he thought—that he had been utterly
forgotten.

'Yes,' he thought, ' they are all alike, and the man
is a fool who stakes his life upon the faith of any one
of them. A woman is like a dog, and a man, to hold
her safe, must be her master.'

Well, he had conquered her at last, but he had not
forgotten her scorn of him, her hauteur, the contempt
she had shown in every look and word. As he stood
thus reviewing the past, he fed his wrath with the
memory of the slights she had put upon him, and
the passion he still felt for her grew into a cruel and
deadly desire. To have her wholly in his power, to
possess her in all her beauty, to humiliate her to his
caprice, to tear her away from the man who had
heaped endless insults upon him, would surely be a

fair revenge! He justified the evil thought within him by his belief in the worthlessness, the stupidity, of women generally, mere bundles of nerves, change-ful, chameleonic, changing with every wind that blew.

'Had she trusted me; had she believed in me,' he thought; 'had she realized the truth—that, what-ever I was to the world, I was loyal to her, it would have been different. It was in her power to save or damn me. She has chosen to do the last! It is not my fault, but hers, that I am what I am—that I have woven around her, and around myself, this network of miserable lies. It was war between us—*guerre à outrance*—and I had to take the weapons nearest to my hand.'

Shut in the gloomy room, he seemed to stifle and pant for air. He walked to the door, and looked out into the corridor: all there was dark and still. Opposite to him, across the corridor, was the door which led upon the old battlement.

He drew the bolt, and passed out into the open moonlight.

CHAPTER XIV.

THE SOMNAMBULIST.

STANDING there on the battlement, suspended, as it were, between earth and heaven, his eyes took in the wonderful beauty of the midnight scene: the heaven sown thick with stars and quick with celestial phosphorescence, the luminous white moon in the midst suffusing the air with quick electric rays, the dim and distant prospect of the park with its great patches of moonlight and its black shadows of woodland, the faint blue stream of light on the edges of the far-off trees.

The wind had fallen ; there was not a sound save that deep stir which is 'less sound than silence audible,' and seems like the still breathing of the sleeping earth, yet the heavens seemed alive to their inmost depths, quickening and kindling ever and anon as a shooting-star fell and was lost in darkness.

He leant over the battlement, looking down, and he could just catch a glimpse of the façade of the mansion and the broad stone terrace which surrounded it.   For some minutes he remained thus ; then the temptation became irresistible, and he began, slowly and cautiously, to descend the steps leading from the battlement to the lower terrace.

It was with no set purpose that he did this ; he was drawn, rather, by some irresistible fascination, to see whether there was a light in Isabel's room, and to discover by that token whether she was awake or sleeping.

But before he reached the terrace, he remembered the promise he had made to Lord Dewsbury—not to seek out Miss Arlington, under any pretext, before he went away. He paused, thinking to himself,. 'Although I am a rogue and a charlatan, he shall not reproach me with having broken my word;' but as he did so, and prepared to retrace his steps, he was startled by the gleam of something white on the terrace beneath him.

Standing moveless on the terrace, looking upward, was the figure of a woman.

He knew in a moment that it was Isabel.

The moonlight fell full upon her, making the white dress that she wore look like marble—and like a marble statue indeed she seemed, as silent and as still.

Quick as thought he crept down the steps and approached her, till he was near enough to see her face; then, hanging in the shadow of the turret, watching her intently, and seeing that her eyes were half closed, he realized that she was fast asleep.

Her face was turned towards the turret, while she stood with outstretched hands, as if listening. Her dark hair was undone, and fell over her shoulders and down to her waist. All that she wore was a night-dress of some white material, which reached to her naked feet.

As he watched her, she sighed deeply, and murmured something to herself. Then, with hands still outreaching, as if to feel her way, she moved slowly away from him, along the terrace.

'Isabel!' he whispered.

She paused a moment, listening, and then came slowly back.

As she did so, he quietly retreated before her, ascending the steps which led to the battlement. Pausing above her, he whispered her name again, and again she listened.

Quickly and silently he reached the battlement, and, gazing down, saw her ascending from step to step, now pausing, now stealing silently on, more like a spirit than a living thing.

Quite heedless now of what might happen, possessed by a certainty of her complete subjection to his will, he crept through the door communicating with the corridor, and waited while the sleeping girl appeared in the full moonlight on the battlement, and stood there as if waiting some further command.

A cold wind stirred the white drapery around her, and she seemed to shiver through and through, but she gave no sign of awakening.

He opened the door of the turret chamber, entered, and blew out the candles burning on the mantelpiece, leaving the room in darkness, save for the dim red light cast by the fire smouldering on the hearth. Then, drawing back into the shadow, and stretching out his hand with a gesture of command, he beckoned to her, and though her eyes were closed she seemed to see and obey.

She flitted through the door beyond the passage, crossed the corridor, and entered the turret chamber.

Pausing just within the threshold, she shivered again, and uttered a deep sigh; then quietly and noiselessly she stole towards the hearth, and, kneeling down, began to warm her hands at the fire.

He watched her breathlessly.

Although she was pale as death, she had never looked so beautiful, and his heart throbbed with smothered passion through all its pulses.

She was *there*, she was *his*, if he dared to do what his mind imagined. He thought of her scorn of him, her falsehood (as he thought it) towards him, and of his oath that she should never become the wife of Dewsbury; and then, creeping from the room on tiptoe, he closed the door leading to the battlement, returned to the room, closed *that* door, and turned the key in the lock.

The sound startled her, and she looked round trembling. He stood with his back to the door, steadfastly regarding her.

The fire flickered up, and illumined her as she knelt from head to feet. She murmured something to herself, and smiled.

Trembling like a leaf, afraid of her, afraid of himself, yet mastered by a wild desire to seize her in his arms, he approached her. Her face was turned again to the fire, and she began singing to herself in a low, soft voice; and though the words were inaudible, the song was the one she had sung on the day of their

11

re-meeting—the strange wild chant of Rubinstein, with its haunting spell.

Did she realize where she was? Did she understand that the man she scorned and dreaded stood so near to her, that they were alone together, while all the household was plunged in sleep? If so, why did she seem so quiet, so self-possessed? Her manner showed no dread whatever; it was rather the manner of a girl peacefully singing to herself in the solitude of her own chamber.

She seemed another creature to the proud, passionate girl he had known hitherto; for she was gentle, subdued, and almost happy.

It was very strange, even to him, the Theosophist, the man who professed to know so much of Nature, of the powers above Nature, and of the human heart. He could understand that his will was controlling hers, that she had come there under the spell of a hypnotic trance. What amazed and troubled him, what was unusual in his experience of the phenomena of hypnotism, was the supreme happiness and peacefulness of her demeanour. Only when some unexpected sound startled her, as when he had turned the key of the door, did she show the slightest sign of nervous fear, and even then the emotion seemed less one of fear than of trembling, listening expectation.

One thing was clear, that she was completely mesmerized.

To test this, Woodville willed silently that she

should cease singing. In a few moments she became silent, the low, monotonous chant growing fainter and fainter, till it died away.

Still with his eyes fixed upon her, he breathed her name:

'Isabel!'

Quick as thought she turned her face towards him with an eager smile, and answered:

'Yes, Philip!'

'Philip!' Never before, in the course of all their meetings, not even in India, when natural sympathy and attraction had first drawn them together, and he had dreamed of winning her love, had she called him by that name; yet it came now from her lips quite naturally, as if she had never called him by any other. As she uttered it her face lighted up with girlish pleasure, and the tone was so quick and clear that it was difficult to realize that she was still asleep.

Woodville was startled—startled almost as much by the tone as by the word. Aware of his evil command over her, he had expected to find himself face to face with a helpless, will-less woman, spell-bound beyond the power of resistance, physical or moral—a woman who, in her waking moments, felt for him nothing but distrust and even dread, and who, even when hypnotized and powerless to resist him, would be conscious only of a dull, numb sense of pain.

How different was the reality! Had he been her dearest and nearest friend, instead of her most dangerous enemy, the sound of his voice could not have awakened in her a more subtle sense of pleasure.

She kept her face turned towards him for some moments, then, as he remained silent, the light on her features gradually died away.

At last he spoke again :

' Isabel !'

Again the sweet responsive cry :

' Yes, Philip ?'

' Can you see me ?'

' No, Philip,' she answered softly ; ' but I hear your voice.'

The answer came slowly from her lips, with a pause between each word.

' Open your eyes !'

She obeyed him instantly, but the large beautiful eyes were quite blank, and seemed to see no more than when they had been closed.

' Do you know where you are ?'

She hesitated for a moment, as if gathering her thoughts together, and then replied in the same sweet, monotonous tone:

' Yes, I am here with *you*.'

' What room is this ?'

' The turret-room.'

' Why did you come here ?'

She hesitated again, and then answered:

' You called me, Philip, and I came.'

Again the name, spoken softly as if the word were

a caress. No wonder the evil spirit in the man was
troubled and disarmed. As she knelt there in her
white dress, pure and spotless as herself, her gentle
face turned to his, her long hair flowing over her
shoulders, she looked more like an innocent child
than like a woman. Like Porphyro in the chamber
of Agnes, Woodville

'—— grew faint ;
She knelt, so fair a thing, so pure from mortal taint !'

His eyes softened, a mist seemed to arise between
him and her, and when he spoke again his voice was
faint and broken.

'Are you not afraid?' he asked. 'Remember
where you are—alone with *me!*—and answer me
truthfully, are you not afraid ?'

'I am not afraid,' she answered.

'Rise up,' he said, approaching close to her, and
looking steadfastly into her face ; then, as she obeyed
him and stood erect without a shadow of fear, her
dark eyes gazing into his, he placed his arm round
her waist and drew her towards him. A tremor ran
through her frame, but she made no resistance, and
her head sank upon his shoulder, while her eyes
closed peacefully.

He had hoped and prayed for this ; he had resolved
with all his soul and all his strength, by fair means
or foul, to hold her in his arms, to become master of
her fate, and so to make her atone for all her scorn
for him, but now that his thought was realized, he

could hardly believe it true. Her breath was upon his cheek, his lips were close to hers, her soft and yielding form was clasped in his embrace, and yet, in the very moment of his triumph he felt guilty and ashamed.

'Isabel!' he whispered.

'Yes, Philip?' she answered, opening her eyes with a restful smile.

'Are you sure, quite sure, that you do not fear me?'

'No, Philip.'

'Nor hate me?'

'No, Philip.'

'In God's name, why?'

She drew closer to him, nestling like a child upon his breast, as she replied:

'Because I *love* you, Philip!'

'You love me? *Me?*' he cried, while once more the mist came between them, and he could not see her face.

'Yes, Philip!'

'Answer me truly. Did you not once *hate* me?'

Again the soft, still, monotonous reply:

'I never hated you.'

'Nor feared me?'

'I never feared you, Philip,' she answered, and added, trembling softly in his embrace, 'I feared *myself!*'

'What did you fear? Answer me truthfully, I command you.'

'I feared my own love for you, Philip. I did not know you. I thought you were false and cruel, but now that you have been so kind to me, now that you have brought my father back to me, I know that you are good, that there is no one like you in all the world !'

As Woodville listened, his emotion mastered him, his voice broke, his eyes were full of tears, and he trembled as if about to fall.

Conscious of his trouble, the girl reached up her little hand, and just touching his eyelids with her finger-tips, murmured softly :

'Why are you crying, Philip ?'

'I am not crying,' he answered, choking down a sob.

It was the supreme moment of his life. Never before had he been so deeply moved, never before had he thought himself capable of such deep feeling. The girl's perfect trust and utter surrender, her complete unconsciousness of any evil, her helplessness, her divine gentleness and affection, stirred his very soul to pity. Often had he dreamed of love, but never of a love like this. It seemed so strange, so unaccountable, that he could scarcely believe it to be real. Yet, for the moment, as always happens in moments of great insight, his own nature became exalted, the passion within him transformed and purified.

As he stood thus, looking sadly down upon her,

and supporting her gently in his arm, a shiver ran
through her frame.

'How cold it is!' she murmured.

'Sit here,' he said, placing her in the settee before
the fire.

CHAPTER XV.

'THE WHITE GAZELLE.'

SEEING that she still shivered, Woodville took a large
travelling cloak, which was lying on a chair close to
the curtained bed, and raising her gently, wrapped it
around her.   Then he placed her softly on the settee,
settling her head back against a pillow, and said to
her: 'Close your eyes, and sleep!'

She obeyed him, smiling like a happy child, and
soon her slow regular breathing showed that she was
slumbering profoundly, quite unconscious of his
presence.

He stood gazing at her, touched to the soul by her
helplessness and her beauty; then, with a deep sigh,
almost a sob, he walked to the window and gazed out
into the night.

And now, for the first time in his life, this man,
who had believed in nothing, who had been trained
to despise all human creatures and regard them as his
dupes, who had regarded all religion as vulgar
superstition, and all morality as only a cloak for

ignorance or hypocrisy, felt ashamed and degraded by his own unbelief. He had spoken truly, however, when he had said that his passion for Isabel would save or damn him; and he asked himself now, was he to be saved or damned? He had prayed, as far as he was capable of prayer, to be revenged on the proud girl for the scorn and insult he had suffered from her. He had sworn, if the opportunity ever came, to drag her down to the level of his own baser nature, and to do this at any risk of dishonour to her and of danger to himself. Well, God had answered his prayer by granting it to the full. The opportunity he sought had come. As helpless as a lamb, spell-bound, sleeping, yet obedient to his slightest wish or will, she was there utterly at his mercy, absolutely and helplessly in his power.

In the story of the White Gazelle, with which he had startled Madame Obnoskin, he had told the tale of himself and Isabel Arlington, and its truth as a parable was now complete. The long and weary chase had ended, the peaks that seemed inaccessible had been reached; his toils, his pains, his doubts, were all over, and the beautiful thing he had sought so long was his at last. It was for him now—for him only—to decide whether it should be destroyed or spared.

Philip Woodville was no sentimentalist. He had been taught, indeed, to despise all deep feeling, both in himself and others. Moreover, he was a man

of strong passions, and his passion for Isabel Arlington had been overpowering since the hour of their
first meeting. But, at the same time, he was no
coward. He loved fighting, he loved victory, but he
was incapable of taking a mean advantage of an enemy
when weak or fallen. He had, in a word, the qualities
of his defects.

It would be false to say that he was not tempted,
that the evil spirit in him did not struggle for the
mastery, as he stood there debating in his own mind
what to do. Had the girl been merely helpless under
hypnotism, had her surrender to him been merely
physical and involuntary, her beauty, which had
never seemed so winsome as it seemed that night,
might have been her destruction. But what he had
seen and heard, what had shone like light in her eyes,
and sounded like music in her voice, was a miracle—
a revelation.

'I *love* you, Philip,' she had said.

Then all her coldness had been a mask, all her
pride unreal. Instead of hating and fearing him as
he had thought, she had feared only her own love
for a man she believed unworthy. From first to last,
if her own words were true, she had loved him and
him only.

Thinking it all over, realizing how he had plotted
to subject her to his influence; knowing, also, that he
was even more base and degraded than she had yet
guessed, could he blame her for having worn the mask

so long? No; his own conscience told him that she had been right and that he was infamous.

Yet the shame he felt was not unmixed with exultation. Whatever happened now, he had triumphed; he had won the sole thing he had thought precious in the world, this pure girl's love. It was for him to decide of what nature his triumph should be, that of the brutes of the field, or that of a man with a living soul.

He gazed across the room to the spot where she was still slumbering peacefully.

'Poor child, poor child!' he murmured. And with that cry of pity, of benediction, came the thought which is born of insight, and he resolved to prove himself worthy of such love.

Up to this moment, strangely enough, he had been so absorbed in the conflict of his own good and evil passions as scarcely to realize the position in which she, an innocent and honourable girl, was already placed. The truth now flashed upon him. If her presence there became known, if any living soul knew or suspected that she had visited him in his room at dead of night, how could he shield her from disgrace? Who would believe that she was pure and innocent, if they found her *there*?

'My God, my God!' he cried to himself in despair. 'What have I done?'

He looked at his watch; it was half-past one o'clock.

He walked on tiptoe to the door, gazed along the

dark corridor, and listened intently. All was perfectly still.

So far everything was safe, and Isabel had not been missed. He knew, however, that Lady Carlotta occupied a room quite close to hers, and at any moment might discover that she had left her bed. If discovery was to be avoided, there was no time to be lost.

He bent over the sleeping girl, and whispered her name again :

'Isabel.'

She stirred, sighed heavily, but scarcely seemed to hear.

'Isabel! Isabel!' he whispered. 'Listen, I command you!'

Her eyes opened, and she looked up at him; but he saw that her trance was still unbroken.

'You must not remain here. You must go away as you came. Do you understand? If you should be found here, a stain will rest for ever on your name.'

Her lips trembled, and a faint tremor ran through her frame.

'Yes, Philip,' she replied.

'But before you go—before you awaken, tell me again that you care for me, that you love me !'

'I love you, Philip !'

'Then why, loving me as you say, did you become betrothed to another man?'

The beautiful face became troubled, but the answer came clearly and truthfully as before :

'I was foolish, I thought you beneath me. My religion taught me that what you did was wicked and profane. I yearned to tell you of my love, but I was too proud. I came to England, but I did not forget you. Day after day I thought of you, and every night you were in my dreams.'

'Are you sleeping or waking now?'

'I do not know.'

'Yet you know where you are?'

'Yes, with you.'

'Will you do as I desire?'

'Yes, Philip.'

'Then you will go at once, quietly, silently. You will return to your room, and when you awaken in the morning you will remember nothing of what you have said to me to-night.'

'I will try not to remember.'

'Yes; try to forget also the love you have felt for me, the kindness you have felt for one who is so unworthy. It will pass away from you like a dream; the thought of me, the memory of me, will also pass away. Now; come, give me your hand, and let me guide you back.'

As she rose, trembling, the cloak which he had placed around her fell from her shoulders. He raised it and wrapped it around her; and then, before he realized what he was doing, placed his arm around her and kissed her on the forehead.

The touch of his lips seemed to break the spell.

She trembled violently, gazed wildly into his face, and with a cry of wonder and terror awakened.

'Hush, for God's sake!' he whispered.

But she freed herself from his embrace, and, shrinking back, gazed wildly around the room. The cloak fell from her, rustling to her naked feet.

'What is this? where am I?' she moaned; then, as if seeing him for the first time, and looking at him in horrified recognition, she cried, 'Mr. Woodville!'

'Calm yourself,' he said. 'You are quite safe. You were walking in your sleep and——'

With another cry she made a movement to pass him and reach the door, but her strength seemed to fail her, and sinking on her knees with a wild sob, she covered her face with her hands.

'For God's sake, Miss Arlington,' he said, 'listen to me! You are in no danger, but you must summon up all your courage, and return as quickly as possible to your own room.'

As she continued to sob loudly, overwhelmed with mingled fear and shame, he made a movement as if to raise her in his arms, but she sprang to her feet with flashing eyes.

'Do not touch me!' she cried. '*You* brought me here! Oh, what will they think of me, what will they think of me?'

'No one will ever know,' he answered sadly. 'What has happened to-night shall be a sacred secret between you and me. Do not think that I shall presume upon it. Do not think that I shall ever take advantage of it in word or deed, although I know now—your own lips have told me—that it was your love for me which brought you here.'

'My love for *you!*' she repeated wildly; 'my love for *you!*'

'Yes, Isabel; it is too late now to wear the mask. I understand now why you were so cruel; but you were right, my child. I am unworthy of your love, even your pity. Before we part for ever, I wish you to understand that clearly. I am at once better and worse than you thought me.'

'Let me go!' she cried. 'I wish to hear nothing —nothing!'

But she did not stir.

'Only a word, and you will understand,' he said. 'I plotted your ruin—that is why I brought you here. That is all. I have lied to you from the beginning. I lied when I pretended to possess supernatural power; I lied when I assumed to be in communication with beings of another world. All my life, all my religion, has only been a lie.'

'So false, so treacherous!' she moaned. 'And what I saw last night——'

'A lie, an imposture, like all the rest. I *knew* your father lived. I used that knowledge to complete my power over you, to subdue your living will. Well, you know me now, and that knowledge will save you.

You will waste no further thought on me; you will blot my image from your memory; you will forget that I ever lived.'

Amazed and almost stupefied, she gazed at him as if fascinated. He moved towards the door, and reached out his hand as if to open it.

'Come!' he whispered.

She made a movement as if to follow, but suddenly, with a quick terrified gesture, he placed his finger on his lips.

Outside, in the corridor, there was the sound of a footfall and a rustling dress, and the next moment someone knocked softly at the door.

CHAPTER XVI.

THE LAST STRUGGLE.

EVEN in her semi-dazed condition, when all she saw and all she heard seemed part of a terrible dream from which she had been rudely awakened, Isabel realized the peril of her situation, and felt the necessity of escaping from it, if possible, without discovery.

She drew back silently, holding her breath and listening in terror.

The knock was repeated—a little more loudly.

Still motioning Isabel to silence, Woodville placed his ear close to the door, and listened intently.

Again the knock was repeated, and Woodville heard again the murmur like the rustling of a dress; then, after a pause, there came the sound of feet retiring along the corridor.

Woodville crept to Isabel, who stood trembling and deadly pale, leaning against the settee.

The fire had now gone out, and the only light in the room was the moonlight streaming in through the window and lighting the dim tapestries on the further wall.

She could not see his face, for the part of the room where they stood was in almost complete darkness.

'You must not go yet,' he whispered. 'I am convinced that the person who knocked is still watching.'

'Who is it?' murmured Isabel.

'I think—I am almost certain it is Madame Obnoskin,' replied Woodville. 'I do not think she would betray you; but you must not, if we can help it, place yourself in the power of that woman.'

He returned to the door and listened again. All was silent, and he was about to turn the key stealthily in the lock, when there was a creaking sound, as of someone moving along the corridor.

'I was right,' he whispered. 'She is there!'

For a moment his impulse was to throw the door open and boldly face the spy, whoever she might be, but he thought of the trembling girl whom he wished

12

to save, and realized the risk of taking any confidant. He knew the Obnoskin too well to think she would believe in the truth if he told it to her, or in any gloss of the truth which he might invent. From that night forward she would hold Isabel's reputation at her mercy, and would use her knowledge, no doubt, without scruple to further her own ends.

There was a possibility, moreover, that the person might not be Obnoskin, after all. In that case, who could it be? Lady Carlotta, if she had discovered Isabel's absence from her room and followed her, would never have gone away so silently and stealthily. No, the watcher, who was certainly a woman—for he had clearly heard the rustle of a woman's dress—was either Madame Obnoskin or one of the female servants of the household. In any case, it was imperative that she should remain in ignorance of Isabel's presence there.

Suddenly he remembered the old disused door which the Earl had shown him underneath the tapestry. Escape was possible that way, as it communicated directly with the old battlement and with the flight of stone steps leading down to the terrace.

He crossed the room on tiptoe, raised the tapestry, and revealed the door; then he tried to turn the key, but at first it resisted his efforts; at last, however, when he used both hands and put out all his strength, it turned slowly with a hard, grating sound, and the door swung open.

'Come!' he whispered, beckoning eagerly.

Isabel did not stir. All he could see was the faint outline of her white dress in the darkness.

'For God's sake, come!' he repeated.

Trembling and tottering as if about to fall, Isabel stole out of the shadows and moved towards him; then, as she reached the moonlit centre of the chamber, she gave a low, piteous cry, and sank forward on her face, in a dead swoon.

'Isabel!' he whispered, kneeling by her and supporting her in his arms.

Moveless and ghastly pale, she lay insensible, like a dead woman in her shroud; but drawing her close to him, he was conscious that she still breathed.

For some minutes he tried to restore her to consciousness, listening eagerly all the time for any sound beyond the corridor. All his efforts were in vain. At last, in sheer despair, he rose to his feet, bent down over her, and lifted her bodily in his arms.

As he did so she stirred, moaned faintly, and clung to him, twining her arms around his neck, as he carried her towards the open door, over which the heavy tapestry had again fallen. He tore the tapestry aside, and bending low with his unconscious burthen (for the doorway was very low) passed out into the moonlight.

Woodville was a man of unusual physical strength. From youth upwards he had hardened his muscles

by constant exercise in the open air; so the girl's
light form was like a feather in his arms. He crossed
the battlement, paused there for a moment to look
round and listen, and then ran, rather than walked,
down the stone steps leading to the terrace.

The terrace once gained, he paused again, and
looked into the girl's face. She was breathing easily
now, as if asleep.

Far away in the east, beyond the park trees, there
were faint red streaks of daylight, a dark cloud
covered the moon, and a thin, misty rain was beginning to fall. The splendour of the night was over,
yielding place to a dull and miserable dawn. The
air had suddenly grown very cold.

The heart of Woodville sank within him. As he
stood gazing at his unconscious burthen, the chillness
of the hour seemed to deepen his own sense of desolation. He almost regretted that he had not, in the
supreme moment of his triumph and opportunity,
acted differently—that he had not taken Isabel to his
heart, and made her his own for ever, despite the
world.

But this feeling lasted only for a moment; it was
lost instantly in a nobler feeling of utter sympathy
and pity. Struck by the chill breath of the dawn,
Isabel shivered in his arms. Her hair, which fell
loose round her shoulders, was damp with dew, and
the thin white raiment she wore was quite wet.

He hastened quickly along the terrace till he

reached the exterior of the room where he had seen her watching on the night of his first arrival at the castle.

The room was an elegantly-furnished boudoir, communicating with Isabel's bedroom and that of Lady Carlotta. The French windows stood wide open, just as Isabel had left them, no doubt, when she wandered out in her sleep.

He was about to enter the room when he was startled by a cry from within, and he found himself confronted by Lady Carlotta, who stood looking at him in terror. A light dressing-gown was thrown around her, and she held a light in her hand.

'Silence, for God's sake!' he said in a low voice.

'Mr. Woodville!'

'Yes,' he replied, entering the room and placing Isabel in an armchair. 'Do not alarm yourself. I found Miss Arlington walking in her sleep. My voice awoke her, and she fainted away.'

'Isabel—Isabel!' cried Lottie, kneeling by the unconscious girl. 'She is wet through! Oh, *where* did you find her?'

'On the terrace, near to the turret-room,' answered Woodville.

Their eyes met, and he saw that Lottie did not believe him. Her face was full of a horrified suspicion.

'Go away!' she said. 'Go away, I implore you! Isabel—Isabel!' And as she clasped Isabel's hand,

and called upon her by her name, Isabel awakened, looked round wildly, and then, seeing Woodville, covered her face with her hands.

'She is safe now,' said Woodville, ' and I will leave her in your care. Be assured, Lady Carlotta, that I shall never speak of what has occurred to-night, and I think that the secret is safe with *you*. Good-night, Lady Carlotta—good-night, Miss Arlington.'

So saying, he left the room.

The moment he had gone, Lottie ran to the windows, closed them, and drew down the blind. It seemed to Woodville as she did so that the light of all the world went out. With a low cry of pain, he passed along the terrace, and returned to the turret-room.

Re-entering the chamber by the opening underneath the tapestry, he locked the door again, and arranged the tapestry over it. There was no moonlight now, and the room was quite dark. He struck a match, lighted a candle, and looked at his watch.

It was nearly three o'clock.

How strangely and rapidly the time had fled ! It seemed that only a few minutes had passed since Isabel and he had stood together there, startled by the mysterious knock. Remembering what had occurred, he unlocked the door leading on to the corridor, and listened. Everything was quite still.

He locked the door again, and began pacing up and down the room.

His first thoughts were of Isabel. He was sure that Lady Carlotta, even if, as he feared, she put the worst construction on what she had seen, would never say or do anything to betray her friend; and, moreover, unless Isabel herself told her, she would never know what had really taken place. The only danger to be apprehended was from the person who had knocked at the door while Isabel was with him in that room; but even she, in all possibility, did not know the truth. If the mysterious visitor was, as he believed, Madame Obnoskin, he would be able, he had no doubt, to disarm her suspicions.

So far, then, Isabel's reputation was safe, sorely as his mad selfishness had put it in peril. But what of herself? What of the physical and mental shock she had sustained that night? Many a woman with far less cause had lost her reason altogether. The strain of the hypnotic spell, the horrible awakening, the agony of the situation in which the girl had found herself, the tension of wonder and terror ending in that long and death-like swoon, must have been terrible to one so highly strung; and its after-consequences might be also terrible. As he thought of all this—as he realized it all—Woodville loathed and hated himself, and cursed the day that he was born.

Then he thought of her wonderful gentleness, her words of ineffable love. Under the hypnotic spell her soul had become like a calm, pellucid water, transparent to the very depths; and he had seen his own image there. Under such conditions, he knew **well**, the spirit does not lie. Isabel had loved him **from** the first—had loved him even when she most feared and doubted him—had loved him in spite of **her** conviction that he was utterly unworthy.

'And now I know, since you have brought **my** father back to me, that there is no one like you in **all** the world!'

Well, he had confessed the shameful fraud; he had torn off the charlatan's mask. She knew now the extent of the deception he had practised upon her, in order to subdue her to his wish and will. ' So far, so well,' he thought. But, having gone so far in self-surrender, the passion for martyrdom urged him to go further still.

With men like Philip Woodville there is no *via media* between good and evil. He was ready to efface himself for the sake of the woman he had wronged. Would that effacement be complete if he left Wanborough Castle without full confession to all those whom he had deceived?

Before the night had passed, his mind was fully made up. He would accept his defeat to the full, with all its humiliation. Only in that way could he prove his devotion and his repentance. When that was done he would leave England for ever.

When daybreak came, it found him still awake, pacing the turret-room. The tempest of his struggle had passed away, but his face looked worn and haggard, like the face of an old man. Nevertheless, he was now quite calm. He had achieved the final victory, and had conquered himself.

CHAPTER XVII.

CONFESSION.

'WELL, Mervyn,' said Lottie, as the Apostle of the New Culture entered the breakfast-room next morning, ' how did you sleep ?'

'Profoundly, as I always do,' said Mervyn.

'I had a dreadful night,' said Lottie. 'I didn't close my eyes till after daybreak, and then I had the most awful dreams. I suppose *you* don't dream ? You'd be above such weakness, naturally.'

'No, I dream occasionally; but when I do so, it is of the serene, the elemental !'

'I don't believe you have any real feeling at all. If you had, you'd have been upset by what happened last night, like the rest of us.'

Mervyn smiled—a languid, tolerating smile.

'My dear Lottie, the New Spirit is never upset. Where is Woodville ?'

'He has asked to be excused from breakfast,' said the Earl. 'Isabel too. Her maid tells me she is unwell.'

'No wonder, after what happened last night,' said Lottie. 'The White Lady is nothing compared to

Mr. Woodville's spooks. He is going to-day, and I
hope he'll pack them up in his portmanteau and take
them away with him.'

The Earl coughed sonorously, and looked severely
at his daughter, who wisely held her peace.

The meal concluded, Lottie, Mervyn, and Frank
strolled out on to the terrace, leaving the Earl and
Madame Obnoskin together. The Earl sat silent,
plunged in deep thought, and the lady watched him,
silent also, until Woodville entered the room.

'I am sorry, Mr. Woodville,' said the old nobleman,
speaking in a fashion as reverent as it was courteous,
'to hear of your indisposition. Cannot I persuade
you to take breakfast?'

'I thank your lordship,' said Woodville, 'but I
would rather eat nothing yet.'

He was unwontedly pale, and there was something
indefinably curious in his manner.

'I should be glad,' he continued, 'if you could
afford me a few minutes' interview. I will not detain
you long.'

'With pleasure,' said the Earl, 'if madame will
excuse us.'

Madame assented with a smiling bow, though she
kept her eyes fixed on Woodville's face, and, afterwards on his retreating figure, with a look of keen
inquiry.

Woodville followed the Earl from the breakfast-
room to the study, and, closing the door, took his

stand upon the hearthrug at a little distance from the armchair, in which the old gentleman sat down with a sigh of weariness.

'I am not very well this morning, Mr. Woodville,' he said. 'The events of last night dwelt so strongly on my mind that I have scarcely slept since, and a sleepless night is a dreadful inconvenience to a man of my years. Well, well,' he continued, with a sigh and a smile together, 'the fleshly envelope decays, but the assurance, the strong and full assurance, of the immortality that awaits us makes amends for all.'

Woodville looked down upon him with eyes in which pity and remorse were both so clearly blended that their expression would not have passed unheeded had the old nobleman looked him in the face. He sat looking before him with a strange, wistful smile.

'I have known it always,' he murmured, more to himself than to his companion. 'I have felt, since I could think at all, that it must be so—that there *must* be other cycles of being than that in which we move at present, other worlds to redress the balance of this. How can a man who thinks at all think otherwise, though so many of the world's greatest *have* thought otherwise, and some think so still? How else could the burden of this existence be borne, if this were all? Life would be too dull and foolish a farce without that hope. Make the hope a certainty, as I feel it now, and the riddle is solved: we have eternity wherein to justify the spiritual Father who, while this life is all He grants to us, seems a crueller tyrant than any that ever reigned on earth.

'Mr. Woodville,' he continued, rising after a short interval of silence, during which Woodville watched him with the same remorseful look, and sought for words to frame the thoughts in his mind, 'the service you have done me must not pass without reward. Nay,' he went on, as Woodville made a motion to speak; 'hear me out. I know you do not look for personal gain. I should not dream of offering to the teacher who has opened to me the vista of immortal life any merely worldly reward. Such happiness as you have brought to me and to that dear child is not to be bought by money. But you have ambition, if not for yourself, for the religion you teach. I am a wealthy man. Take what you need of my substance; it is freely yours. Take all you need to help you in your holy crusade against ignorance and false science —to spread to other minds the light you have poured on mine. Whatever help I can give, count upon it, be it much or little. I shall hold myself only too fortunate if I can, at any mere pecuniary cost, help in your glorious championship of eternal truth.'

He had spoken most of this address while walking excitedly about the room, but the delivery of the last few words brought him close to the man he addressed. There was such strange matter readable in Woodville's pale face, that the Earl started as he saw it.

'Mr. Woodville, are you ill?'

'No, my lord; I am well in health. When you granted me the honour of this interview, I told you I had something to tell you.'

'True, true!' said the Earl. 'I beg your pardon. I am so excited by what occurred last night, that I seem unable to think of anything else. Won't you take a seat? Pray go on, Mr. Woodville; I am all attention.'

'I am afraid, my lord, that the communication I am about to make will be a heavy blow to you. If it were possible to spare you, I would do so; but there is no other course possible than that I have determined to take.'

His lordship looked at him at first with an expression of pure surprise, which changed as he proceeded to one of growing agitation.

'Mr. Woodville, you alarm me. Pray speak plainly; suspense is always painful.'

'The more plainly the better, my lord. Your suspense and my shame will be over the quicker.'

'Your shame!' echoed his lordship.

'I am here,' said Woodville, 'to make a shameful confession. I have deceived you. I am not what you believe me; I possess nothing of the power or the knowledge I claimed.'

The shock was, for the moment, too much for the old nobleman. He seemed unable to grasp the meaning of the words he listened to. Still with his eyes remorsefully fixed on his face, Woodville proceeded:

'I have deceived you throughout. I am what Lord Dewsbury proclaimed me to be—a charlatan, an impostor, who has practised on your desire for knowledge, on the need of your assurance of immortality. It was to tell you this that I asked for this interview.'

The Earl glared at him like a man distraught, with a face whiter than Woodville's own, struggling to grasp the gist of this amazing self-indictment.

'I must be mad or dreaming!' he murmured, pressing his hand across his eyes with the gesture of a man waking from a narcotic sleep in some strange place.

'Neither, my lord,' said Woodville quietly.

'Then *you* are mad!' cried the Earl, his stunned senses beginning to recover a little from the prodigious shock of Woodville's first words. 'An impostor, a charlatan, a pretender to occult power, after your marvellous manifestation of last night!'

'Imposture, like the rest,' said Woodville. 'I knew that Colonel Arlington was alive. My friends in Thibet have tracked him for months past in all his movements, and have kept me informed!'

'But the apparition——'

'Imposture again. An optical delusion—a juggler's trick.'

The perfect quiet of Woodville's manner puzzled and amazed the old gentleman beyond description,

He started from his chair, and paced the room in a fever-heat of perplexity, with broken exclamations of wonder and surprise. Woodville stood quietly on the spot where he had remained during the entire interview, following him with his eyes.

'Am I to understand your words in their absolute, literal significance?' he asked at last.

'Absolutely and literally,' rejoined Woodville; 'I have spoken the truth.'

'Then, sir,' said the Earl, 'you are a villain, a scoundrel—as low and base a scoundrel as ever disgraced humanity!'

Woodville went paler yet, but stood silent, with only an acquiescent gesture of the hands in answer to the charge.

'But why—why, in the name of heaven!' broke out the Earl again—'why this deception, practised on people who never injured you? What purpose does it serve? What object did you hope to gain?'

'That,' said Woodville, 'is a question I must leave unanswered. If the secret were mine you should know it; but it affects another person, and I cannot in honour reveal it.'

'In honour!' said the Earl, with concentrated scorn and amazement mingled in his voice. 'With one breath you denounce yourself as a rogue, an impostor, and with the next you prate about your honour!'

Woodville answered only by the same dumb gesture.

'Great heaven!' cried the Earl, half staggering as the thought struck him. 'That woman—Madame Obnoskin—must have been in league with you!'

'She was,' said Woodville. 'We were in correspondence before I came here, and so she was able to predict my coming.'

It took the Earl another minute or two of disordered walking about the room to digest this last communication.

'And now,' he said, turning upon Woodville, 'why this confession? You had succeeded in your conspiracy—why do you throw away the results of success?'

'To explain that fully,' returned Woodville, 'would touch on the secret I have spoken of.'

The Earl stared at him in silence for awhile, and then angrily demanded:

'Well, sir! Have you anything more to tell me? Is there any further villainy or baseness behind all this?'

'Nothing,' said Woodville; 'I have said all I had to say.'

Amazement and anger, quite beyond words to express, set the Earl striding again about the room.

Presently he tugged furiously at the bell. Before the servant had time to answer the call, he tore open the study door, crossed the corridor, and walked into the breakfast-room.

As the Earl left the room with Woodville behind him, Madame Obnoskin watched them with a quick, piercing, sidelong glance. Woodville's manner, so unusual that even she, with her long and close knowledge of him, joined to all her natural keenness of intelligence, could read nothing of its meaning, his guarded speech, and the unwonted pallor of his face, all tended to warn her of some hidden mystery.

'What can he be going to say to the Earl?' she asked herself.

They had left the door open behind them in passing out, and the door of the study, to which they had retired, was just opposite on the other side of the corridor. She strained her ears as she sat, but could catch nothing but the murmur of leaves and the light buzz of insects from the creepers on the terrace. Maddened by curiosity, she rose and stole to the door of the study, listening there intently, but all she could hear was the monotonous hum of one voice—whether Woodville's or the Earl's she could not tell. A light, quick step approaching her along the corridor startled her from her listening place. She assumed a *degagé* air, and strolled back into the breakfast-room as Lottie came in sight.

'Have you happened to see papa, Madame Obnoskin?' the latter asked.

'Yes. He is in the study. I would not disturb him yet, if I may make a suggestion. He is engaged

13

on particular business with Mr. Woodville, who starts for London by an early train, as you know.'

'All right,' responded Lottie, 'it isn't of much consequence,' and passed on.

Madame was about to resume her listening when a sudden staccato interjection from Lord Wanborough, so loud as to be clearly audible through the closed door, came to her ears, succeeded by a violent ringing at a bell. Immediately after the door was flung open, and Lord Wanborough issued from the study, crossed the corridor, and entered the breakfast-room. He was in a condition of violent agitation, evidenced by his rapid movement and abrupt exclamation.

'Atrocious abuse of my hospitality! Heartless deception! Charlatan! Impostor! Blackguard!' he muttered, as he strode about the room, unwitting of madame's presence there.

A moment later, Woodville made his appearance. He was deadly pale, and his expression might have been that of a man walking resolutely to the gallows.

'You deserve no consideration at my hands,' said the Earl, turning upon him with scorn and anger in his voice, 'and you shall receive none. Send Lord Dewsbury here to me at once!' he said to the servant who had answered his loud summons on the study bell.

'He is here, my lord,' answered the man, as Dewsbury entered the room from the terrace.

'Good! Go!' said the Earl. 'Dewsbury,' he

continued, 'look at this man! You were right concerning him. I have it from his own lips. My God! to think that I should have been cheated; that I should have been miserably duped by such an impostor.'

'I knew it all along,' said Dewsbury. 'I never doubted it for a moment.'

'Conceive my position,' continued the Earl. 'Put yourself in my place, Dewsbury. I must either admit that I have been fooled, or must hold my tongue and let this scoundrel go unpunished. How Marrables will smile, how the Dean will chuckle, over my infirmity!'

So far, neither of the three had noticed the presence of Madame Obnoskin, who had taken her stand quietly beside the window. The Earl, taking short, sharp strides about the apartment, came suddenly upon her, glared at her in furious silence for a second, and turned away.

'My dear friend,' said madame, in her silkiest voice, 'you are agitated. May I ask——'

'If you desire any information, madame, ask your confederate for it. Yes, madame, your confederate, for, if *he* is an impostor, *you* must have been in his confidence.'

'There is some mistake,' she began.

'There is no mistake, madame, or if there be one, it is *you* who have made it.'

The Obnoskin slipped her mask. She bore down

on Woodville with tight clenched hands and blazing eyes, unrecognisable, in her sudden rage, as the sleek purring creature she had hitherto seemed.

'What have you said to the Earl?' she cried hoarsely. 'I *will* know!'

'I have simply informed Lord Wanborough of the facts of the case; that the manifestations he has seen were not genuine, and that I had imposed upon his credulity—that, to use his own words, I was a charlatan, an impostor.'

The Obnoskin's reception of this utterance seemed, for the moment, strange to all who witnessed it. She went as suddenly calm as she had the moment before become excited, and walking to a little side table, took her seat there, with her feet crossed, and her head resting on her hand in an attitude of calm patience, keeping her glittering eyes fixed on Woodville's face.

'May I ask you to leave us, madame?' said Dewsbury. 'We wish to speak to Mr. Woodville alone.'

'I shall not leave you,' said madame, speaking very clearly and calmly, without taking her eyes from Woodville's face. 'I shall remain here.'

'In that case,' said Dewsbury, 'we may, I presume, take it for granted that between yourself and Mr. Woodville there are no secrets.'

'None whatever,' returned the Obnoskin. 'None in the world, I assure you.'

'Am I to understand,' Dewsbury asked the Earl, 'that you do me the honour to ask my advice in this affair ?'

'Yes,' said the Earl. 'I need advice. My mind seems unhinged by the shock. Nothing on earth but this man's direct confession would have made me believe such baseness possible!'

'My advice,' said Dewsbury, 'is simple, and easily followed. It will be best for all parties concerned to let this man go, on certain definite conditions. What are your intentions regarding the future, Mr. Woodville ?'

'I am about to leave England.'

'For what period ?'

'For good and all. I shall never return here again.'

'Will you give your promise to hold no communication with any member of this household, by any means whatsoever, henceforth ?'

'Yes. My written promise, if you care to have it ?'

'Your word will do, in this matter,' said Dewsbury, with a cold scorn, far harder to bear than the Earl's angry denunciations. 'What you have told the Earl, and repeated in my presence, is true ?'

'It is true.'

'Men of your kind do not act without a motive. May I ask what was the motive which inspired you to make this confession at the last moment ?'

'A motive,' replied Woodville, 'which your lordship will think highly improbable. I thought it my *duty*.'

'In that one respect,' said Dewsbury, after a short pause spent in close scrutiny of Woodville's face, and speaking with great dryness, 'you have certainly behaved like an honest man.'

'Thank you,' said Woodville quietly.

'You have nothing more to say?' inquired Dewsbury.

'Nothing.'

'Then we need detain you no longer.'

'A moment longer, if you please,' said Madame Obnoskin, rising from her seat. '*I* should like to say a few words.'

'You, madame!' cried the Earl. 'We are fully aware of the nature of the conspiracy between you.'

'Yet,' said madame, quietly still, 'in justice to yourself and to the young lady whom Lord Dewsbury proposes to marry——'

Woodville gave an irrepressible start, and turned his eyes on madame's face.

'Leave Miss Arlington's name out of the question,' said Lord Dewsbury sharply. 'She is not concerned in the discussion.'

'On the contrary,' said madame, 'she is very deeply concerned in it. It is on Miss Arlington's account that Mr. Woodville has rushed into so extraordinary a confession.'

'For God's sake,' cried Woodville, 'be silent!'

'I will not be silent!' she answered. 'I do not propose to spare *you* or *her*.'

'What does all this mean?' asked Dewsbury.

'Mr. Woodville,' continued madame, 'has been candour itself, save on one point, the relations existing between himself and Miss Arlington. When he entered this house it was in pursuit of her. Now he is leaving, it is because he and Miss Arlington have come to a perfect understanding.'

'Take care what you say,' said Dewsbury, losing somewhat of his habitual self-control. 'If you insinuate that between this man and Miss Arlington——'

'I insinuate nothing,' cried madame, rising with a sounding blow on the table beside her. 'I *know*! If you do not believe me, ask him why Miss Arlington visited him alone last night in the turret-chamber!'

'It was she who knocked!' murmured Woodville.

'Is this true?' demanded Dewsbury, turning threateningly on Woodville. 'Does this lady speak the truth? Answer! Deny it!'

'He cannot!' cried madame. 'You see now how candid he has been! I have nothing more to say; my work here is done. Many thanks, my lord, for your hospitality.'

She swept him a curtsey, and with a look of unutterable loathing and contempt at Woodville, left the room.

'My lord,' cried Woodville, 'don't believe that woman! Publish my shame to all the world! Denounce me! Heap what humiliation you will upon me! I will bear it all. But do not believe one word against Miss Arlington!'

'Did you meet last night, as she declares?' demanded Dewsbury, in a white heat of passion by this time. 'Answer me, or——'

'Take care, my lord, take care!' cried Woodville, as the young peer came towards him with his hand raised.

'Dewsbury!' cried the Earl. 'For God's sake, no violence here!'

'She came to you at midnight, to your room. You were alone there together! Deny it!'

A calm voice, which made them all start and turn, broke on their ears.

'Do not trouble to deny it, Mr. Woodville. It is true.'

Isabel Arlington came forward, looking very pale and resolute.

'For God's sake, Miss Arlington——' began Woodville

'Let me speak!' she said quietly. 'Lord Dewsbury has a right to an explanation. I walked last night in my sleep. Awakening, I found myself in Mr. Woodville's room.'

'Isabel!' exclaimed the Earl. 'What are you saying?'

'Only the truth. I was there. Then Mr. Woodville told me what he has told you, that he was in-

famous and unworthy, and that he asked my pardon
for the deception he had practised on me.'

'You were alone, in this man's room at midnight,
in his company?' said Dewsbury.

'I was there!' repeated Isabel. 'And, being there,
I learned that he was not infamous, but noble; not
unworthy, but capable of sacrificing his name, his
honour, his very life, to save me from reproach, and
to repair his fault.'

'Is this your only explanation?' asked Dewsbury.

'Yes,' said Isabel; 'it is the only one, and the
true one.'

'And you, sir?' continued his lordship, turning
to Woodville. 'Have you no better one to offer?'

'Miss Arlington has spoken the truth. I have
nothing to add to her statement of the facts.'

'The whole truth?' asked Dewsbury.

'The whole truth,' repeated Woodville.

'And you expect two men of the world to believe
it?'

'If you doubt it, Dewsbury, I do not,' said the Earl.
'Isabel, my child, I believe every word that you
have said. For you, sir,' he continued to Woodville,
'follow your accomplice, and never let me see your
face again.'

Woodville bent his head in silence, and left the
room, not daring to direct a glance towards Isabel,
who, before his footsteps had ceased to sound in the
corridor, fell insensible into her guardian's arms.

CHAPTER XVIII.

'MR. PHILLIPS.'

WOODVILLE's first impulse on quitting Wanborough Castle had been to leave England immediately, returning to India *via* Paris and Trieste. On arriving in London, however, he remembered that it was necessary to see his bankers, and also to transact some other business for friends in the East—business which he had postponed from time to time, and which would occupy several days.

Instead of returning to the fashionable rooms in Albemarle Street, where he had resided before his expedition into the country, he sought out quarters in the very heart of Soho, saying to himself with a bitter laugh, 'Since I am now labelled rogue and vagabond for ever, I had better consort with my kind.'

His chief desire was to escape observation, and especially to avoid the few men whom he knew in the Metropolis. With that view he changed his name for the time being, and was known in the hotel which he had selected for his hiding-place as 'Mr. Phillips,' a gentleman on a visit from Bombay.

The place, like the neighbourhood, was dull and gloomy, but it suited his gloomy mood. It was kept by an old Italian who had escaped from the Sardinian mines, and was a favourite resort of all sorts of

mysterious foreigners, who gathered every evening to
the cheap *table d'hôte*, and filled the air with a confusion of tongues reminiscent of the Tower of Babel.

Of these people, however, Woodville saw little or
nothing. He occupied rooms, a sitting-room and a
bedroom communicating, on the first-floor, and such
meals as he took in the house were served privately.
For this accommodation he paid liberally enough;
so the landlord, though he was puzzled a little by his
guest's superior manners and mysterious ways,
evinced no curiosity and asked no questions.

The business he had to do occupied him very little,
and he had plenty of spare time on his hands between
the date of his arrival in London and the date he
had fixed for his final departure. So it came to
pass that he yielded, as so many weary men have
done, to the strange fascination of the great city, and
spent many hours after nightfall in lonely wanderings
from street to street.

It was a comfort to him in his utter despair and
humiliation to feel swallowed up in the great ocean
of life, to know no one, and yet to be a part of an
ever busy multitude of souls. In the remotest solitude
he had never felt so completely alone as he did now,
surrounded by men, living shadows of himself, toiling,
striving, suffering, coming they knew not whence, and
going they knew not whither.

It was something in his wretchedness to see so
many whose wretchedness far exceeded his own—lost

london

waifs of humanity, struggling miserably in the **very**
slough of existence. At that time many a **poor**
creature had cause to bless the liberal hand of **Philip**
Woodville.

It is a truism to say that in self-sacrifice is to be
found the highest good, and that virtue is its own
reward. Like most truisms, however, it needs a very
liberal interpretation. At any rate, it would be absurd
to say that this man was happy. He had obeyed his
conscience; he had given up without hesitation everything that he held most precious in the world; he
had put on sackcloth and cast dust and ashes on his
head in obedience to the living voice within him. *conscience*
Après ?

He was an outcast from humanity, or from all he
held precious in humanity, and he had not even to
help him—the comfort given to so many of the out-
casts around him—some dim belief in a beneficent
God, some feeble faith that the sorrows of this world
would be mended in a better world to come.

He had never felt any faith, and he was not likely
to feel it now. On the contrary, he had been persuaded, since first he began to think, that human life
was at best a miserable business. The cry for personal
continuance had always seemed to him an infant's
cry for the moon—too foolish for serious consideration; and who were those who uttered it? In what
respect were the majority of them more worthy of
perpetuation than the beasts of the field?

Sometimes, in his mood of bitter scorn for humanity, he felt that only one thing was certain—a horrible and ever-present hell; and as he walked through the streets and alleys, swarming with unclean creatures, full of the wails of broken lives, he seemed to be wandering through hell indeed. And his soul rose in revolt against the idea of a personal Creator who could boast Himself the author of the world, and yet leave it so foul and incomplete.

There were moments, however, when he was more peaceful and acquiescent, when he forgot the evil in the world, and remembered only the good. These were the moments when he thought of Isabel.

If he was lost, she was saved. His dark shadow had passed away from her life, which thenceforward he prayed might be sunshine. If that was so, he was content, or so he thought. Yet he knew that he would yearn for her presence, grow mad at times with the memory of her beauty, think of her, dream of her, be possessed by her, so long as he walked erect and drew this mortal breath.

Never much interested in the ordinary affairs of the world, Woodville read no newspapers. If he glanced at one, it was only to throw it aside in contempt for the ignorance and folly it represented. So he missed the advertisement which Mervyn Darrell had inserted in the agony column. Even had he done so, he would not have responded to it in any way, for the Apostle of Culture was the very last person in whom he would have confided at that sorrowful epoch of his life.

During the day he seldom left his rooms. His time was chiefly occupied in writing and in making preparations for his departure. But one night, as he strolled among the dark streets in the neighbourhood of Drury Lane, he was attracted to the theatre, where an enterprising manager was giving a season of German opera. A crowd was entering the doors, he joined it, paid his money, and found a place at the back of the pit.

How he came to enter the building, he could hardly tell, for he was not a playgoer, and he had no curiosity of any kind to see the performance. In view of what occurred afterwards, it seemed that he was drawn thither by some occult influence. Be that as it may, there he was, seated in shadow under the dress circle, in the midst of the crowd.

The opera was a masterpiece—Wagner's 'Der Fliegende Holländer'—a work which, through its very simplicity and power of purpose, represents a great musician at his highest and best. Before the wonderful overture was ended, Woodville was listening like a man bewitched, and when the opera itself began he was spellbound.

Such a theme, treated by a master, seemed a splendid adumbration of Woodville's own life. The storm of wind and wave, the elemental anarchy, the terror of mystery, were all familiar; he was a waif

tossed on the great waters, like the doomed outcast of
the story. Then the storm subsided, and out of the
depths came, white and dove-like, the form of Signa,
the one woman, the *ewigweibliche*, the very soul of
human love. Her first song at the spinning-wheel,
her deep emotion when the tumultuous music died
away, and in deep awful silence the wayfarer of the
ocean first appeared, the gust of passion that drew
them together, her dread of him, her attraction to
him, the conflict of their living wills, culminating in
supreme sympathy and self-abnegation, were all
familiar to him, were all things he had known and
felt, were a part of his existence. The Flying
Dutchman was himself, and the Signa of his salvation
was Isabel Arlington.

Never had he been so moved by any production of
human genius; yet there seemed something mysterious
and inexplicable in the impression which it made
upon him. At last his emotion grew almost too
painful to bear. As the curtain fell on the second
act, and he sat dazed and wonderstruck amid the
applauding audience, he was startled by a voice
moaning in his ears, 'Philip, Philip!' He rose to his
feet with a startled cry and looked round the crowded
house. His eyes fell on a box on the pit tier, close to
the stage, and there, with her face turned to the
curtain, was Isabel!

His heart leapt within him, and for a moment he
seemed to totter and fall. Collecting his faculties, he

continued to watch her, fixing his eyes intently on her face. Yes, it was no dream, no fancy! there she sat, with Lady Carlotta and the Earl.

Suddenly, as if startled, she turned her face from the stage and seemed searching the audience for some familiar face. The place where he stood was in deep shadow, but slowly, involuntarily, her gaze seemed drawn that way. The Earl spoke to her; she did not answer. The next moment she rose with a terrified look, leant out of the box, and with eyes dilated, and face pale as death, continued to gaze towards him!

Woodville hardly knew what followed. His head swam, and a mist rose before his eyes. When he looked again, the box was empty, and Isabel was gone.

Eager to know what had happened, he made his way out of the theatre. His progress was slow, owing to the crowd, and it was some minutes before he reached the front of the building. When he did so, he saw a closed carriage driving away, and just caught a glimpse of Isabel's face flashing by in the lamplight; but their eyes met, and he knew that he was recognised.

Was it witchery, or mere accident, that had brought about this meeting? Under what spell had he entered the theatre that night? Was the link between them so strong that it was not yet broken? These were among the questions which he asked himself, in his mad agitation, as he walked along the dismal streets.

There was no rest that night for Woodville. He

wandered about for hours like a restless spirit, and then made his way to the gloomy hotel in Soho. A sleepy boots admitted him. Instead of going upstairs, he strolled into the empty salle-à-manger, where a solitary gas-jet was still burning, and ordered the boots to bring him a glass of brandy. While the man was procuring it, he listlessly took up a newspaper —*The Observer* of the previous Sunday. Was it accident again, or some witchcraft, that drew his eyes to the fashionable intelligence, where he read the following words?—

'The Earl of Wanborough, accompanied by Lady Carlotta Deepdale and Miss Arlington, has arrived at his town mansion in Grosvenor Square.'

Then he had not been dreaming! The night's experience, which still seemed so fantastic and strange, was a reality, and Isabel was in London.

He drank his brandy, lit a cigar, and went up to his rooms.

Sceptical as he was concerning most occult influences, there was one power in which experience had taught him faith, and that was the power of hypnotism. He himself had exerted it over Isabel, with extraordinary results; through it he had subdued her will, and brought her in the trance condition to the turret-tower. Had the slave suddenly become the master? Was the power which he had used so long against others being at last exerted over himself?

14

He sat asking himself that question, and pondering over the events of the night.

So far as he could recollect, he had not even been thinking of Isabel when he was drawn into the theatre. Even during the performance he had been unconscious of any influence but the spell of the musician and the interest of the theme. How, then, account for the voice which he had suddenly heard, for the spell which drew his eyes to the box, and for Isabel's evident consciousness of his presence in the theatre, although it was impossible for her to distinguish his form or face? Was it all this hypnotism, or some cognate influence, and, if so, were not the cases this time reversed, and he himself the person hypnotized?

Whatever the explanation might be, he was conscious more than ever of some power beyond himself conditioning his life—some power from which he could never escape, and from which, indeed, he would never escape willingly.

Under its influence his passion for the woman he loved rose again to fever-heat. Again he held her in his arms, and looked with mad yearning into her face. Again he remembered her sweet words, her tenderness, her devotion. As he sat in the lonely room, thinking it all over, he heard once more the music of the master-musician, surging up into all the tumult of the tempest, and dying away in all the ecstasies of love; and he, Philip Woodville, was the outcast of the sea, despised by man, rejected by God, but saved, for time and eternity, by the love of a woman!

CHAPTER XIX.

MERVYN IN A NEW CHARACTER.

WITHIN a very few days after Woodville's confession Wanborough Castle was deserted, save by its owner, his daughter, and Isabel. Madame Obnoskin, after a pathetic scene with the Earl, in the course of which she promised faithfully to be silent on the subject of Isabel's visit to the turret-chamber, had vanished into space, taking with her (if the proverbial small bird is to be trusted) a certain solatium in the shape of a little cheque, payable to 'bearer.' Lord Dewsbury had returned to London, leaving behind him a letter, in which he formally renounced all hope of Isabel— not, he explained, because he had ceased to respect and esteem her, whom he begged to forgive the angry words he had spoken, but because he felt now convinced that she herself was eager to be set free. Mervyn Darrell had gone back to Oxford, where he was busy doing the honours to a certain German Professor, who, having proved by metaphysics the absolute non-existence of a personal God, had followed up his argument by proving that the invention of one by man was a political necessity.

The Earl remained in a sort of moral stupefaction, seeing no one, refusing himself to all comers, even to his old friend the Dean, who constantly left his card. One of his first proceedings, after Woodville's departure, had been to shut up and double-padlock the turret-chamber.

'For the future,' he said, 'the White Lady shall have it to herself. It shall never again be occupied by any human being—certainly not during my lifetime.'

Despite all that had happened, he still clung to a belief in supernaturalism.

'Every religion,' he argued, 'had its impostors, and Theosophy was no more discredited by Philip Woodville and Madame Obnoskin than true Christianity had been by scoundrels like Pope Innocent and Louis XI.'

He turned again with eagerness to his library, and soon forgot his dishallucination in the old enchantment of occult books.

And Isabel?

For a time it seemed as if Woodville's fears might turn out true, and that her strength would break down utterly under the cruel mental strain. For days she kept her room, seldom speaking a word, and lost in quiet thought; but when Lottie wanted her to see a doctor, she only smiled and shook her head.

'No doctor can do me any good,' she said. 'Besides, I am quite well, and I never felt so peaceful in my life.'

Peaceful, indeed, she seemed—in a dull, listless, dreamy sort of way. Lottie was fairly puzzled.

'She can't be fretting about Frank,' Lottie reflected,

'for I feel sure that she is glad the engagement is broken off. Can she still be thinking of that man? Oh, if I knew what really took place that dreadful night!'

At last, one lovely morning, as the two girls sat together at the open window of the boudoir, Isabel broke the silence which she had kept so long:

'Do you know,' she asked quietly, 'whether Mr. Woodville has left England?'

'No, dear,' answered Lottie; 'I've heard nothing whatever about him, and, frankly, I don't want to. I fervently trust that I shall never see his face again.'

Isabel only smiled.

'With you it is different, dear,' she said gently. 'His coming here meant nothing in your life; but with me it meant so much! I have tried very hard to forget him, but you see it is impossible. You remember that night when he brought me here in his arms? He thought I was asleep, and so, perhaps, I was, but even in sleep one is conscious, and I knew what was happening, and I felt so happy; and always now, when I close my eyes, I seem to be there still, supported in his arms, and being carried, in a dream as it were, I knew not whither!'

'Oh, Isabel,' said Lottie, kneeling by her and looking up in her face; 'I understand now! What a goose I was not to understand before! You love him!'

'Yes, Lottie.'

'Thank heaven he never knew it!' exclaimed Lottie.

'He did know it, dear, and it was because he knew it that he went away. I don't think that we shall ever meet again in life, but we are nearer to each other now than ever; and perhaps—perhaps—if there is a hereafter——'

Her eyes filled with tears, and she could say no more.

Two days after this interview Mervyn Darrell, sitting in his rooms at Oxford, received the following message, short and incisive, like its sender:

'Come here at once.—LOTTIE.'

The Apostle of Culture obeyed the mandate, took the train, and arrived at Wanborough Castle that evening. He found Lottie alone in the drawing-room, looking very pale and troubled, but still preserving her brisk, imperative manner.

'I'm glad you've come,' she said, giving him the tips of her fingers. 'Sit down.'

Mervyn smiled and obeyed. She looked at him thoughtfully for some minutes, and then said:

'Mervyn, have you ever in all your life been of the slightest use to anybody?'

The question was a startling one, but it did not disconcert Mervyn in the least.

'Never,' he answered, with his usual superior smile. 'I have a constitutional objection to useful things and people. A donkey is useful—so, I presume, is a clergyman; but I hope I resemble neither.'

'Humph!' muttered Lottie, continuing to regard him thoughtfully.

'Is anything the matter?' he inquired, after a pause. 'In *your* case, Lottie, I might strain a point, and endeavour to be of assistance.'

'You'd very likely make a bungle of the whole affair,' returned Lottie; 'you're so impossible.'

'In that case, why did you send for me? Surely not to tell me what I already know!'

'You were the only person I could think of. I've no brothers, and no friends. Papa is in a state of moral collapse, and Frank has gone back to his politics. Oh, Mervyn,' she added, with a sudden change of manner, 'do be sensible, and help me if you can!'

'My dear Lottie,' said Mervyn, 'I can't promise to be sensible. But tell me what it is you want.'

'A man of the world, a man of tact, a diplomatist. One who will do whatever I tell him, and do it judiciously.'

'Dear me!' exclaimed Mervyn. 'I'm afraid——'

'Don't say you refuse!' cried Lottie, stamping her little foot; 'and don't pretend to be more perfectly imbecile than you are!'

'On my word!' said Mervyn, leaning back in his chair with a yawn and folding his arms behind his head, 'energy suits some people tremendously well. You look awfully nice when you're excited, Lottie!'

'Oh, Mervyn,' pleaded the girl, 'can you be serious just for once?'

'I hardly know,' said the young man meditatively. 'I suppose I might be, under sufficient provocation. I think,' he added, 'that I haven't been really serious since I had that turn-up with the bargee at Iffley.'

'What was that?' asked Lottie. 'A fight? *You* fought somebody, Mervyn?'

'Thrashed him, too!'

'Oh!' cried Lottie, with beaming eyes, 'how splendid! I love a fighting man! I should have admired you then, Mervyn!'

'My dear Lottie, I was a most disgusting exhibition! I went about for a fortnight with one eye closed and a nose like a pumpkin!'

'I shouldn't have cared for your nose,' said Lottie. 'Who ever thinks about a hero's nose? But now, Mervyn,' she went on, dropping back to gravity again, 'let us be serious. Really and truly, I need your help. I know you're clever, though you do try so hard to hide it, and I believe you have a good heart.'

'Highly flattered, I'm sure,' said Mervyn. 'Well? I'm listening.'

'It's about Isabel,' said Lottie, lowering her voice and looking cautiously round, though she knew they were alone together. 'Mervyn, I don't know what

to do; it's terrible!   She is getting thinner and paler
every day; she doesn't eat as much as one of my
canaries; she takes no interest in anything, and
wanders about the place like a ghost.   Not even the
knowledge of her father's return, and the hope of
seeing him in a week or two, seems to do her any
good.   Mervyn,' she continued, laying her hand on
her companion's, and speaking brokenly and with
wet eyes, 'there are moments when I fear she may
not live to see him!'

'Bless my soul!' cried Mervyn, for once startled
out of his affected languor.   'Lottie, my dear child,
what are you saying?'

'It's true, Mervyn,' she continued, 'and you would
think so too if you saw her.'

'But what use can *I* be here?' asked the young
man.   'I'm not a doctor.'

'It's no case for doctors,' said Lottie.   'All the
drugs in the what-d'ye-call-it couldn't do the poor
darling any good.   Listen!   Have you seen or heard
anything of Mr. Woodville since he left the castle?'

'Nothing,' answered Mervyn, obviously surprised by
Lottie's apparent inconsequence.

'You must find him,' said the girl emphatically.
'You must find that man, if he's above ground.'

Mervyn stared at her in silence, with a completely
blank visage, for at least thirty seconds; then suddenly
started and emitted a long, low whistle.   'By Jove!'

he murmured to himself. 'I say, Lottie, you can't mean—confound it!—you can't mean that Isabel——

'I mean,' said Lottie, 'that she's in love with him I mean that she'll die if he leaves England and they are parted for ever. Yes, yes,' she cried, answering the expression of Mervyn's face, 'I know. I should have said just the same myself a month ago. I should have laughed at anyone who told me that anybody ever died for love. But that is what Isabel is dying of, Mervyn. Her life is bound up in that terrible man. You must find him!' She rose. 'I don't want to hear you say anything,' she continued, as Mervyn opened his lips. 'It's absurd and silly and impossible, and all that, for a girl who might have been a peeress to fall in love with a conjurer, but that's what happened, and we've just got to make the best of it. You must go to London, Mervyn, and find Mr. Woodville. It's a thousand to one he's there, for he can't have sailed for India yet; there has been no ship since he left here. Go, and be of some use for once in your life. Find that man, or never show your face in Wanborough Castle again.'

The girl's enthusiasm, the novelty of the quest on which she sent him, fired Mervyn with a sudden zeal. As he rose and took her hand there was a look on his face which Lottie had never seen there before, a look which would have surprised his fellow Apostles of the New Spirit more even than it surprised her. He cared vastly more for Lottie than he liked to admit, even to himself, and she looked delightfully winning as she imperiously requisitioned his services in her-cousin's cause.

'I'll go,' he said. 'I'll be off by the next train, and if Woodville's above ground I'll find him. By Jove! Lottie, energy isn't such a bad thing, after all, just as an occasional tonic. Do you know, I feel as if another set-to, such as I had with the bargee, would do me good.'

'You're a good fellow, Mervyn,' said the girl, 'when you aren't posing and pretending to be something that you're not. There, there!' she said, extricating her fingers from his grasp as he bent down to kiss them. 'Don't be silly. Go and find Mr. Woodville, and there will be plenty of time for nonsense afterwards.'

Mervyn drove back to the station just in time to catch the early afternoon train to St. Pancras. Man-hunting is always the most fascinating of pursuits, and the condition of excitement into which he worked himself about Lottie's commission surprised him. As he sat in the train he found two advertisements of Private Inquiry Offices, the chief of each establish-ment boasting a former connection with Scotland Yard. He took a cab at the station and rattled off to their various addresses, leaving at each a detailed account of Woodville's appearance, and what he knew or could guess of his haunts and habits. Next he drove to a big advertisement agent's in the Strand, and insured the appearance in every leading London daily of the following announcement :

'Mr. Philip Woodville is urgently desired to communicate at once with M. D., Poste Restante, Oxford.'

Before he went to bed, thoroughly tired out, he had made inquiries at the Travellers' and Sports' Clubs, and at many of the hotels most patronized by Anglo-Indian travellers.   Next day saw him at the twin-villas rented by the Theosophical Society in Finchley Road, and he scoured London east, west, north and south to inquire for any possible news of the missing man at the private addresses of the devotees of the faith.

But there was nothing to be heard. Woodville's presence in England was known. His arrival from India and his sojourn at Wanborough Castle had been chronicled in the gossiping prints, in which also had appeared various more or less mutilated accounts of the *séance;* but Woodville appeared to have held no communication with any person interested in theosophy since his leaving the castle. The detective agencies drew blank also. No person answering the description given had been remarked at the shipping offices or railway stations, and on the third day of the appearance of Mervyn's advertisements no answer had been received.

It was on the afternoon of that day that Fortune first favoured him in his quest.   He was strolling dejectedly along Bond Street, when a lady emerged from a shop, the door of which was held obsequiously open by one of the attendants.

'I thank you, sir,' said the lady.

Mervyn started at the voice, and, turning, found himself face to face with Madame Obnoskin. She answered his gaze with an aspect of such perfect self-possession that no onlooker could have thought for a moment that they had ever met before—so perfect that Mervyn was for a moment staggered by the idea that he had been deceived by a chance resemblance. She would have passed him, but, uncovering politely, he barred her path.

'Will you grant me the favour of a word, Madame Obnoskin?' She made no answer, and he continued: 'I want particularly to learn the whereabouts of our common friend, Mr. Woodville.'

'I know nothing of Mr. Woodville or his where-abouts,' she answered curtly. 'Have the kindness to stand aside, sir.'

It was perfectly obvious that, whether she spoke the truth or not, Mervyn would get no information from her, and a squabble with a lady in a West-end thoroughfare was neither to his taste nor his interest. He stepped aside with a second salute, and madame entered a neat little one-horse brougham, the door of which was held open by a well-appointed page-boy. It moved away; and Mervyn, after waiting for a second, hailed a hansom, and bade the driver follow it. The brougham stopped at a house in Clarges Street. Mervyn gave his cabman the word to drive straight on, marked the number of the house in

passing, and stopped his vehicle at the further corner
of the street, in time, himself unseen, to see madame
descend and enter. The shades of evening had
fallen pretty thickly by this time, so Mervyn felt
secure in keeping in sight of the house. He had been
in watching for a half-hour or so, when a servant-
maid came up the area-steps and directed her footsteps towards Piccadilly. He followed and accosted
her, soothing her initial alarm by the gift of half-a-
sovereign and the assurance that all he needed was a
little information. The lady he had just seen enter
the house was a foreign lady, of the name of Obnoskin.
Did she live there? Yes; she had lived there, on the
drawing-room floor, for the last two or three days.
Did she receive visitors? Yes; two people had called
upon her. Was one of them a young, handsome man
with a very dark complexion, dark eyes, and black
curly hair? No, the maid said; nobody answering
to that description had called. Mervyn let the girl
go, she promising to tell no one of his inquiries, and
strolled back along the street. Over the fanlight of
a house, immediately facing that in which Madame
Obnoskin had taken up her quarters, was a card
announcing apartments to let. Struck by a sudden
inspiration, Mervyn knocked. The rooms to be let
were on the second floor in front of the house, and so
suited his purpose, which was to dog madame on her
every visit to the outward world until he could establish the truth or falsehood of her ignorance of Wood-

ville's hiding-place. He watched from his window till long after midnight, but though many persons left or entered the house opposite, he caught no further glimpse of madame. He was beginning to think further watching useless for that night, when a vehicle drew up at the door, and he recognised it as the carriage in which madame had driven home in the afternoon. He seized his hat and umbrella, dashed downstairs, and, cautiously keeping in the shadow of the lintel of the front-door, saw madame emerge from the house, give a short direction to the coachman, and enter the vehicle. He walked quickly into Piccadilly, the carriage overtaking him before he gained the corner. He ran behind it noiselessly until he met an empty cab, sprang in and instructed the driver. The brougham rolled rapidly to a little back street in Soho, where madame alighted before a tall narrow-fronted house, and, after knocking and holding a short conference with a servant, was admitted. It was raining heavily, and Mervyn's watch, as he tramped backwards and forwards just out of the range of the windows of the house, was anything but comfortable. Twice the church bells clamorously answered each other overhead, telling the hour, but he stuck to his task with a constancy he felt to be heroic. The third hour was far gone before the door of the house opened, revealing two people, a woman and a man. He walked rapidly past them, his face hidden by his umbrella, and put all his soul into his ears. Madame's voice, angry and excited, reached him first, speaking in a language of which he had no knowledge; and Philip Woodville's voice, soft and languidly monotonous, answered her petulant phrases.

'Tout vient à point à celui qui sait attendre,' murmured Mervyn; 'I have found him at last!'

CHAPTER XX.

INTERCESSION.

MERVYN lingered in the rainy street until Madame Obnoskin, returning to her carriage, was driven away and Woodville had retreated to the house and closed the door behind him. Then, after carefully registering in his mind the number of the house and the name of the street, he betook himself to his hotel, leaving word with the night porter that he was to be called at a sufficiently early hour to enable him to catch the morning train to Wanborough. He apprised Lottie by telegram of the satisfactory conclusion, so far, of his quest, and he was in no measure surprised to find that energetic young lady awaiting him just within the park gates. He dismissed his fly, and they walked side by side along the avenue, while he recounted to her his experience of the chase after Woodville.

'You've managed very well,' said Lottie, 'all things considered.' She never paid Mervyn an undiluted compliment. 'But I don't know, after all, if our trouble will be of much use. Isabel puzzles me dreadfully. This last day or two her manner has changed completely.'

'How changed?' asked Mervyn.

'The day you went to London she came down to dinner in the highest spirits. She has been running all over the place, laughing and singing, gayer than I ever saw her before.'

'That's a good symptom, surely,' said Mervyn; 'it looks as if she had made up her mind to forget the fellow.'

'Yes,' said Lottie, 'but there are other symptoms that I don't like nearly so well. She doesn't eat any more than she did when she was moping herself to death. And she doesn't sleep well. I have heard her crying in the night, and when I went to her room to try to comfort her, I found her pretending to be fast asleep. Her gaiety isn't real, and you can't help feeling that she might break down at any moment.'

'What are you going to do in reference to Mr. Woodville?' asked Mervyn, after a pause.

'I don't know yet,' Lottie answered.

'If anything at all is going to be done,' answered Mervyn, 'it should be done quickly. He might leave England at any moment.'

'He mustn't go without our knowledge,' said

15

Lottie. 'If Isabel can cure herself of the infatuation
she has for him, well and good, but if she can't——'

She left the remainder of her thought unspoken.

'You must be in touch with him, Mervyn, or at
least keep your eye upon him, and be able to communicate with him if it should prove necessary.' She
mused for a little while. 'I'll tell you what we will
do. He knows your handwriting, I suppose.'

'Yes,' said Mervyn. 'We have had some little
correspondence together.'

'He doesn't know mine,' said Lottie. 'I shall
write him a line telling him not to leave England for
another week, and to hold himself in readiness for
a summons, and sign it, "A Friend." You can post
the letter in London, and tell one of the detectives to
keep him in view and report his actions. I think I
shall be able to tell finally in a day or two whether
Isabel is going to get over this folly or not.'

They reached the house, and found Isabel sitting in
the drawing-room alone. She had not noticed their
approaching footsteps, and Mervyn had time to
observe her. She was sitting in an attitude of
fatigue and dejection, with her chin sunk upon her
breast, and her eyes bent upon the carpet at her feet.
Her cheeks had a hectic, unhealthy flush, and her
eyes, unnaturally large and bright, were ringed by
dark circles. Mervyn was shocked at the alteration
in her appearance. When she became conscious of
their presence, she rose to her feet with a quick,

nervous shudder, instantly suppressed, and approached them.

'Good news!' she cried, with a feverish gaiety. 'I have persuaded uncle to take us all to London. It is terribly dull here; one is bored to death.'

'I am afraid you won't find London much better,' said Mervyn, 'the season is over, and there is nothing doing.'

'Oh!' cried Isabel, sitting at the piano and rattling at the keys, 'London is never dull. There are always more or less people in town, and there are the theatres, and picture galleries, and lots of things to amuse one. And I like the crowd. I hate solitude. I feel as if I should like to pass the rest of my life driving about the streets in a swift carriage, looking at the shops and at the people. I want life, move-ment, excitement! This place stifles me. I've had enough of vegetating.'

Lottie and Mervyn interchanged a quick look of intelligence. Isabel's manner was as unlike her usual style of speech as could be imagined and the new idea of enjoyment she propounded was startlingly distinct from any she had ever spoken of before. She had never cared for the crowded gaieties of London, and had always been happy to leave them for the tranquillity of country life. Her very voice was changed. Its melancholy, musical softness was gone; there was a haggard, defiant ring of forced jollity in it far more painful to hear.

'When do we go?' asked Lottie.

'This afternoon by the 3.10,' answered Isabel. 'Fifine is packing our things; I think I'll go and look after her.'

She flitted off, humming a tune.

'You see,' said Lottie to Mervyn, 'how changed she is.'

Mervyn nodded with a grave face.

'You had better stay and have lunch with us, and we will all go to London together.'

It was a dull party which travelled that afternoon. Isabel's mood had changed to a petulant silence, and she sat at the window of the train looking out on the flying landscape without speaking a word to her companions. The Earl was glad to get away from the castle for a time, but had no great expectation of pleasure from the excursion to London.

Isabel's silence lasted till she was seated in the carriage which they found waiting at the station in readiness to convey them to Grosvenor Square.

'At last!' she said, looking out on the bustle of the streets. 'Now we're going to enjoy ourselves. Where shall you take us to-night, Mervyn?'

'I really didn't know that you would like to go anywhere,' he replied.

'Of course I want to go somewhere,' said Isabel irritably. 'Do you think I've come to London to bury myself alive? What are they doing at the theatres?'

'Well,' said Mervyn, consulting the advertisement column of a newspaper, 'there's "Olivia" at the Lyceum.'

'No, I don't care for the Lyceum,' said Isabel; 'it's too slow. Find something else.'

'There's a melodrama at the Princess's.'

'That sounds better; but isn't there anything funny?'

'Burlesque at the Gaiety,' said Mervyn.

'The very thing!' cried Isabel, clapping her hands. 'You must go and dress and get a box. I've never seen a burlesque.'

'Had you not better rest to-night, my dear,' asked Lottie, 'and begin pleasure-seeking to-morrow?'

'I don't want to rest,' said Isabel; 'I want to enjoy myself and see everything I can. You must find out anything that is going on, Mervyn, and let us know each morning.'

The Earl looked at her wonderingly. He was not a very keen or observant old gentleman, but Isabel's change of manner was too marked to escape his attention. To find this reticent and retiring girl out-Lottieing Lottie, in her thirst for frivolous amusement was a curious experience. He put it down to the excitement occasioned by the expected return of her father, and a natural desire to abridge the period of waiting for the earliest news at hand. This burst of feverish pleasure-seeking lasted for two or three days, during which time Mervyn and Lottie were both hard

put to it to keep pace with Isabel.   It ended with that
night at Drury Lane already spoken of, and the girl
fell back into the dark, listless, uninterested mood
which had frightened her friend aforehand.   After
this had lasted for a couple of days, Lottie summoned
Mervyn to secret council.

'Mervyn,' she asked, 'is that man still in London?'

'Yes; my men are watching him.   He not only
hasn't gone, but, so far as they can make out, he has
no immediate intention of going; at least, he is
making no preparation.'

Lottie sat silent for a minute, obviously, from her
intent and troubled look, thinking hard.

'Yes,' she said aloud, speaking to herself, 'there
might be a way.   I suppose,' she continued, addressing her companion, 'that you have studied this
hypnotic business, and know all about it.'

'I have read a little about it,' replied Mervyn, with
a great deal more modesty than he usually displayed
in claiming acquaintance with a subject.   'Why do
you ask?'

'I want you to tell me something.   Can a person
who has hypnotized another person take off the
influence if he chooses to do so?'

'I should suppose so,' replied Mervyn, 'though I
really couldn't say for certain.   But I suppose that
because you have been subjugated by the power of a
certain personality, it does not follow that you need
be the lifelong slave of that personality, unless the

hypnotic force is constantly renewed by the will of the hypnotizer. He could remove the influence by the mere fact of ceasing to continue it.'

Lottie rose to her feet with a sudden air of determination.

'I'll do it !' she cried, ' it's the only way.'

'Do what ?' asked Mervyn.

'I shall go and see Mr. Woodville,' said Lottie, ' and make him leave Isabel alone.'

' What do you mean ?'

'I mean,' said Lottie, ' that I have thought the whole business out and got to the bottom of it. That man has cast a spell on Isabel ; he has hypnotized her, and he must be made to take his spell off her.'

' My dear Lottie,' cried Mervyn, ' what nonsense are you talking ?'

'I'm not talking nonsense at all,' said Lottie ; ' that's *your* province. If you knew all that I know, you would see this matter as I see it.'

For a moment she was on the point of telling him what she had witnessed on that eventful night when Isabel's sleeping feet had borne her to the turret-chamber, but she refrained. That was not her secret, but Isabel's, and Lottie was loyalty incarnate.

' I'll go at once,' said Lottie, ' and you must go with me. We've got time before lunch, and nobody will miss us. Isabel is out, and papa is busy in the study. Ring for a hansom while I get my jacket on.

Never mind making any objections; my mind is
made up.'

She left the room, and Mervyn, after some mutter-
ings and pulling at his moustache, ordered the cab,
which was announced as Lottie bustled back into the
room, completely equipped for out of doors.

'You had better send up your own name, and say
nothing about me,' said Lottie, breaking silence for
the first time as the vehicle entered the street in
which Woodville had taken up his quarters. 'He
won't want to see me.'

They entered the restaurant on the ground-floor of
the hotel, where half a dozen groups of swarthy,
ear-ringed Continental gentlemen were consuming
cigarettes and *petits verres* over their newspapers and
dominoes at the little marble-topped tables, and a
waiter came forward to inquire their needs.

'You have a gentleman staying in the house,' said
Mervyn, and described Woodville. The waiter hesitated, shrugged, changed colour a little, and finally,
with a word of excuse, crossed the room to confer
with the patron.

'You know the gentleman's orders,' said the latter
in Italian. 'Say there is no such person here.'

'You may spare yourself the trouble,' said Mervyn,
also in Italian, which language he spoke fluently.
'I know that he is here. Give him this card, if you
please, and say that my business is of the most
pressing importance,'

The waiter shrugged again, and glared inquiringly at the landlord.

'Take the gentleman's card,' said the landlord. 'You will understand, signor, that we but obey the orders of the dark signor in refusing him.'

'I quite understand. Say nothing about the lady who accompanies me,' said Mervyn, and returned to Lottie's side as the waiter vanished with his card. He reappeared a minute or two later, and requested Mervyn to follow him, which he did, followed in turn by Lottie.

They found Woodville alone in a little sitting-room, furnished more in the Continental than in the English style. He looked pale and worn, and was markedly thinner than when Lottie had last seen him. He evinced no surprise at her appearance, and not the slightest curiosity as to how his retreat had been discovered.

'This is an unexpected pleasure, Lady Carlotta,' he said, as he set a chair for her. 'You are well, I hope, Mr. Darrell?'

Mervyn, with considerably less aplomb than he ordinarily showed, replied that he was very well indeed.

'To what, may I ask, do I owe this honour?'

'I don't know, Mr. Woodville,' Lottie began, 'whether I am quite the right person to intrude on your privacy, to ask a favour, but that is the object with which I asked Mr, Darrell to bring me here,'

She paused, and Woodville slightly inclined his head in token of attention.

'You may not be particularly anxious to oblige me, but when I tell you that it is on Miss Arlington's account that I have come, perhaps you will listen.'

'I will listen to any communication you may do me the honour to make,' said Woodville. 'None the less willingly,' he added, 'because it is you who make it.'

'What are you doing to Miss Arlington?' asked Lottie, with sudden sharpness of voice and manner.

Woodville looked from her to Mervyn and back again, puzzled by the curious character and manner of the question.

'I beg your pardon, Lady Carlotta; I am afraid that I scarcely understand you.'

'Pardon me, Mr. Woodville,' said Lottie, 'but you understand me perfectly. This is no time for beating about the bush, and if I am impolite I am very sorry, but I can't help it. Ever since you came to Wanborough Castle Isabel has been a changed being. I had hoped that when you went away the trouble would be over, but instead of that it has become worse and worse. You are killing her, Mr. Woodville! Killing her as certainly as you would kill her if you shot or poisoned her!'

Woodville was looking at her with a white scared face.

'You have established some sort of influence over

her, of what kind I don't know, though I suppose it is what you call hypnotism. I have heard you say that you possess that power, and I believe—*you* will understand what I mean if Mr. Darrell does not—that I have seen you exercise it on Miss Arlington.'

'I do possess the power,' said Woodville, 'and I do not deny—it would be useless to deny it to you—that I have exercised it on Miss Arlington, but not since I left the castle. I swear to you that what I say is true. I have exercised no control over Miss Arlington's acts or thoughts since then by any voluntary movement of my will. I hope, I am sure, that your fears for your friend are exaggerated.'

'And I am sure that they are not,' replied Lottie; 'she is fretting herself into her grave,' she went on, rising, with the tears running down her face. 'I have said all I have to say, sir. If you are practising those wicked arts on Isabel you are a murderer, and her death will lie at your door. Come, Mervyn!'

She left the room, and Woodville turned his white face on Mervyn, with a wild question in his eyes.

'Lady Carlotta,' said the latter, answering the dumb question thus addressed to him, 'has said nothing more than the truth about Miss Arlington's condition. It is a very grave business, Mr. Woodville. It was I who introduced you to the castle, and the responsibility rests partly upon me. Can nothing be done?'

Woodville sank trembling into a chair, staring

straight before him. 'My God!' he murmured in a voice so low that it scarcely reached Mervyn's ears.

'Can you suggest nothing?' asked Mervyn again. 'If you have done the evil, is it beyond your power to cure it?'

'For God's sake,' said Woodville, 'leave me to myself awhile; let me think in peace. Yes,' he cried, rising from his seat and gripping Mervyn's hand; 'it shall be cured, though it costs me my life.'

CHAPTER XXI.

FASCINATION.

As the reader already knows, Woodville had been visited, shortly after his arrival in the hotel in Soho, by Madame Obnoskin. He himself had written to her, under care of a certain Theosophical Society, of which they were both members, requesting an interview, and telling her his reasons for remaining incognito during the short period that he remained in London.

She had come to him at once, still furious at the failure of her designs on the Earl of Wanborough, and at her ignominious expulsion from the castle. In no measured terms, but with all the spitefulness of an angry woman, she had reproached him for his treachery to herself and to what she called 'the cause.'

He had listened to her quietly, with an air of ineffable weariness, until the moment when, trembling with passion, she touched again upon his relations with Isabel.

'Stop there, if you please!' he said, with a terrible look. 'Neither of us is fit to breathe that lady's name. Think what you like of me, denounce and insult me in whatever way you please, but be silent concerning Miss Arlington — for your own sake be silent.'

'Why should I spare her?' cried the Obnoskin; 'neither she nor you have spared me. I have been degraded, insulted, ruined, and you are the cause.'

'You have escaped very lightly, my dear Obnoskin,' said Woodville, with a touch of his old sarcastic manner. 'For less than you and I have done many an unfortunate thaumaturgist has stood in the felon's dock. I should be sorry to see so charming a lady there,' he added, smiling darkly; 'but stranger things have happened.'

'I shouldn't care,' she exclaimed fiercely, 'if I had taken my revenge!'

'Oh yes, you would care—a prison dress would not become you, and you, who are so fond of luxury, would object to the prison fare. You are safe now, my dear Obnoskin, and I advise you to be discreet. If you are not, I shall take care that the world knows what you have done. I shall denounce myself, and, in doing so, denounce my charming fellow-conspirator.'

Cowed at last by his determination, and well aware
that he would hesitate at nothing if it once became a
case of open war, she had taken her departure on the
evening when Mervyn Darrell was on the watch.
Since then she had made no sign.   But on the
morning after Woodville's adventure at the opera she
came again.

Woodville sat writing at an escritoire, and the
moment her eyes fell upon his face she was startled
by its haggard expression and ghastly pallor.   She
closed the door softly behind her, and advanced
smiling, with outstretched hand.

'My dear Woodville,' she said, 'I have come with
a flag of truce!   I was angry when we last met; but
I am cooler now, and I wish to say, " Let bygones be
bygones."   After all, what is done cannot be undone,
so let us shake hands.'

She took his hand in hers, and then sat down.

'After all,' she continued, with a cat-like purr,
'my matrimonial designs, as you called them, were
unworthy of me, and I could never have settled down
with that benevolent old imbecile.   I am going to
Vienna, to interview a circle there.'

'Alone?' asked Woodville, smiling.

'The Count von Mozer—a charming man—will
escort me.   He is a believer, and fabulously rich,'
she replied, showing her white teeth and flashing her
eyes.

'I see—another conquest!   Well, I wish you luck.'

'But you, my dear Woodville, what will become of you? Shall you, like myself, become philosophical, and seek fresh fields of activity?'

'I am returning to India,' said Woodville quietly.

'Cured, I hope, of your infatuation. My dear friend, oil and vinegar will never mix, and you and I have nothing in common with these cold English. I am sorry,' she added, ' to see you looking so ill.'

'I am well enough,' he answered.

'Humph! What would you say to me if I gave you a piece of news? Miss Arlington is in London!'

'I know that,' replied Woodville.

'You have seen her—you have met again?'

'I have seen her, but we have not spoken,' he said, rising and holding out his hand.

She laughed and said ' Good-bye,' tripping out of the room with the light step of a girl of seventeen. He turned to the window, and saw at the door an open carriage drawn by two fine horses. A liveried coachman sat on the box and a footman stood at the door, and in the carriage was seated a stout elderly gentleman with a white moustache.

'The happy Count von Mozer !' thought Woodville, as Madame Obnoskin entered the carriage and seated herself by the elderly gentleman's side. As they drove off she looked up, nodded, and playfully kissed her hand.

For days after his meeting with Isabel, Philip Wood-

ville remained <u>like a man under a charm</u>. He could
do nothing and plan nothing, and he could think of
nothing except Isabel. <u>Under this enchantment, the</u>
<u>great City itself became transformed.</u> His walks
through the dark streets were no longer solitary;
the thought of her was comfort and companionship.
Again and again he asked himself: 'What is she
doing now? Is she thinking of me? Is she conscious of the sympathy which seems to link us together, and am I forgiven?'

For two nights and days he fought against the
influence which drew him towards the place which
sheltered her. On the third night, unable to resist it
any longer, he walked in the direction of Grosvenor
Square.

Wandering out of Soho, and turning into Coventry
Street, he mixed with the crowds returning from the
theatres and with the idlers lingering along the pavement; crossed Piccadilly Circus, where the nightly
saturnalia of painted women was beginning; pushed
his way through the obscene throngs outside the
St. James's Restaurant, and gained the quieter pave-
ments of Piccadilly. The rattle of innumerable cabs,
the sound of voices, the flashing of the lamps in the
street and the lamps of the moving vehicles, all
seemed strange and afar off, like lights and sounds in
a dream.

It was a fine night, but the skies overhead were
covered with clouds, through which a stormy moon

was sailing, now hidden, now seen, and casting
flying gleams on the streets and housetops.

He turned out of Piccadilly, and followed the street
which leads into Berkeley Square. All was quiet here,
save for an occasional hansom driving by, and the
foot passengers were very few. A few minutes later
he reached Grosvenor Square.

Ignorant of the number of the Earl's residence, he
walked quietly round the narrow pavement underneath
the trees. The square was perfectly deserted, and
there were few lights in the houses, for the season
was almost completely over, and the fashionable exit
was in full swing. At long intervals a carriage would
draw up at one of the houses, discharge its load of
cloaked and hooded women and shirt-fronted men,
and drive away again, leaving the deep silence deeper
still. The leaves rustled gently overhead in the
central garden, and now and then, when the autumnal
breeze rocked their branches with greater force, a few
of them flitted to the ground.

The season and the time of night were consonant
with the feelings uppermost in Woodville's mind.
The moist air, prophetic of coming rain, fanned his
hot brow and soothed the tension of his nerves. As
he strolled round and round under the murmuring
leaves, he watched the windows in which a light still
lingered. The wild passion, the mad desire of
possession, had died out of his heart, he thought of
her now always with a tender pity and remorse.

16

Why had he obeyed the foolish impulse to follow her
to England ?   It would have been so much better, so
much braver and tenderer in him to have accepted
the decree of fate, to have beaten down his passion for
her, and to have let her go away, to forget him.

'She will forget me in time,' he told himself, and
found comfort in the thought; for he was purified,
and the good in his nature, which for so many years
he had sedulously suppressed, had asserted itself, and
triumphed over the cynicism he had fostered.   He
could think of her, happy in the life-long society of
another man, nursing his children, without any dis-
turbing pang of jealousy.   Self was forgotten, his only
desire was for her happiness, his only sentiment pity
for the tender heart he had bruised.   He would never
see her again, he knew, and that knowledge, which
would have been the very quintessence of sorrow to
him only so short a time before, had no power to stir
him from his calm.

'She will learn to forgive me,' he told himself, ' and
then to forget me, and in a little time I shall be nothing
but a memory.'   He bowed to his fate and accepted
his sentence with quietude, almost with cheerfulness.

Three o'clock had struck, and still he wandered
round and round the railings.   The lights had died
out from most of the windows of the square, and for
the last half-hour the only sound which had broken
its silence had been the measured tramp of the police-
man as he paced upon his beat.   The whirr of wheels

and hum of voices came faintly from the great
thoroughfares of Piccadilly and Oxford Street, dead-
ened by the moist air. A carriage rounded the
corner of a street leading into the square. Idly,
Woodville watched its gleaming lights as they neared
him, till they stopped before the door of one of the
mansions. A footman descended from the box and
roused the sleepy echoes with a thunderous summons
on the knocker. The door of the house opened, and in
the flood of crude light shed by the hall lamp, Woodville saw a well-known figure trip up the steps and
into the house. Lady Carlotta ! His breath came
thick ; he advanced quickly into the horse road, as
Lord Wanborough followed with a second female
figure on his arm.

'Isabel !' he breathed, scarcely above a whisper.

Was it fancy or reality ? The girl shrank nearer to
the old man, and threw a quick glance behind her as
she entered the house.

The door closed and the carriage rolled away.

CHAPTER XXII.

THE LAST RESOLVE.

It was clear at last to Philip Woodville that there
was only one way.

So far his sacrifice had been useless ; it had neither
saved Isabel from the consequences of his sin, nor

ensured his own moral redemption. *She* was still the slave of his evil power; *he* was still the slave of his own overmastering passion. The inexorable laws of Nature, which he had ignored or defied, were exacting the full retribution for a broken commandment.

It is part of the mystery of existence that the punishment of sin does not end with the guilty: it extends to the innocent, even to the remotest generation; and this fact, though it has made many thinking men doubt the beneficence of God, often multiplies tenfold the sinner's sense of responsibility. Philip Woodville was no longer a casuist; he had escaped from the atmosphere of intellectual casuistry into the clearer air of spiritual insight. He understood, therefore, that Isabel, though wholly innocent of all blame, was reaping the harvest of *his* sin.

And so long as he *lived* she must suffer. The wicked magic of his hypnotism would continue to possess her, so long as he remained capable of thought and passion.

He might school himself to resignation, he might efface himself from her knowledge, he might fly to the furthest ends of the earth, but it would be all of no avail. Here, again, the charlatan was hoist with his own petard. He had played with things superhuman and supernatural, he had juggled with the machinery of Nature, and at last he had lived to discover that these things were not chimeras, but terrible realities.

Now, his knowledge of hypnotism, altogether empirical, taught him that its influence was <u>funda-mentally a physical influence</u>, dependent on the living body, the seat of the living will. With the death of the body, that influence ceased. <u>In order to free Isabel Arlington, he had only to die.</u>

Death had never had much terror for this man, for he had never been much in love with life, and he was not troubled with any misgivings about a hereafter. He determined, therefore, to complete his sacrifice without delay in the only way possible.

Having once made up his mind to this course, which was to be the solution of all his sorrow, he quietly and deliberately made his preparations. He completed the business which he had undertaken on behalf of others ; and placed in the care of his bankers a brief will, which left such property as he possessed to his Indian relations on the mother's side. He explained, as his reason for depositing the will, that he was going on a long and dangerous journey, from which he might never return.

All his worldly affairs being thus arranged, he deliberated for some time as to the method by which he would put an end to his existence.

If he committed suicide in the ordinary way, the usual vulgar formalities would be gone through over his dead body, and the horrible truth might be conveyed, by some accident or another, to Isabel. He would spare her this, as well as all other, sorrow.

He would quietly disappear, and destroy himself in such a way as to leave no trace whatever.

He occupied many hours in destroying all such papers or articles of property as might tend to establish his identity. He then conveyed the greater part of his luggage to one of the great railway-stations, and left it in 'the cloak-room' to be called for. Among all this luggage there was no article whatever which could furnish any clue to the owner. He retained only a small dressing-bag, which he proposed taking with him when he left London, and which (if his plan did not fail) would soon be lying, like himself, at the bottom of the ocean.

His plan was simple enough. He would go quietly on board one of the great sea-going steamers, pay for his passage under an assumed name, and then—well, the rest would be easy. On some stormy night, when there was confusion on board, a passenger would disappear into the darkness without being missed, and his fate would only be another of the many secrets of the sea.

It needed a stony heart and an iron will to carry out this programme, but these Woodville possessed. When everything was ready, he sat down to his desk and wrote the following words:

'By the time you read these lines, if you ever read them, I shall have left England, never to return. After you have read them, please destroy them, and with them obliterate if you can all memory of one who has brought you so much sorrow.

'It would be better, perhaps, if I went away without a word; and even now, though I am writing out of the fulness of an over-burdened heart, though I cannot resist the impulse to set down my thoughts, I am not quite sure that I shall ever send you what is so written. Yet I want you to know, to realize, that evil as I am, I am not altogether evil; that thanks to you, and to you only, I have risen out of the ashes of my dead self, and am another, perhaps a better, man.

'My child—dare I call you *that*, and be forgiven? It is strange, but now all is over, now my angry passions are hushed to sleep, now my last struggle with my baser nature is ended, I feel as if you were a child only, for whom I had only felt a father's holy love. Though I am not yet old in years, I feel like a gray-haired man, blessing a dear little one whom he is never to see again.

'Isabel, my child, you have brought me at least one thing—to believe in human goodness, in human purity and love. It has been a hard lesson, but I have learned it well. Do not think that I shall ever forget it! When my eyes close for ever, I shall die with that knowledge. If God is Goodness, if God is Purity and Love, then, for the first and last time, I believe in God.

'This is *your* victory, my child. If there be any

comfort to you in having converted a soul so worthless, may it comfort you.

'But I must not leave you with a lie upon my lips, or what is the shadow of a lie. I still believe that, if there be a God, He is powerless to undo the sorrow of this world; I still believe that no Omnipotence could have created evil; I still believe that Death is silence and the end of all.

'Alas! I am preaching, where I meant only to pray. My prayer is for your forgiveness—better still, for your happiness, my child.

'May all good spirits watch over you! May all pure thoughts and gracious hopes sustain you! May love and happiness dwell with you and bless you, now and until life is done.

'PHILIP WOODVILLE.'

The letter written, he read it again and again without tears, but with a despair so deep, so absolute, as almost to dry up the fountain of all emotion. At last he folded it up and placed it in an envelope, which he carefully sealed and addressed to Miss Arlington, care of the Earl of Wanborough, Grosvenor Square. Still hesitating whether or not to send the letter at all, he placed it in his pocket-book, to await his final determination.

Two days afterwards Woodville called at the London office of the Peninsular and Oriental Steamship Company, and took an intermediate passage in one of

the company's vessels, the *Semiramis*, which was to sail from Southampton next morning. He avoided engaging a berth in the saloon, lest he might stumble on any friend or acquaintance among the cabin passengers, and he gave the name which he had temporarily adopted, ' Mr. Phillips.'

He left by the night train for Southampton and went on board under cover of the darkness. Before leaving the shore, he posted the letter of adieu which he had written to Isabel.

Few would have recognised Philip Woodville in the sad, worn-looking man who stood almost alone, on the fore part of the vessel, in the dim gray light of the following dawn. He was disguised to no little extent, moreover, by a short black beard, which he had suffered to grow during the past fortnight. Clad in a dark suit of blue serge, and wearing a soft low-crowned hat which was drawn well down over his forehead and partially concealed his face, he looked more like a foreign sailor than a man accustomed to mix in good society.

The deck was almost deserted, for a thin drizzly rain was falling. Clammy white vapours hung over the sea, which was deep inky black and glassy calm.

Leaning over the bulwarks, he watched the white shores of England disappearing in the mist. When they vanished altogether, his eyes grew dim, and something rose in his throat; for with them vanished, swallowed up for ever, the one light that had shone upon his lonely life.

Although the sea was smooth, it was full of vague trouble and unrest. As the ship toiled up and down the great mounds of waves it seemed like a living thing, and the throb of the engines was like the monotonous beating of its heart.

One of the hands, a grizzly seaman, who had just finished helping to wash and scrub the decks, came to the spot where Woodville stood, and hung over the bulwarks, looking down at the water. Then he glanced at Woodville, and said phlegmatically:

'There'll be dirty weather afore long, sir.'

'Why do you think so?'

'Well, it ain't what *I* thinks, neither,' answered the man, squirting a mouthful of tobacco-juice into the water; 'it's what the *sea* thinks. You ain't a sailor, I suppose, sir, or maybe you'd know?'

He paused a moment reflectively, and then continued:

'The sea's like a live critter, and knows long before any mortal man what kind o' storm's comin'. Sometimes, when it knows there's going to be a capful o' wind, or maybe half a fresh gale, it jumps about like a dog a-wagging its tail, and cocks up its head to the sky, like a dog to its master; but sometimes it tumbles about in a lump, and trembles, and feels afraid. Look at it now, sir! Though there ain't a breath blowin', it's shiverin' through and through.

It knows dirty weather's comin'; and what's more, it tells the wessel, and the wessel gets kind o' narvous too. Just you watch her! She's like a chap in a cold perspiration, and there ain't a timber in her as don't shake!'

'Many passengers?' asked Woodville, smiling at the old man's explanation.

'Plenty on 'em aft,' was the reply. 'We don't see much on 'em for the first few days, for most on 'em keeps their berths unless the weather's extra fine. You see, many on 'em is heavy-hearted at leaving old England and their friends. Goin' far with us, sir?'

'I've taken my passage to Bombay,' said Woodville.

At that moment there was a call of 'All hands aft!' and he was left alone.

As he looked at the heaving waters, he realized more and more the meaning of the old man's words. There was something sentient in their ominous unrest. He strained his eyes downward, trying to penetrate the glassy gloom, and there was a moan in his ears as of many stifled voices, while the ship seemed to answer with a troubled groan.

As the day advanced, the steerage and intermediate passengers began to creep on deck—men and women of all nationalities, soldiers, sailors, landsmen, little children, and shivering ayahs. Everyone seemed cheerless and depressed, like the weather; for heavy mists and clouds continued to hang over the sea, and there was no sign of the sun.

The dreary day passed, and evening came.

Like a man under sentence of death, Woodville watched for the night. Nothing had shaken his purpose—nothing was likely to shake it. He was only waiting for a favourable opportunity; then, quietly, silently, unseen, unheard, he would disappear over the vessel's side, and so return to the troubled elements from which he came.

Never for a moment did it occur to him that such a suicide might be evil; on the contrary, he justified it to his conscience as supremely sane and good. He felt no superstitious dread. He believed in nothing, hoped for nothing, prayed for nothing, beyond death.

Towards nightfall the old sailor's prophecy seemed likely to be fulfilled. The barometer fell suddenly, and shortly afterwards it began to blow great gusts from the north-west. The waves grew mountainous, broken from ridge to ridge with white breakers, and the trumpets of the storm began to blow.

From time to time the waves broke heavily on the vessel and deluged the decks, which were already wet with flying foam. With panting breath and straining sides, the *Semiramis* laboured heavily through the surging seas.

It had grown pitch-dark. Not a gleam was seen, save the lights of the vessel, rising and falling. The passengers had crowded below, and Woodville was the only one left on deck.

He leant over the bulwarks for one last look at the element which was to engulf him. Brave as he was, he felt at that moment a thrill of hopeless anguish, almost of fear. But if he was to carry out his terrible purpose that night, the time had surely come.

He had set his teeth together and clenched his hands, preparing to leap into the sea, when a hand was laid upon his arm, and, turning wildly, he saw the old sailor who had spoken to him in the morning. He was wrapped from head to foot in oilskins, and carried a ship's lanthorn.

'Best get below, sir,' said the old man. 'We'll be battening down hatches soon, if this goes on. What did I tell ye?' he added, with a grim chuckle. 'It's comin' now, and no mistake.'

Woodville did not reply, but stood trembling, like a man just snatched from death—as, indeed, he had been. The old man raised the lanthorn, and flashed the light into his face.

'Lord love ye!' he cried, 'you look as white as a ghost! Take my advice, and turn in. You'll soon have enough o' this.'

Forcing a laugh, Woodville turned away, and staggered, rather than walked, towards the after-part of the ship, as if he were making for his cabin; but instead of turning in, he made for the darkness amidships, under the hurricane deck. The vessel rolled and lurched under him so that he could scarcely keep his feet. He was close under the hurricane deck, when a great sea struck the ship, and he was flung helplessly towards the bulwarks aft, where he stood soaked from head to foot, clinging to the main rigging.

He was nerving himself for a fresh effort, and looking wildly round to make sure that he was unobserved, when he was startled by a voice sounding out of the darkness close to him:

'Isabel, are you there? Isabel!'

'Yes, here I am,' answered another voice, the sound of which caused his heart to cease beating and his brain to swim round and round.

'Do come in,' said the first voice.

'I am coming, dear,' was the reply; 'but I should love to stay here all night and watch the sea.'

Was he dreaming? Was it indeed Isabel who spoke? Had Destiny by some mysterious means brought her there?

Clinging to the bulwarks for support, and deep in the darkness, he crept slowly towards the spot whence the voices had come.

A few steps brought him within sight of the open door of one of the deck cabins, and standing in the doorway, her pale face dimly illumined by the light of the cabin lamp, and her eyes looking out eagerly the tumultuous sea, was Isabel.

He had just time to catch a glimpse of her, and to recognise her, when she drew back into the cabin and closed the door.

CHAPTER XXIII.

THE GREAT WATERS.

By what miracle, Woodville asked himself, had Isabel come there? It seemed like enchantment, and for a long time he could not believe that it was real.

Were his wits wandering at last under the awful tension of his despair, and before the prospect of annihilation?

Dazed and stupefied, like a man who has seen an apparition, he remained in the darkness, clinging to the rigging, swept this way and that by the plunges of the storm-tossed ship, soaked from head to foot with foam and spray, thinking no more of death, but thrilling through and through with a new and tumultuous sense of life.

At last, fain to convince himself that what he had seen and heard was no delusion, he released his hold of the rigging and crept towards the cabin door; reaching which, he clung for support to the brass stanchions which were fixed on the cabin. Listening intently, he again heard the sound of voices—a whispered sound almost lost in the shrieking of the 'orm, but he clearly distinguished the voice of Isabel.

It was no dream, then—no illusion. Isabel was there!

Certain of this, conscious once more of her near presence, he forgot altogether the purpose which had brought him on shipboard. The warm blood coursed again through his veins, and a burthen seemed lifted from his soul. Fate, more potent than any human will, had decreed that they should again be thrown together. The hour of sacrifice and martyrdom had passed; he was saved for one supreme joy, that of looking again in the face of the woman he loved.

It was something, moreover, to feel that they had been swept, by accident or miracle, out of the ordinary world of men and women, and into the great darkness where the elements were at strife—that they were lifted up, as it were, like Francesca and Paolo, and mysteriously brought together. Might not Fate, which had done so much already, eventually do more? Might he not again hold her in his arms, hear her sweet words of love, feel her kisses on his face, and know that even in death they could not be divided?

Meantime the storm was growing.

For two nights and days the tempest lasted, but the *Semiramis* crawled upon its way, like a bird with broken wings. On the second day and night all the passengers were kept below, and the hatches were battened down. From time to time it seem those listening below as if the last crash had

and the ship, rent open or crushed amidships, was
about to founder; then wild shrieks would come
from the darkness, and die away amid the roar of
wind and sea.

Woodville had gone to his cabin, where he remained
a prisoner, calmly awaiting the event. More than
once, in the utter selfishness of love, he wished that
the end might come, and that Isabel and he might
perish together; but then he hated himself for the
wish, and prayed, in deep contrition, that *she* might
be spared.

On the third day the strength of the storm was
broken. The sea still rolled mountains high, but the
wind veered round the north and fell there to half a
gale, with occasional hurricanes, squalls of sleet and
hail. The captain, after taking their bearings, went
below to snatch a little hard-earned rest; he had been
on the bridge, with only a few minutes' respite, for
forty-eight consecutive hours.

In the dim cold light of the afternoon a few
straggling passengers began to creep on deck. Among
them was Woodville, who went forward and leant over
the forecastle bulwarks, watching the sea.

As he stood thus he was accosted by his former
acquaintance, the grim old sailor who had prophesied
the storm.

'All right now, sir?' asked Neptune, with a grin.
'I warn't far wrong, wur I, when I said as how the
was afraid o' sutthin' coming? It's had its

17

bellyful this time, anyhow, but I reckon we've seen the worst on it *this* bout.'

His attention was attracted at that moment by the figure of a man in a travelling-cap and a long ulster, who came lurching along the decks from the after-cabin, and who looked the picture of utter misery and desolation.

'Hold up, sir!' cried the sailor, catching him just as he seemed on the point of pitching head forward into the scuppers. 'You're out of your bearing, I fancy? Shall I help 'ee back to the saloon?'

'Thank you,' said a faint voice. 'I came on deck for a little air, and——'

'That's all right,' replied Neptune, still supporting him. 'It's more airier forward, as you say. Sit down here, sir, and I'll get ye a tarpaulin to wrap round your legs.'

So saying, he deposited the passenger on a seat close to the fore cabin, and ran off to fetch the tarpaulin. The passenger groaned dolefully, and Woodville, for the first time, looked round.

He recognised the passenger in a moment. It was Mervyn Darrell. Their eyes met, and he saw in a moment that he, too, was recognised.

'Good heavens!' gasped Mervyn. 'Is it possible?'

Woodville motioned him to silence as the sailor came up with the tarpaulin and wrapped it round his legs.

'Shall I get ye anything? Ye look as if a drop of summat would do ye good!'

'I have been exceedingly unwell,' answered Mervyn. 'I am an excellent sailor, as a rule, but the cabin was like the Black Hole of Calcutta. If you could get me a little brandy I should feel obliged.'

The sailor nodded approvingly, and walked off to the cabin. Then Mervyn looked again at Woodville, as if deeply perplexed.

'You quite startled me, Mr. Woodville,' he said. 'Am I to understand that you knew we were here, that you have followed us from England, that——'

'I knew Miss Arlington was on board,' interrupted Woodville. 'I knew it two nights ago. My own presence is purely accidental. I am returning to Bombay.'

'And Miss Arlington is going to Aden to meet her father, who is on his way home. She was far from well, you will be sorry to hear, and I—well, as you see, I am in attendance,' he added nervously, looking at Woodville with a helpless expression. 'Really, this is most unfortunate!'

'We must make the best of the inevitable,' replied Woodville. 'There is no necessity whatever that Miss Arlington should know that I am so near her— it is far better, indeed, that she should never know.'

'Quite so,' murmured Mervyn.

'She is well, I trust? She has not suffered much during the storm?'

'To be quite candid, I really don't know—I've been suffering so dreadfully myself. But I *think* she's all right—indeed, Lady Carlotta says so. For myself, I feel humiliated, degraded. Sea-sickness is so un-beautiful!'

Here Neptune brought the brandy, which Mervyn drank at once.

'Where are we now, my good man?' he asked.

'Somewheres near the Bay o' Biscay,' replied the sailor.

'A dreadful place, I have heard, where it is always blowing. Ah, well, I suppose there is no longer any danger?'

The sailor shook his head with a grin, and then walked away.

'My dear Woodville,' said Mervyn, after a pause, leaning his head against the cabin and rocking up and down with the motion of the ship, 'this meeting, extraordinary as it is, is only an instance of what a contemporary writer calls the long arm of coincidence. Seen philosophically, however, everything is coincidence; without it evolution would be impossible.'

'You will keep my secret?' demanded Woodville—'from Miss Arlington, I mean?'

'Certainly. The knowledge, I am afraid, would only distress her. She has a sincere regard for you, my dear Woodville, and is quite superior, as you know, to the usual prejudices of her sex; but, of course, under all the circumstances——'

He did not complete the sentence, but sighed and shrugged his shoulders.

Later in the afternoon, when Mervyn returned to the saloon, it was quite understood between the two men that Isabel should be kept in complete ignorance of Woodville's presence in the ship. Mervyn promised to say nothing, and Woodville, on his part, undertook to keep to his cabin as much as possible, and never, at any time, to approach the saloon part of the vessel.

It would have been strange indeed, in view of the subtle influence which Woodville had exercised over her life, if Isabel had been altogether unaffected by the near presence of one who was thinking of her so continually. That same evening, when the storm was well over, she ventured out on the after-deck, whither Lottie presently followed her, and found her sitting alone, with that strange far-off look in her eyes which she had so often dreaded.

'What is the matter, dear?' asked Lottie, sitting by her side and taking her hand.

'Listen!' said Isabel, trembling.

'I can hear nothing except the waves breaking and that horrible wind whistling. What is that you think you hear?'

'I'm sure it is no fancy, I have heard it so often,' answered Isabel, as if to herself. 'Always when the wind falls for a moment I seem to hear a voice calling my name. All through the storm I heard it crying, and once, last night, I saw something like a hand beckoning.'

'Of course, it is only your fancy,' said the practical Lottie. 'You're nervous—and no wonder! The weather has been simply awful!'

Isabel leant back with a sigh, closing her eyes. Suddenly she started, listened again, and rose to her feet, gazing intently towards the bows of the vessel. Then, as if sleep-walking, she began moving slowly in that direction.

'Isabel!' cried Lottie, embracing her and holding her back.

'He is calling me!' sighed the girl, with a vacant look. 'Let me go to him! let me go to him!'

'She is not well,' said Lottie to Mervyn, who came up at that moment. 'Help me to take her back to the cabin.'

They led her softly back, and she made no resistance, though she still seemed conscious of some influence apart from theirs. When they reached the small deck-cabin she sank on the seat with a low cry, and began hysterically sobbing. Presently, however, she became quite calm.

'Forgive me,' she said, smiling faintly up at Lottie. 'I'm better now; but I thought—I thought——'

The end of the sentence died away unspoken in a gush of tears.

Mervyn beckoned Lottie out of the cabin, and told her in whispers what had occurred that afternoon.

'Here—on board the ship!' cried Lottie, aghast.

'Quite by accident, he says. He is returning to India. But he has promised me faithfully not to approach her, or to let her know.'

'But she does know!' said Lottie, in despair. 'He is bewitching her still, as he bewitched her on land. He is a demon, a wizard, or something equally diabolical, and it is a wonder he hasn't sent the ship to the bottom of the sea!'

She decided, nevertheless, not to breathe one word of the truth to Isabel.

As the night advanced the wind fell still more, and a bright, cold moon rose over the western horizon and shone upon the sea. As it climbed higher and higher into the heavens, it seemed to still the water with its rays, as with the touch of an enchanter's wand. All grew hushed and peaceful. The only sound that broke the silence was the monotonous throb of the engines, and even this seemed subdued as the ship stole swiftly on.

Soon after midnight the moon had ceased to shine, and deep darkness enveloped sea and land. Presently the shrill shriek of the fog-horn broke the silence, and was repeated again and again at intervals. The ship was surrounded on every side by a thick mist.

The engines went at half-speed, the look-outs were doubled, and the ship crept slowly through the darkness, as if groping her way.

Lottie had been asleep for some hours, when she

suddenly awakened, and saw Isabel standing in the
centre of the cabin. Her eyes were wide open, but
Lottie saw in a moment that she was fast asleep.

Somnambulism

Slowly and silently she moved towards the cabin
door, and was about to open it and pass out, when
Lottie sprang from her berth and gently drew her
back. She hesitated and trembled, endeavouring to
set herself free.

'Let me go! Do you not hear him calling me?'
she whispered. And then cried eagerly, reaching out
her hands: 'Philip! Philip!'

At that moment the fog-horn shrieked loudly, and
was answered by the loud shriek of human voices.
There was a roar, a crash, and the ship shook through
and through, as if a thunderbolt had rent it asunder.

Isabel awoke screaming, and clung to Lottie. The
shriek of voices was repeated; then over it all rose
the captain's loud voice of command, followed by
the sound of feet rushing along the decks. The
monotonous pulsation of the cylinders now ceased;
the engines had stopped.

CHAPTER XXIV.

THE LAST LOOK.

LOTTIE opened the cabin door and peered out into the night.

At first she could see nothing, for it was pitch-dark; then, raising her eyes, she saw near to her and close to the bridge something like a dense black cloud, and above it a great ball of light.

The great hull and masthead-light of another ship!

Lottie understood at a glance what had happened. The strange ship, a steamer also, had collided with the *Semiramis* in the darkness, smiting her almost amidships with savage force, and cutting into her steel sides like a jagged knife. Its own bows were shattered with the shock, and there, like a great living monster clutching its prey, it clung on, quivering through and through convulsively, and vomiting clouds of black smoke into the air.

Meantime the tumult of disaster had begun. From both ships rose the cry of seamen, the shrieks of passengers crowding the decks, mingled with the roaring of water, the hiss of escaping steam, the crashing and rending of planks and masts. Lights moved here and there in the strange ship, and from time to time there was a ghastly flash from the engine fires.

Horrified by what she saw, Lottie fell back and almost swooned away.

And now a strange metamorphosis occurred in the two girls. The delicate and nervous Isabel, sensitive as a leaf to every nervous impression, became cool and collected in face of their great peril, while Lottie, for the first time in her life, was hysterical with fear.

change in Isabel

Amid the deafening din around them, they dressed rapidly, and prepared to leave the cabin, when there was a sharp knock at the door.

'You must dress at once!' cried the voice of Mervyn. 'We may have to leave the ship.'

At that moment an order was given in the strange ship to reverse the engines, and, quivering through and through with the slow strokes of the propeller, she began to back away. As her cut-water was drawn out like a jagged knife from the wounded sides of the *Semiramis*, the waves rushed in with a dull roar, and the stricken vessel heaved over as if about to sink, while her funnel-stays and rigging, clinging like fingers to the bows of the other vessel, were cut away with axes to set her free.

Slowly the black hull receded, and the *Semiramis* heeled over to the water-line and floated helplessly on the black waves. When she was about fifty yards away, the strange vessel stood stationary, letting off steam. She was a great iron steamship, several thousand tons bigger than the *Semiramis*, and her black hull towered far above the water-line, as if she was in ballast.

Rocket signals were now rapidly exchanged between the two ships, the stranger intimating that she would stand by until daybreak, and send assistance if necessary. The clamour was now hushed. The captain and chief engineer had gone below to ascertain the extent of the damage done. The passengers crowded the decks and waited in terror, while the crew gathered amidships, and whispered together.

The darkness was now partially broken by the dim ghostly gleam of the coming dawn. Dark clouds of vapour still hung over the sea, but between them crept feeble shafts of light, falling coldly on the heaving black waters of the sea. The figures of men were now clearly visible on the strange ship, crowding in the bows and gazing towards the *Semiramis*. Above the water-line of the hull was a great jagged gap or wound, where the iron bows had been torn open by the force of the collision.

The captain and engineer now emerged from the hold of the *Semiramis*, and orders were immediately given to 'man the pumps.' This was done, and after a little time the men seemed to gain on the water, and the ship seemed to float more buoyantly. It had been found impossible, however, to ascertain the exact extent of the damage.

The great ship looked like a wreck. One of the funnels had toppled over, crushing in its fall two of

the boats, and splitting open the hurricane deck. The
mainmast had gone by the board, swinging by the
shrouds and stays until they cut it away. That the
worst was still apprehended was evident from the
fact that a portion of the men were piped away to
prepare the remaining boats.

Pale as death, but still quite calm and collected,
Isabel stood close to the cabin door, gazing at the
scene of disaster and desolation. Lottie had sunk in
a seat, hiding her face in her hands.

'I knew it!' she cried, clinging to Mervyn, who
was trying in vain to console her. 'I knew it from
the moment you told me that that man was on
board!'

Isabel did not seem to hear the words. Her eyes
had fallen on the man himself, who suddenly rose
before her. He was bareheaded, his face was grimed
with smoke and soot, he had thrown off his coat and
waistcoat to work at the pumps, and stood in his
shirt sleeves, but she knew him in a moment, and
uttered a low cry of recognition.

'There is a chance for the ship yet,' he said quickly
without pausing to give any explanation of his
presence; 'and in any case, *you* will be quite
safe.'

At the sound of his voice, she tottered and seemed
about to fall. He caught her in his arms.

'Courage, Miss Arlington!' he cried.

She released herself gently, and, looking into his

face, gave him her hand. The action was so sweet, so gentle, that his heart overflowed with love and gratitude.

'How strange that we should meet,' she said; 'and yet—I *thought* that you were near—I have thought it ever since we left land—and I am glad, very glad, to find it true.'

'Stand by the boats!' cried the captain's voice from above them. 'Make ready to lower away!'

'Aye, aye, sir!' came the answer from below.

A wild cry came from the passengers crowding the fore part of the vessel:

'She's sinking! God help us!'

'Silence there!' cried the captain's voice again. 'She's floating yet, and may float for hours. Silence those lubbers forward,' he continued, 'and pass the word round to women and children.'

A heavy tremor ran through and through the ship, and she rolled on the black waves like a thing in pain. There was a tumult forward as the passengers made for the boats which had been lowered; then a shriek of agony, as one of the boats, swamped with its sudden load, heeled over and sank.

'Come!' cried Woodville, placing his arm round Isabel and hurrying her forward; then, turning to Mervyn, he added, 'Bring Lady Carlotta!'

The bulwarks were open forward, and the long boat, manned, and already half filled, was rocking wildly alongside. As the crowd of panic-stricken passengers crushed forward, the captain faced them revolver in hand.

'The women and children first,' he said. 'I'll shoot the first man that comes this way!'

One by one the children and women were lifted forward, and dropped into the boat, till it was crowded with moaning creatures.

'Push off!' cried the captain, and the long boat, loaded almost to the water's edge, was rowed away.

A second boat took its place. There was another rush of the terrified passengers, and again the captain kept the men back.

All this time Woodville had been vainly trying to force his way through the crowd. Suddenly Isabel held him back.

'Philip,' she whispered, clinging to him.

'Yes?'

'Let us stay here! I do not wish to live. Let us die together!'

He looked at her in wonder. Her face was smiling, her eyes were full of deep and unutterable love. With a sob he drew her to his bosom, and kissed her on the forehead. No one looked at or heeded them. Every soul there was struggling towards the boats, and praying to be spared from death.

'No, my darling,' he whispered, 'you will live. But God bless you for your love! You have made me very happy!'

The last boat was rocking at the vessel's side, and it was nearly full of men.

'Make way there!' cried Woodville, struggling forward.

The captain saw him approaching with Isabel in his arms, and waved back the men who were crowding to the boat.

'This way, sir!' he cried.   'Room there!'

In another moment Woodville had placed her in the captain's arms, and she was helped down into the boat.   Woodville then turned, and handed forward Lady Carlotta.   Mervyn sprang down after her, and some half dozen men followed.   A few still remained, and tried to follow, but the captain pushed them fiercely back, as the boat was already dangerously full.

'Away with you, lads!   Quick, for God's sake!'

The last boat left the vessel's side.

Some dozen passengers, several of the engineers and crew, and the old captain, now remained with Woodville on the *Semiramis*.   There was a chance of rescue yet, for the other ship was launching its boats to come to their assistance.

It was now broad daylight.

Leaning against the foremast with folded arms, Philip Woodville quietly watched the last boat rising and falling on the black waves, and he could see distinctly the form of Isabel, standing up and gazing towards him.

' Philip, Philip !' she cried.

He heard the cry, and murmured her name in answer. As he did so, he felt the decks sinking beneath him, and knew that the ship was going down.

A minute afterwards no sign of her remained upon the lonely waters; she had sunk like lead, drawing all on board with her in the whirlpool of her descent.

The ship's boats still floated on the sea, and from one of them rose again that cry of passionate farewell :

' Philip ! Philip !'

THE END.

BILLING AND SONS, PRINTERS, GUILDFORD.

CHATTO & WINDUS'S
LIST OF CHEAP POPULAR NOVELS

BY THE BEST AUTHORS.

Picture Covers, TWO SHILLINGS each.

BY EDMOND ABOUT.
The Fellah.

BY HAMILTON AIDE.
Carr of Carrlyon.
Confidences.

BY MARY ALBERT.
Brooke Finchley's Daughter.

BY MRS. ALEXANDER.
Maid, Wife, or Widow?
Valerie's Fate.

BY GRANT ALLEN.
Strange Stories.
Philistia.
Babylon.
The Beckoning Hand.
In All Shades.
For Maimie's Sake.
The Devil's Die.
This Mortal Coil.
The Tents of Shem.
The Great Taboo.
Dumaresq's Daughter.
The Duchess of Powysland.
Blood Royal.
Ivan Greet's Masterpiece.
The Scallywag.

BY EDWIN LESTER ARNOLD.
Phra the Phœnician.

BY FRANK BARRETT.
A Recoiling Vengeance.
For Love and Honour.
John Ford; and His Helpmate.
Honest Davie.
A Prodigal's Progress.
Folly Morrison.
Lieutenant Barnabas.
Found Guilty.
Fettered for Life.
Between Life and Death.
The Sin of Olga Zassoulich.
Little Lady Linton.

BY SHELSLEY BEAUCHAMP.
Grantley Grange.

BY BESANT & RICE.
Ready-Money Mortiboy.
With Harp and Crown.
This Son of Vulcan.
My Little Girl.
The Case of Mr. Lucraft.
The Golden Butterfly.
By Celia's Arbour.
The Monks of Thelema.
'Twas in Trafalgar's Bay.
The Seamy Side.
The Ten Years' Tenant.
The Chaplain of the Fleet.

BY WALTER BESANT.
All Sorts and Conditions of Men.
The Captains' Room.
All in a Garden Fair.
Dorothy Forster.
Uncle Jack.
Children of Gibeon.
The World went very well then
Herr Paulus.
For Faith and Freedom.
To Call her Mine.
The Bell of St. Paul's.
The Holy Rose.
Armorel of Lyonesse.
St. Katherine's by the Tower.
The Ivory Gate.
Verbena Camellia Stephanotis.
The Rebel Queen.

BY AMBROSE BIERCE.
In the Midst of Life.

BY FREDERICK BOYLE.
Camp Notes.
Savage Life.
Chronicles of No-Man's Land.

BY HAROLD BRYDGES.
Uncle Sam at Home.

London: CHATTO & WINDUS, 214 Piccadilly, W.

BY ROBERT BUCHANAN.
The Shadow of the Sword.
A Child of Nature.
God and the Man.
Annan Water.
The New Abelard.
The Martyrdom of Madeline.
Love Me for Ever.
Matt: a Story of a Caravan.
Foxglove Manor.
The Master of the Mine.
The Heir of Linne.

BY HALL CAINE.
The Shadow of a Crime.
A Son of Hagar.
The Deemster.

BY COMMANDER CAMERON.
The Cruise of the 'Black Prince.'

BY MRS. LOVETT CAMERON.
Deceivers Ever.
Juliet's Guardian.

BY EX-CHIEF INSPECTOR CAVANAGH.
Scotland Yard, Past and Present.

BY AUSTIN CLARE.
For the Love of a Lass.

BY MRS. ARCHER CLIVE.
Paul Ferroll.
Why Paul Ferroll Killed his Wife

BY MACLAREN COBBAN.
The Cure of Souls.
The Red Sultan.

BY C. ALLSTON COLLINS.
The Bar Sinister.

BY WILKIE COLLINS.
Armadale.
After Dark.
No Name.
A Rogue's Life.
Antonina.
Basil.
Hide and Seek.
The Dead Secret.
Queen of Hearts.
My Miscellanies.
The Woman in White.
The Moonstone.
Man and Wife.
Poor Miss Finch.

BY WILKIE COLLINS—*continued.*
Miss or Mrs.?
The New Magdalen.
The Frozen Deep.
The Law and the Lady.
The Two Destinies.
The Haunted Hotel.
The Fallen Leaves.
Jezebel's Daughter.
The Black Robe.
Heart and Science.
'I say No.'
The Evil Genius.
Little Novels.
The Legacy of Cain.
Blind Love.

BY MORTIMER COLLINS.
Sweet Anne Page.
Transmigration.
From Midnight to Midnight.
A Fight with Fortune.

MORTIMER & FRANCES COLLINS.
Sweet and Twenty.
Frances.
The Village Comedy.
You Play Me False.
Blacksmith and Scholar.

BY M. J. COLQUHOUN
Every Inch a Soldier.

BY DUTTON COOK.
Leo.
Paul Foster's Daughter.

BY C. EGBERT CRADDOCK.
The Prophet of the Great Smoky Mountains.

BY MATT CRIM.
Adventures of a Fair Rebel.

BY B. M. CROKER.
Pretty Miss Neville.
Proper Pride.
A Bird of Passage.
Diana Barrington.
'To Let.'
A Family Likeness.

BY WILLIAM CYPLES.
Hearts of Gold.

BY ALPHONSE DAUDET.
The Evangelist.

London: *CHATTO & WINDUS*, 214 *Piccadilly, W.*

BY ERASMUS DAWSON.
The Fountain of Youth.

BY JAMES DE MILLE.
A Castle in Spain.

BY J. LEITH DERWENT.
Our Lady of Tears.
Circe's Lovers.

BY CHARLES DICKENS.
Sketches by Boz.
Oliver Twist.
Nicholas Nickleby.

BY DICK DONOVAN.
The Man-hunter.
Caught at Last!
Tracked and Taken.
Who Poisoned Hetty Duncan?
The Man from Manchester.
A Detective's Triumphs.
In the Grip of the Law.
Wanted!
From Information Received.
Tracked to Doom.
Link by Link.
Suspicion Aroused.
Dark Deeds.
The Long Arm of the Law.

BY MRS. ANNIE EDWARDES.
A Point of Honour.
Archie Lovell.

BY M. BETHAM-EDWARDS.
Felicia.
Kitty.

BY EDWARD EGGLESTON.
Roxy.

BY G. MANVILLE FENN.
The New Mistress.
Witness to the Deed.

BY PERCY FITZGERALD.
Bella Donna.
Polly.
The Second Mrs. Tillotson.
Seventy-five Brooke Street.
Never Forgotten.
The Lady of Brantome.
Fatal Zero.

BY PERCY FITZGERALD and Others.
Strange Secrets.

BY ALBANY DE FONBLANQUE.
Filthy Lucre.

BY R. E. FRANCILLON.
Olympia.
One by One.
Queen Cophetua.
A Real Queen.
King or Knave.
Romances of the Law.
Ropes of Sand.
A Dog and his Shadow.

BY HAROLD FREDERIC.
Seth's Brother's Wife.
The Lawton Girl.

Prefaced by Sir H. BARTLE FRERE
Pandurang Hàrl.

BY HAIN FRISWELL.
One of Two.

BY EDWARD GARRETT.
The Capel Girls.

BY GILBERT GAUL.
A Strange Manuscript found in
a Copper Cylinder.

BY CHARLES GIBBON.
Robin Gray.
For Lack of Gold.
What will the World Say?
In Honour Bound.
In Love and War.
For the King.
Queen of the Meadow.
In Pastures Green.
The Flower of the Forest.
A Heart's Problem.
The Braes of Yarrow.
The Golden Shaft.
Of High Degree.
The Dead Heart.
By Mead and Stream.
Heart's Delight.
Fancy Free.
Loving a Dream.
A Hard Knot.
Blood-Money.

London: CHATTO & WINDUS, 214 *Piccadilly, W.*

BY WILLIAM GILBERT.
James Duke.
Dr. Austin's Guests.
The Wizard of the Mountain.

BY ERNEST GLANVILLE.
The Lost Heiress.
The Fossicker.
A Fair Colonist.

BY REV. S. BARING GOULD.
Eve.
Red Spider.

BY HENRY GREVILLE.
Nikanor.
A Noble Woman.

BY CECIL GRIFFITH.
Corinthia Marazion.

BY SYDNEY GRUNDY.
The Days of his Vanity.

BY JOHN HABBERTON.
Brueton's Bayou.
Country Luck.

BY ANDREW HALLIDAY.
Every-Day Papers.

BY LADY DUFFUS HARDY.
Paul Wynter's Sacrifice.

BY THOMAS HARDY.
Under the Greenwood Tree.

BY BRET HARTE.
An Heiress of Red Dog.
The Luck of Roaring Camp.
Californian Stories.
Gabriel Conroy.
Flip.
Maruja.
A Phyllis of the Sierras.
A Waif of the Plains.
A Ward of the Golden Gate.

BY J. BERWICK HARWOOD.
The Tenth Earl.

BY JULIAN HAWTHORNE.
Garth.
Ellice Quentin.
Sebastian Strome.
Dust.
Fortune's Fool.
Beatrix Randolph.
Miss Cadogna.

BY J. HAWTHORNE—continued.
Love—or a Name.
David Poindexter's Disappearance.
The Spectre of the Camera.

BY SIR ARTHUR HELPS.
Ivan de Biron.

BY HENRY HERMAN.
A Leading Lady.

BY HEADON HILL.
Zambra the Detective.

BY JOHN HILL.
Treason-Felony.

BY MRS. CASHEL HOEY.
The Lover's Creed.

BY MRS. GEORGE HOOPER.
The House of Raby.

BY TIGHE HOPKINS.
'Twixt Love and Duty.

BY MRS. HUNGERFORD.
In Durance Vile.
A Maiden all Forlorn.
A Mental Struggle.
Marvel.
A Modern Circe.
Lady Verner's Flight.

BY MRS. ALFRED HUNT.
Thornicroft's Model.
The Leaden Casket.
Self-Condemned.
That Other Person.

BY JEAN INGELOW.
Fated to be Free.

BY WILLIAM JAMESON.
My Dead Self.

BY HARRIETT JAY.
The Dark Colleen.
The Queen of Connaught.

BY MARK KERSHAW.
Colonial Facts and Fictions.

BY R. ASHE KING.
A Drawn Game.
'The Wearing of the Green.'
Passion's Slave.
Bell Barry.

London : *CHATTO & WINDUS,* 214 *Piccadilly, W.*

BY JOHN LEYS.
The Lindsays.

BY E. LYNN LINTON.
Patricia Kemball.
The Atonement of Leam Dundas.
The World Well Lost.
Under which Lord?
With a Silken Thread.
The Rebel of the Family.
'My Love!'
Ione.
Paston Carew.
Sowing the Wind.

BY HENRY W. LUCY.
Gideon Fleyce.

BY JUSTIN McCARTHY.
Dear Lady Disdain.
The Waterdale Neighbours.
My Enemy's Daughter.
A Fair Saxon.
Linley Rochford.
Miss Misanthrope.
Donna Quixote.
The Comet of a Season.
Maid of Athens.
Camiola: a Girl with a Fortune.
The Dictator.
Red Diamonds.

BY HUGH MacCOLL.
Mr. Stranger's Sealed Packet.

BY MRS. MACDONELL.
Quaker Cousins.

BY KATHARINE S. MACQUOID.
The Evil Eye.
Lost Rose.

BY W. H. MALLOCK.
The New Republic.
A Romance of the Nineteenth Century.

BY FLORENCE MARRYAT.
Fighting the Air.
Written in Fire.
A Harvest of Wild Oats.
Open! Sesame!

BY J. MASTERMAN.
Half-a-dozen Daughters.

BY BRANDER MATTHEWS.
A Secret of the Sea.

BY LEONARD MERRICK.
The Man who was Good.

BY JEAN MIDDLEMASS.
Touch and Go.
Mr. Dorillion.

BY MRS. MOLESWORTH.
Hathercourt Rectory.

BY J. E. MUDDOCK.
Stories Weird and Wonderful.
The Dead Man's Secret.
From the Bosom of the Deep.

BY D. CHRISTIE MURRAY.
A Life's Atonement.
Joseph's Coat.
Val Strange.
A Model Father.
Coals of Fire.
Hearts.
By the Gate of the Sea.
The Way of the World.
A Bit of Human Nature.
First Person Singular.
Cynic Fortune.
Old Blazer's Hero.
Bob Martin's Little Girl.
Time's Revenges.
A Wasted Crime.

BY D. CHRISTIE MURRAY AND HENRY HERMAN.
One Traveller Returns.
Paul Jones's Alias.
The Bishops' Bible.

BY HENRY MURRAY.
A Game of Bluff.
A Song of Sixpence.

BY HUME NISBET.
'Bail Up!'
Dr. Bernard St. Vincent.

BY ALICE O'HANLON.
The Unforeseen.
Chance? or Fate?

London: CHATTO & WINDUS, 214 Piccadilly, W.

BY GEORGES OHNET.
Doctor Rameau.
A Last Love.
A Weird Gift.

BY MRS. OLIPHANT.
Whiteladies.
The Primrose Path.
The Greatest Heiress in England

BY MRS. ROBERT O'REILLY.
Phœbe's Fortunes.

BY OUIDA.
Held in Bondage.
Strathmore.
Chandos.
Under Two Flags.
Idalia.
Cecil Castlemaine's Gage.
Tricotrin.
Puck.
Folle Farine.
A Dog of Flanders.
Pascarèl.
Signa.
In a Winter City.
Ariadnê.
Moths.
Friendship.
Pipistrello.
Bimbi.
In Maremma.
Wanda.
Frescoes.
Princess Napraxine.
Two Little Wooden Shoes.
A Village Commune.
Othmar.
Guilderoy.
Ruffino.
Syrlin.
Santa Barbara.
Wisdom, Wit, and Pathos.

BY MARGARET AGNES PAUL.
Gentle and Simple.

BY JAMES PAYN.
Lost Sir Massingberd.
A Perfect Treasure.

BY JAMES PAYN—*continued.*
Bentinck's Tutor.
Murphy's Master.
A County Family.
At Her Mercy.
A Woman's Vengeance.
Cecil's Tryst.
The Clyffards of Clyffe.
The Family Scapegrace.
The Foster Brothers.
The Best of Husbands.
Found Dead.
Walter's Word.
Halves.
Fallen Fortunes.
What He Cost Her.
Humorous Stories.
Gwendoline's Harvest.
Like Father, Like Son.
A Marine Residence.
Married Beneath Him.
Mirk Abbey.
Not Wooed, but Won.
Two Hundred Pounds Reward.
Less Black than We're Painted.
By Proxy.
High Spirits.
Under One Roof.
Carlyon's Year.
A Confidential Agent.
Some Private Views.
A Grape from a Thorn.
From Exile.
Kit: A Memory.
For Cash Only.
The Canon's Ward.
The Talk of the Town.
Holiday Tasks.
Glow-worm Tales.
The Mystery of Mirbridge.
The Burnt Million.
The Word and the Will.
A Prince of the Blood.
Sunny Stories.
A Trying Patient.

BY C. L. PIRKIS.
Lady Lovelace.

BY EDGAR A. POE.
The Mystery of Marie Roget.

London : CHATTO & WINDUS, 214 Piccadilly, W.

BY MRS. CAMPBELL PRAED.
The Romance of a Station.
The Soul of Countess Adrian.
Outlaw and Lawmaker.

BY E. C. PRICE.
Valentina.
Gerald.
Mrs. Lancaster's Rival.
The Foreigners.

BY RICHARD PRYCE.
Miss Maxwell's Affections.

BY CHARLES READE.
It is Never Too Late to Mend.
Hard Cash.
Peg Woffington.
Christie Johnstone.
Griffith Gaunt.
Put Yourself in His Place.
The Double Marriage.
Love Me Little, Love Me Long.
Foul Play.
The Cloister and the Hearth.
The Course of True Love.
The Autobiography of a Thief.
A Terrible Temptation.
The Wandering Heir.
A Simpleton.
A Woman-Hater.
Singleheart and Doubleface.
Good Stories of Men and other
The Jilt.   [Animals.
A Perilous Secret.
Readiana.

BY MRS. J. H. RIDDELL.
Her Mother's Darling.
The Uninhabited House.
Weird Stories.
Fairy Water.
Prince of Wales's Garden Party.
The Mystery in Palace Gardens.
The Nun's Curse.
Idle Tales.

BY AMÉLIE RIVES.
Barbara Dering.

BY F. W. ROBINSON.
Women are Strange.
The Hands of Justice.

BY JAMES RUNCIMAN.
Skippers and Shellbacks.
Grace Balmaign's Sweetheart.
Schools and Scholars.

BY W. CLARK RUSSELL.
Round the Galley Fire.
On the Fo'k'sle Head.
In the Middle Watch.
A Voyage to the Cape.
A Book for the Hammock.
Mystery of the 'Ocean Star.'
The Romance of Jenny Harlowe
An Ocean Tragedy.
My Shipmate Louise.
Alone on a Wide Wide Sea.

BY ALAN ST. AUBYN.
A Fellow of Trinity.
The Junior Dean.
The Master of St. Benedict's.
To his Own Master.

BY GEORGE AUGUSTUS SALA.
Gaslight and Daylight.

BY JOHN SAUNDERS.
Guy Waterman.
The Lion in the Path.
The Two Dreamers.

BY KATHARINE SAUNDERS.
Joan Merryweather.
The High Mills.
Margaret and Elizabeth.
Sebastian.
Heart Salvage.

BY GEORGE R. SIMS.
Rogues and Vagabonds.
The Ring o' Bells.
Mary Jane's Memoirs.
Mary Jane Married.
Tales of To-day.
Dramas of Life.
Tinkletop's Crime.
Zeph: a Circus Story.
My Two Wives.
Memoirs of a Landlady.
Scenes from the Show.

BY ARTHUR SKETCHLEY.
A Match in the Dark.

BY HAWLEY SMART.
Without Love or Licence.

London: CHATTO & WINDUS, 214 Piccadilly, W.

BY T. W. SPEIGHT.
The Mysteries of Heron Dyke.
The Golden Hoop.
By Devious Ways.
Hoodwinked.
Back to Life.
The Loudwater Tragedy.
Burgo's Romance.
Quittance in Full.

BY R. A. STERNDALE.
The Afghan Knife.

BY R. LOUIS STEVENSON.
New Arabian Nights.

BY BERTHA THOMAS.
Proud Maisie.
The Violin-player.
Cressida.

BY WALTER THORNBURY.
Tales for the Marines.
Old Stories Re-told.

BY ANTHONY TROLLOPE.
The Way We Live Now.
Mr. Scarborough's Family.
The Golden Lion of Granpère.
The American Senator.
Frau Frohmann.
Marion Fay.
Kept in the Dark.
The Land-Leaguers.
John Caldigate.

BY FRANCES E. TROLLOPE.
Anne Furness.
Mabel's Progress.
Like Ships upon the Sea.

BY T. ADOLPHUS TROLLOPE.
Diamond Cut Diamond.

BY J. T. TROWBRIDGE.
Farnell's Folly.

BY IVAN TURGENIEFF, etc.
Stories from Foreign Novelists.

BY MARK TWAIN.
Tom Sawyer.
A Tramp Abroad.
The Stolen White Elephant.
A Pleasure Trip on the Continent of Europe.

BY MARK TWAIN—continued.
The Gilded Age.
Huckleberry Finn.
Life on the Mississippi.
The Prince and the Pauper.
Mark Twain's Sketches.
A Yankee at the Court of King Arthur.
The £1,000,000 Bank-note.

BY SARAH TYTLER.
Noblesse Oblige.
Citoyenne Jacqueline.
The Huguenot Family.
What She Came Through.
Beauty and the Beast.
The Bride's Pass.
Saint Mungo's City.
Disappeared.
Lady Bell.
Buried Diamonds.
The Blackhall Ghosts.

BY C. C. FRASER-TYTER.
Mistress Judith.

BY ALLEN UPWARD.
The Queen against Owen.

BY ARTEMUS WARD.
Artemus Ward Complete.

BY AARON WATSON AND LILLIAS WASSERMANN.
The Marquis of Carabas.

BY WILLIAM WESTALL.
Trust-Money.

BY MRS. F. H. WILLIAMSON.
A Child Widow.

BY J. S. WINTER.
Cavalry Life.
Regimental Legends.

BY H. F. WOOD.
Passenger from Scotland Yard.
Englishman of the Rue Cain.

BY LADY WOOD.
Sabina.

BY CELIA PARKER WOOLLEY.
Rachel Armstrong.

BY EDMUND YATES.
Castaway.
Land at Last.
The Forlorn Hope.

London: CHATTO & WINDUS, 214 Piccadilly, W.

LIST OF BOOKS PUBLISHED BY

CHATTO & WINDUS

214 PICCADILLY, LONDON, W.

About (Edmond).—The Fellah: An Egyptian Novel. Translated by Sir RANDAL ROBERTS. Post 8vo, illustrated boards, 2s.

Adams (W. Davenport), Works by.
A Dictionary of the Drama: being a comprehensive Guide to the Plays, Playwrights, Players, and Playhouses of the United Kingdom and America, from the Earliest Times to the Present Day. Crown 8vo, half-bound, 12s. 6d.　　　　　　　　　　　　　　[*Preparing.*
Quips and Quiddities. Selected by W. DAVENPORT ADAMS. Post 8vo, cloth imp, 2s. 6d.

Agony Column (The) of 'The Times,' from 1800 to 1870. Edited, with an Introduction, by ALICE CLAY. Post 8vo, cloth limp, 2s. 6d.

Aidé (Hamilton), Novels by. Post 8vo, illustrated boards, 2s. each.
Carr of Carrlyon. | Confidences.

Albert (Mary).—Brooke Finchley's Daughter. Post 8vo, picture boards, 2s. ; cloth limp, 2s. 6d.

Alden (W. L.).—A Lost Soul: Being the Confession and Defence of Charles Lindsay. Fcap. 8vo, cloth boards, 1s. 6d.

Alexander (Mrs.), Novels by. Post 8vo, illustrated boards, 2s. each.
Maid, Wife, or Widow? | Valerie's Fate.

Allen (F. M.).—Green as Grass. With a Frontispiece. Crown 8vo, cloth, 3s. 6d.

Allen (Grant), Works by.
The Evolutionist at Large. Crown 8vo, cloth extra, 6s.
Post-Prandial Philosophy. Crown 8vo, art linen, 3s. 6d.
Moorland Idylls. With numerous Illustrations. Large crown 8vo, cloth, 6s.　　　　[*Shortly.*

Crown 8vo, cloth extra, 3s. 6d. each ; post 8vo, illustrated boards, 2s. each.

Philistia.	In all Shades.	Dumaresq's Daughter.
Babylon. 12 Illustrations.	The Devil's Die.	The Duchess of Powysland
Strange Stories. Frontis.	This Mortal Coil.	Blood Royal.
The Beckoning Hand.	The Tents of Shem. Frontis.	Ivan Greet's Masterpiece.
For Maimie's Sake.	The Great Taboo.	The Scallywag. 24 Illusts.

Crown 8vo, cloth extra, 3s. 6d. each.
At Market Value. | Under Sealed Orders.　　　[*Shortly.*

Dr. Palliser's Patient. Fcap. 8vo, cloth boards, 1s. 6d.

Anderson (Mary).—Othello's Occupation: A Novel. Crown 8vo, cloth, 3s. 6d.

Arnold (Edwin Lester), Stories by.
The Wonderful Adventures of Phra the Phœnician. Crown 8vo, cloth extra, with 12 Illustrations by H. M. PAGET, 3s. 6d. ; post 8vo, illustrated boards, 2s.
The Constable of St. Nicholas. With Frontispiece by S. L. WOOD. Crown 8vo, cloth, 3s. 6d.

Artemus Ward's Works. With Portrait and Facsimile. Crown 8vo, cloth extra, 7s. 6d.—Also a POPULAR EDITION, post 8vo, picture boards, 2s.
The Genial Showman: The Life and Adventures of ARTEMUS WARD. By EDWARD P. HINGSTON. With a Frontispiece. Crown 8vo, cloth extra, 3s. 6d.

Ashton (John), Works by. Crown 8vo, cloth extra, 7s. 6d. each.
History of the Chap-Books of the 18th Century. With 334 Illustrations.
Social Life in the Reign of Queen Anne. With 85 Illustrations.
Humour, Wit, and Satire of the Seventeenth Century. With 82 Illustrations.
English Caricature and Satire on Napoleon the First. With 115 Illustrations.
Modern Street Ballads. With 57 Illustrations.

Bacteria, Yeast Fungi, and Allied Species, A Synopsis of. By
W. B. GROVE, B.A. With 87 Illustrations. Crown 8vo, cloth extra, 3s. 6d.

Bardsley (Rev. C. Wareing, M.A.), Works by.
English Surnames: Their Sources and Significations. Crown 8vo, cloth, 7s. 6d.
Curiosities of Puritan Nomenclature. Crown 8vo, cloth extra, 6s.

Baring Gould (Sabine, Author of 'John Herring,' &c.), Novels by.
Crown 8vo, cloth extra, 3s. 6d. each; post 8vo, illustrated boards, 2s. each.
Red Spider. | Eve.

Barr (Robert: Luke Sharp), Stories by. Cr. 8vo, cl., 3s. 6d. each.
In a Steamer Chair. With Frontispiece and Vignette by DEMAIN HAMMOND.
From Whose Bourne, &c. With 47 Illustrations by HAL HURST and others.

Crown 8vo, cloth extra, 6s. each.
A Woman Intervenes. With 8 Illustrations by HAL HURST.   [Shortly.
Revenge! With numerous Illustrations.   [Shortly.

Barrett (Frank), Novels by.
Post 8vo, illustrated boards, 2s. each; cloth, 2s. 6d. each.

Fettered for Life.	A Prodigal's Progress.
The Sin of Olga Zassoulich.	John Ford; and His Helpmate.
Between Life and Death.	A Recoiling Vengeance.
Folly Morrison.	Honest Davie.	Lieut. Barnabas.	Found Guilty.
Little Lady Linton.	For Love and Honour.

The Woman of the Iron Bracelets. Crown 8vo, cloth, 3s. 6d.

Barrett (Joan).—Monte Carlo Stories. Fcap. 8vo, cl., 1s. 6d. [Shortly.

Beaconsfield, Lord. By T. P. O'CONNOR, M.P. Cr. 8vo, cloth, 5s.

Beauchamp (Shelsley).—Grantley Grange. Post 8vo, boards, 2s.

Beautiful Pictures by British Artists: A Gathering of Favourites
from the Picture Galleries, engraved on Steel. Imperial 4to, cloth extra, gilt edges, 21s.

Besant (Sir Walter) and James Rice, Novels by.
Crown 8vo, cloth extra, 3s. 6d. each; post 8vo, illustrated boards, 2s. each; cloth limp, 2s. 6d. each.

Ready-Money Mortiboy.	By Celia's Arbour.
My Little Girl.	The Chaplain of the Fleet.
With Harp and Crown.	The Seamy Side.
This Son of Vulcan.	The Case of Mr. Lucraft, &c.
The Golden Butterfly.	'Twas in Trafalgar's Bay, &c.
The Monks of Thelema.	The Ten Years' Tenant, &c.

*** There is also a LIBRARY EDITION of the above Twelve Volumes, handsomely set in new type on a large crown 8vo page, and bound in cloth extra, 6s. each; and a POPULAR EDITION of **The Golden Butterfly**, medium 8vo, 6d.; cloth, 1s.—NEW EDITIONS, printed in large type on crown 8vo laid paper, bound in figured cloth, 3s. 6d. each, are also in course of publication.

Besant (Sir Walter), Novels by.
Crown 8vo, cloth extra, 3s. 6d. each; post 8vo, illustrated boards, 2s. each; cloth limp, 2s. 6d. each.
All Sorts and Conditions of Men. With 12 Illustrations by FRED. BARNARD.
The Captains' Room, &c. With Frontispiece by E. J. WHEELER.
All in a Garden Fair. With 6 Illustrations by HARRY FURNISS.
Dorothy Forster. With Frontispiece by CHARLES GREEN.
Uncle Jack, and other Stories. | Children of Gibeon.
The World Went Very Well Then. With 12 Illustrations by A. FORESTIER.
Herr Paulus: His Rise, his Greatness, and his Fall. | The Bell of St. Paul's.
For Faith and Freedom. With Illustrations by A. FORESTIER and F. WADDY.
To Call Her Mine, &c. With 9 Illustrations by A. FORESTIER.
The Holy Rose, &c. With Frontispiece by F. BARNARD.
Armorel of Lyonesse: A Romance of To-day. With 12 Illustrations by F. BARNARD.
St. Katherine's by the Tower. With 12 Illustrations by C. GREEN.
Verbena Camellia Stephanotis, &c. With a Frontispiece by GORDON BROWNE.
The Ivory Gate. | The Rebel Queen.

Beyond the Dreams of Avarice. Crown 8vo, cloth extra, 6s.
In Deacon's Orders, &c. With Frontispiece by A. FORESTIER. Crown 8vo, cloth, 6s.
The Master Craftsman. 2 vols., crown 8vo, 10s. net.   [Shortly.
Fifty Years Ago. With 144 Plates and Woodcuts. Crown 8vo, cloth extra, 5s.
The Eulogy of Richard Jefferies. With Portrait. Crown 8vo, cloth extra, 6s.
London. With 125 Illustrations. Demy 8vo, cloth extra, 7s. 6d.
Westminster. With Etched Frontispiece by F. S. WALKER, R.P.E., and 130 Illustrations by WILLIAM PATTEN and others. Demy 8vo, cloth, 18s.
Sir Richard Whittington. With Frontispiece. Crown 8vo, art linen, 3s. 6d.
Gaspard de Coligny. With a Portrait. Crown 8vo, art linen, 3s. 6d.
As we Are: As we May Be: Social Essays. Crown 8vo, linen, 6s.   [Shortly.

Bechstein (Ludwig).—As Pretty as Seven, and other German
Stories. With Additional Tales by the Brothers GRIMM, and 98 Illustrations by RICHTER. Square
8vo, cloth extra, 6s. 6d.; gilt edges, 7s. 6d.

Beerbohm (Julius).—Wanderings in Patagonia; or, Life among
the Ostrich-Hunters. With Illustrations. Crown 8vo, cloth extra, 3s. 6d.

Bellew (Frank).—The Art of Amusing: A Collection of Graceful
Arts, Games, Tricks, Puzzles, and Charades. With 300 Illustrations. Crown 8vo, cloth extra, 4s. 6d.

Bennett (W. C., LL.D.).—Songs for Sailors. Post 8vo, cl. limp, 2s.

Bewick (Thomas) and his Pupils. By AUSTIN DOBSON. With 95
Illustrations. Square 8vo, cloth extra, 6s.

Bierce (Ambrose).—In the Midst of Life: Tales of Soldiers and
Civilians. Crown 8vo, cloth extra, 6s.; post 8vo, illustrated boards, 2s.

Bill Nye's History of the United States. With 146 Illustrations
by F. OPPER. Crown 8vo, cloth extra, 3s. 6d.

Biré (Edmond). — Diary of a Citizen of Paris during 'The
Terror.' Translated by JOHN DE VILLIERS. Two Vols., demy 8vo, cloth extra, 21s.   [*Shortly.*

Blackburn's (Henry) Art Handbooks.

Academy Notes, 1875, 1877-86, 1889, 1890, 1892-1895, Illustrated, each 1s.	**Grosvenor Notes,** Vol. II., 1883-87. With 300 Illustrations. Demy 8vo, cloth, 6s.
Academy Notes, 1875-79. Complete in One Vol., with 600 Illustrations. Cloth, 6s.	**Grosvenor Notes,** Vol. III., 1888-90. With 230 Illustrations. Demy 8vo, cloth, 3s. 6d.
Academy Notes, 1880-84. Complete in One Vol., with 700 Illustrations. Cloth, 6s.	**The New Gallery, 1888-1895.** With numerous Illustrations, each 1s.
Academy Notes, 1890-94. Complete in One Vol., with 800 Illustrations. Cloth, 7s. 6d.	**The New Gallery,** Vol. I., 1888-1892. With 250 Illustrations. Demy 8vo, cloth, 6s.
Grosvenor Notes, 1877. 6d.	**English Pictures at the National Gallery.** With 114 Illustrations. 1s.
Grosvenor Notes, separate years from 1878-1890, each 1s.	**Old Masters at the National Gallery.** With 128 Illustrations. 1s. 6d.
Grosvenor Notes, Vol. I., 1877-82. With 300 Illustrations. Demy 8vo, cloth, 6s.	**Illustrated Catalogue to the National Gallery.** With 242 Illusts. Demy 8vo, cloth, 3s.

The Paris Salon, 1895. With 300 Facsimile Sketches. 3s.

Blind (Mathilde), Poems by.
The Ascent of Man. Crown 8vo, cloth, 5s.
Dramas in Miniature. With a Frontispiece by F. MADOX BROWN. Crown 8vo, cloth, 5s.
Songs and Sonnets. Fcap. 8vo, vellum and gold, 5s.
Birds of Passage: Songs of the Orient and Occident. Second Edition. Crown 8vo, linen, 6s. net.

Bourget (Paul).—Lies. Translated by JOHN DE VILLIERS. Crown
8vo, cloth, 6s.   [*Shortly.*

Bourne (H. R. Fox), Books by.
English Merchants: Memoirs in Illustration of the Progress of British Commerce. With numerous
Illustrations. Crown 8vo, cloth extra, 7s. 6d.
English Newspapers: Chapters in the History of Journalism. Two Vols., demy 8vo, cloth, 25s.
The Other Side of the Emin Pasha Relief Expedition. Crown 8vo, cloth, 6s.

Bowers (George).—Leaves from a Hunting Journal. Coloured
Plates. Oblong folio, half-bound, 21s.

Boyle (Frederick), Works by. Post 8vo, illustrated bds., 2s. each.
Chronicles of No-Man's Land. | **Camp Notes.** | **Savage Life.**

Brand (John).— Observations on Popular Antiquities; chiefly
illustrating the Origin of our Vulgar Customs, Ceremonies, and Superstitions. With the Additions of Sir
HENRY ELLIS, and numerous Illustrations. Crown 8vo, cloth extra, 7s. 6d.

Brewer (Rev. Dr.), Works by.
The Reader's Handbook of Allusions, References, Plots, and Stories. Seventeenth
Thousand. Crown 8vo, cloth extra, 7s. 6d.
Authors and their Works, with the Dates: Being the Appendices to 'The Reader's Hand-
book,' separately printed. Crown 8vo, cloth limp, 2s.
A Dictionary of Miracles. Crown 8vo, cloth extra, 7s. 6d.

Brewster (Sir David), Works by. Post 8vo, cloth, 4s. 6d. each.
More Worlds than One: Creed of the Philosopher and Hope of the Christian. With Plates.
The Martyrs of Science: GALILEO, TYCHO BRAHE, and KEPLER. With Portraits.
Letters on Natural Magic. With numerous Illustrations.

Brillat-Savarin.— Gastronomy as a Fine Art. Translated by
R. E. ANDERSON, M.A. Post 8vo, half-bound, 2s.

Brydges (Harold).—Uncle Sam at Home. With 91 Illustrations.
Post 8vo, illustrated boards, 2s.; cloth limp, 2s. 6d.

Buchanan (Robert), Works by. Crown 8vo, cloth extra, 6s. each.
Selected Poems of Robert Buchanan. With Frontispiece by T. DALZIEL.
The Earthquake; or, Six Days and a Sabbath.
The City of Dream: An Epic Poem. With Two Illustrations by P. MACNAB.
The Wandering Jew: A Christmas Carol.

The Outcast: A Rhyme for the Time. With 15 Illustrations by RUDOLF BLIND, PETER MACNAB, and HUME NISBET. Small demy 8vo, cloth extra, 8s.
Robert Buchanan's Poetical Works. With Steel-plate Portrait. Crown 8vo, cloth extra. 7s. 6d

Crown 8vo, cloth extra, 3s. 6d. each; post 8vo, illustrated boards, 2s. each.

The Shadow of the Sword.	**Love Me for Ever.** With Frontispiece.
A Child of Nature. With Frontispiece.	**Annan Water.** | **Foxglove Manor.**
God and the Man. With 11 Illustrations by	**The New Abelard.**
FRED. BARNARD.	**Matt:** A Story of a Caravan. With Frontispiece.
The Martyrdom of Madeline. With	**The Master of the Mine.** With Frontispiece.
Frontispiece by A. W. COOPER.	**The Heir of Linne.**

Crown 8vo, cloth extra, 3s. 6d. each.

Woman and the Man. |	**Red and White Heather.** |	**Rachel Dene.**

Lady Kilpatrick. Crown 8vo, cloth extra, 6s.

The Charlatan. By ROBERT BUCHANAN and HENRY MURRAY. With a Frontispiece by T. H. ROBINSON. Crown 8vo, cloth, 3s. 6d. [*Shortly.*

Burton (Richard F.).—The Book of the Sword. With over 400 Illustrations. Demy 4to, cloth extra, 32s.

Burton (Robert).—The Anatomy of Melancholy. With Translations of the Quotations. Demy 8vo, cloth extra, 7s. 6d.
Melancholy Anatomised: An Abridgment of BURTON'S ANATOMY. Post 8vo, half-bd., 2s. 6d.

Caine (T. Hall), Novels by. Crown 8vo, cloth extra, 3s. 6d. each.; post 8vo, illustrated boards, 2s. each; cloth limp, 2s. 6d. each.
The Shadow of a Crime. \| **A Son of Hagar.** \| **The Deemster.**
A LIBRARY EDITION of **The Deemster** is now ready; and one of **The Shadow of a Crime** is in preparation, set in new type, crown 8vo, cloth decorated, 6s. each.

Cameron (Commander V. Lovett).—The Cruise of the 'Black Prince' Privateer. Post 8vo, picture boards, 2s.

Cameron (Mrs. H. Lovett), Novels by. Post 8vo, illust. bds. 2s. ea.
Juliet's Guardian. \| **Deceivers Ever.**

Carlyle (Jane Welsh), Life of. By Mrs. ALEXANDER IRELAND. With Portrait and Facsimile Letter. Small demy 8vo, cloth extra, 7s. 6d.

Carlyle (Thomas).—On the Choice of Books. Post 8vo, cl., 1s. 6d.
Correspondence of Thomas Carlyle and R. W. Emerson, 1834-1872. Edited by C. E. NORTON. With Portraits. Two Vols., crown 8vo, cloth, 24s.

Carruth (Hayden).—The Adventures of Jones. With 17 Illustrations. Fcap. 8vo, cloth, 2s.

Chambers (Robert W.), Stories of Paris Life by. Long fcap. 8vo, cloth, 2s. 6d. each.
The King in Yellow. \| **In the Quarter.**

Chapman's (George), Works. Vol. I., Plays Complete, including the Doubtful Ones.—Vol. II., Poems and Minor Translations, with Essay by A. C. SWINBURNE.—Vol. III., Translations of the Iliad and Odyssey. Three Vols., crown 8vo, cloth, 6s. each.

Chapple (J. Mitchell).—The Minor Chord: The Story of a Prima Donna. Crown 8vo, cloth, 3s. 6d.

Chatto (W. A.) and J. Jackson.—A Treatise on Wood Engraving, Historical and Practical. With Chapter by H. G. BOHN, and 450 fine Illusts. Large 4to, half-leather, 28s.

Chaucer for Children: A Golden Key. By Mrs. H. R. HAWEIS. With 8 Coloured Plates and 30 Woodcuts. Crown 4to, cloth extra, 3s. 6d.
Chaucer for Schools. By Mrs. H. R. HAWEIS. Demy 8vo, cloth limp, 2s. 6d.

Chess, The Laws and Practice of. With an Analysis of the Openings. By HOWARD STAUNTON. Edited by R. B. WORMALD. Crown 8vo, cloth, 5s.
The Minor Tactics of Chess: A Treatise on the Deployment of the Forces in obedience to Strategic Principle. By F. K. YOUNG and E. C. HOWELL. Long fcap. 8vo, cloth, 2s. 6d.
The Hastings Chess Tournament Book (Aug.-Sept., 1895). Containing the Official Report of the 231 Games played in the Tournament, with Notes by the Players, and Diagrams of Interesting Positions; Portraits and Biographical Sketches of the Chess Masters; and an Account of the Congress and its surroundings. Crown 8vo, cloth extra, 7s. 6d. net. [*Shortly*

Clare (Austin).—For the Love of a Lass. Post 8vo, 2s.; cl., 2s. 6d.

Clive (Mrs. Archer), Novels by. Post 8vo, illust. boards, 2s. each.
Paul Ferroll. | Why Paul Ferroll Killed his Wife.

Clodd (Edward, F.R.A.S.).—Myths and Dreams. Cr. 8vo, 3s. 6d.

Cobban (J. Maclaren), Novels by.
The Cure of Souls. Post 8vo, Illustrated boards, 2s.
The Red Sultan. Crown 8vo, cloth extra, 3s. 6d.; post 8vo, Illustrated boards, 2s.
The Burden of Isabel. Crown 8vo, cloth extra, 3s. 6d.

Coleman (John).—Players and Playwrights I have Known. Two
Vols., demy 8vo, cloth, 24s.

Coleridge (M. E.).—The Seven Sleepers of Ephesus. Cloth, 1s. 6d.

Collins (C. Allston).—The Bar Sinister. Post 8vo, boards, 2s.

Collins (John Churton, M.A.), Books by.
Illustrations of Tennyson. Crown 8vo, cloth extra, 6s.
Jonathan Swift: A Biographical and Critical Study. Crown 8vo, cloth extra, 8s.

Collins (Mortimer and Frances), Novels by.
Crown 8vo, cloth extra, 3s. 6d. each; post 8vo, Illustrated boards, 2s. each.
From Midnight to Midnight. | Blacksmith and Scholar.
Transmigration. | You Play me False. | A Village Comedy.
Post 8vo, illustrated boards, 2s. each.
Sweet Anne Page. | A Fight with Fortune. | Sweet and Twenty. | Frances.

Collins (Wilkie), Novels by.
Crown 8vo, cloth extra, 3s. 6d. each; post 8vo, illustrated boards, 2s. each; cloth limp, 2s. 6d. each.
Antonina. With a Frontispiece by Sir JOHN GILBERT, R.A.
Basil. Illustrated by Sir JOHN GILBERT, R.A., and J. MAHONEY.
Hide and Seek. Illustrated by Sir JOHN GILBERT, R.A., and J. MAHONEY.
After Dark. With Illustrations by A. B. HOUGHTON. | The Two Destinies.
The Dead Secret. With a Frontispiece by Sir JOHN GILBERT, R.A.
Queen of Hearts. With a Frontispiece by Sir JOHN GILBERT, R.A.
The Woman in White. With Illustrations by Sir JOHN GILBERT, R.A., and F. A. FRASER.
No Name. With Illustrations by Sir J. E. MILLAIS. R.A., and A. W. COOPER.
My Miscellanies. With a Steel-plate Portrait of WILKIE COLLINS.
Armadale. With Illustrations by G. H. THOMAS.
The Moonstone. With Illustrations by G. DU MAURIER and F. A. FRASER.
Man and Wife. With Illustrations by WILLIAM SMALL.
Poor Miss Finch. Illustrated by G. DU MAURIER and EDWARD HUGHES.
Miss or Mrs.? With Illustrations by S. L. FILDES, R.A., and HENRY WOODS, A.R.A.
The New Magdalen. Illustrated by G. DU MAURIER and C. S. REINHARDT.
The Frozen Deep. Illustrated by G. DU MAURIER and J. MAHONEY.
The Law and the Lady. With Illustrations by S. L. FILDES, R.A., and SYDNEY HALL.
The Haunted Hotel. With Illustrations by ARTHUR HOPKINS.
The Fallen Leaves. | Heart and Science. | The Evil Genius.
Jezebel's Daughter. | 'I Say No.' | Little Novels. Frontis.
The Black Robe. | A Rogue's Life. | The Legacy of Cain.
Blind Love. With a Preface by Sir WALTER BESANT, and Illustrations by A. FORESTIER.
POPULAR EDITIONS. Medium 8vo, 6d. each; cloth, 1s. each.
The Woman in White. | The Moonstone.

Colman's (George) Humorous Works: 'Broad Grins,' 'My Night-
gown and Slippers,' &c. With Life and Frontispiece. Crown 8vo, cloth extra, 7s. 6d.

Colquhoun (M. J.).—Every Inch a Soldier. Post 8vo, boards, 2s.

Colt-breaking, Hints on. By W. M. HUTCHISON. Cr. 8vo, cl., 3s. 6d.

Convalescent Cookery. By CATHERINE RYAN. Cr. 8vo, 1s.; cl., 1s. 6d.

Conway (Moncure D.), Works by.
Demonology and Devil-Lore. With 65 Illustrations. Two Vols., demy 8vo, cloth, 28s.
George Washington's Rules of Civility. Fcap. 8vo, Japanese vellum, 2s. 6d.

Cook (Dutton), Novels by.
Paul Foster's Daughter. Crown 8vo, cloth extra, 3s. 6d.; post 8vo, illustrated boards, 2s.
Leo. Post 8vo, illustrated boards, 2s.

Cooper (Edward H.).—Geoffory Hamilton. Cr. 8vo, cloth, 3s. 6d.

Cornwall.—Popular Romances of the West of England; or, The
Drolls, Traditions, and Superstitions of Old Cornwall. Collected by ROBERT HUNT, F.R.S. With
two Steel Plates by GEORGE CRUIKSHANK. Crown 8vo, cloth, 7s. 6d.

Cotes (V. Cecil).—Two Girls on a Barge. With 44 Illustrations by
F. H. TOWNSEND. Post 8vo, cloth, 2s. 6d.

Craddock (C. Egbert), Stories by.
The Prophet of the Great Smoky Mountains. Post 8vo, illustrated boards, 2s.
His Vanished Star. Crown 8vo, cloth extra, 3s. 6d.

Crellin (H. N.) Books by.
Romances of the Old Seraglio. With 28 Illustrations by S. L. WOOD. Crown 8vo, cloth, 3s. 6d.
Tales of the Caliph. Crown 8vo, cloth, 2s.
The Nazarenes: A Drama. Crown 8vo, 1s.

Crim (Matt.).—Adventures of a Fair Rebel. Crown 8vo, cloth
extra, with a Frontispiece by DAN. BEARD. 3s. 6d.; post 8vo, illustrated boards, 2s.

Crockett (S. R.) and others.—Tales of Our Coast. By S. R.
CROCKETT, GILBERT PARKER, HAROLD FREDERIC, 'Q.,' and W. CLARK RUSSELL. With 12
Illustrations by FRANK BRANGWYN. Crown 8vo, cloth, 3s. 6d.   [Shortly.

Croker (Mrs. B. M.), Novels by. Crown 8vo, cloth extra, 3s. 6d.
each; post 8vo, illustrated boards 2s. each; cloth limp, 2s. 6d. each.

Pretty Miss Neville.	Diana Barrington.	A Family Likeness.
A Bird of Passage.	Proper Pride.	'To Let.'

Crown 8vo, cloth extra, 3s. 6d. each.

Village Tales and Jungle Tragedies.	
Mr. Jervis.	The Real Lady Hilda.

Married or Single? Three Vols., crown 8vo, 15s. net.   [Shortly.

Cruikshank's Comic Almanack. Complete in Two SERIES: The
FIRST, from 1835 to 1843; the SECOND, from 1844 to 1853. A Gathering of the Best Humour of
THACKERAY, HOOD, MAYHEW, ALBERT SMITH, A'BECKETT, ROBERT BROUGH, &c. With
numerous Steel Engravings and Woodcuts by GEORGE CRUIKSHANK, HINE, LANDELLS, &c.
Two Vols., crown 8vo, cloth gilt, 7s. 6d. each.
The Life of George Cruikshank. By BLANCHARD JERROLD. With 84 Illustrations and a
Bibliography. Crown 8vo, cloth extra, 6s.

Cumming (C. F. Gordon), Works by. Demy 8vo, cl. ex., 8s. 6d. ea
In the Hebrides. With an Autotype Frontispiece and 23 Illustrations.
In the Himalayas and on the Indian Plains. With 42 Illustrations.
Two Happy Years in Ceylon. With 28 Illustrations.
Via Cornwall to Egypt. With a Photogravure Frontispiece. Demy 8vo, cloth, 7s. 6d.

Cussans (John E.).—A Handbook of Heraldry; with Instructions
for Tracing Pedigrees and Deciphering Ancient MSS., &c. Fourth Edition, revised, with 408 Woodcuts
and 2 Coloured Plates. Crown 8vo, cloth extra, 6s.

Cyples (W.).—Hearts of Gold. Cr. 8vo, cl., 3s. 6d.; post 8vo, bds., 2s.

Daniel (George).—Merrie England in the Olden Time. With
Illustrations by ROBERT CRUIKSHANK. Crown 8vo, cloth extra, 3s. 6d.

Daudet (Alphonse).—The Evangelist; or, Port Salvation. Crown
8vo, cloth extra, 3s. 6d.; post 8vo, illustrated boards, 2s.

Davenant (Francis, M.A.).—Hints for Parents on the Choice of
a Profession for their Sons when Starting in Life. Crown 8vo, 1s.; cloth, 1s. 6d.

Davidson (Hugh Coleman).—Mr. Sadler's Daughters. With a
Frontispiece by STANLEY WOOD. Crown 8vo, cloth extra, 3s. 6d.

Davies (Dr. N. E. Yorke-), Works by. Cr. 8vo, 1s. ea.; cl., 1s. 6d. ea.
One Thousand Medical Maxims and Surgical Hints.
Nursery Hints: A Mother's Guide in Health and Disease.
Foods for the Fat: A Treatise on Corpulency, and a Dietary for its Cure.
Aids to Long Life. Crown 8vo, 2s.; cloth limp, 2s. 6d.

Davies' (Sir John) Complete Poetical Works. Collected and Edited,
with Introduction and Notes, by Rev. A. B. GROSART, D.D. Two Vols., crown 8vo, cloth, 12s.

Dawson (Erasmus, M.B.).—The Fountain of Youth. Crown 8vo,
cloth extra, with Two Illustrations by HUME NISBET, 3s. 6d.; post 8vo, illustrated boards, 2s.

De Guerin (Maurice), The Journal of. Edited by G. S. TREBUTIEN.
With a Memoir by SAINTE-BEUVE. Translated from the 20th French Edition by JESSIE P. FROTH-
INGHAM. Fcap. 8vo, half-bound, 2s. 6d.

De Maistre (Xavier).—A Journey Round my Room. Translated
by Sir HENRY ATTWELL. Post 8vo, cloth limp, 2s. 6d.

De Mille (James).—A Castle in Spain. Crown 8vo, cloth extra, with
a Frontispiece, 3s. 6d.; post 8vo, illustrated boards, 2s.

━━━━ (The): The Blue Ribbon of the Turf. With Brief Accounts
━. By LOUIS HENRY CURZON. Crown 8vo, cloth limp, 2s. 6d.

Derwent (Leith), Novels by. Cr. 8vo, cl., 3s. 6d. ea.; post 8vo, 2s. ea.
Our Lady of Tears. | Circe's Lovers.

Dewar (T. R.).—A Ramble Round the Globe. With 220 Illustrations. Crown 8vo, cloth extra, 7s. 6d.

Dickens (Charles), Novels by. Post 8vo, illustrated boards, 2s. each.
Sketches by Boz. | Nicholas Nickleby. | Oliver Twist.

About England with Dickens. By ALFRED RIMMER. With 57 Illustrations by C. A. VANDERHOOF, ALFRED RIMMER, and others. Square 8vo, cloth extra, 7s. 6d.

Dictionaries.
A Dictionary of Miracles: Imitative, Realistic, and Dogmatic. By the Rev. E. C. BREWER, LL.D. Crown 8vo, cloth extra, 7s. 6d.
The Reader's Handbook of Allusions, References, Plots, and Stories. By the Rev. E. C. BREWER, LL.D. With an ENGLISH BIBLIOGRAPHY. Crown 8vo, cloth extra, 7s. 6d.
Authors and their Works, with the Dates. Crown 8vo, cloth limp, 2s.
Familiar Short Sayings of Great Men. With Historical and Explanatory Notes by SAMUEL A. BENT, A.M. Crown 8vo, cloth extra, 7s. 6d.
The Slang Dictionary: Etymological, Historical, and Anecdotal. Crown 8vo, cloth, 6s. 6d.
Words, Facts, and Phrases: A Dictionary of Curious, Quaint, and Out-of-the-Way Matters. By ELIEZER EDWARDS. Crown 8vo, cloth extra, 7s. 6d.

Diderot.—The Paradox of Acting. Translated, with Notes, by WALTER HERRIES POLLOCK. With Preface by Sir HENRY IRVING. Crown 8vo, parchment, 4s. 6d.

Dobson (Austin), Works by.
Thomas Bewick and his Pupils. With 95 Illustrations. Square 8vo, cloth, 6s.
Four Frenchwomen. With Four Portraits. Crown 8vo, buckram, gilt top, 6s.
Eighteenth Century Vignettes. TWO SERIES. Crown 8vo, buckram, 6s. each.—A THIRD SERIES is in preparation.

Dobson (W. T.).—Poetical Ingenuities and Eccentricities. Post 8vo, cloth limp, 2s. 6d.

Donovan (Dick), Detective Stories by.
Post 8vo, illustrated boards, 2s. each; cloth limp, 2s. 6d. each.
The Man-Hunter. | Wanted. | A Detective's Triumphs.
Caught at Last. | In the Grip of the Law.
Tracked and Taken. | From Information Received.
Who Poisoned Hetty Duncan? | Link by Link. | Dark Deeds.
Suspicion Aroused. | The Long Arm of the Law. [Shortly.

Crown 8vo, cloth extra, 3s. 6d. each; post 8vo, illustrated boards, 2s. each; cloth, 2s. 6d. each.
The Man from Manchester. With 23 Illustrations.
Tracked to Doom. With Six full-page Illustrations by GORDON BROWNE.

The Mystery of Jamaica Terrace. Crown 8vo, cloth, 3s. 6d. [Shortly.

Doyle (A. Conan).—The Firm of Girdlestone. Cr. 8vo, cl., 3s. 6d.

Dramatists, The Old. Crown 8vo, cl. ex., with Portraits, 6s. per Vol.
Ben Jonson's Works. With Notes, Critical and Explanatory, and a Biographical Memoir by WILLIAM GIFFORD. Edited by Colonel CUNNINGHAM. Three Vols.
Chapman's Works. Three Vols. Vol. I. contains the Plays complete; Vol. II., Poems and Minor Translations, with an Essay by A. C. SWINBURNE; Vol. III., Translations of the Iliad and Odyssey.
Marlowe's Works. Edited, with Notes, by Colonel CUNNINGHAM. One Vol.
Massinger's Plays. From GIFFORD'S Text. Edited by Colonel CUNNINGHAM. One Vol.

Duncan (Sara Jeannette: Mrs. EVERARD COTES), Works by.
Crown 8vo, cloth extra, 7s. 6d. each.
A Social Departure. With 111 Illustrations by F. H. TOWNSEND.
An American Girl in London. With 80 Illustrations by F. H. TOWNSEND.
The Simple Adventures of a Memsahib. With 37 Illustrations by F. H. TOWNSEND.

Crown 8vo, cloth extra, 3s. 6d. each.
A Daughter of To-Day. | Vernon's Aunt. With 47 Illustrations by HAL HURST.

Dyer (T. F. Thiselton).—The Folk-Lore of Plants. Cr. 8vo, cl., 6s.

Early English Poets. Edited, with Introductions and Annotations, by Rev. A. B. GROSART, D.D. Crown 8vo, cloth boards, 6s. per Volume.
Fletcher's (Giles) Complete Poems. One Vol.
Davies' (Sir John) Complete Poetical Works. Two Vols.
Herrick's (Robert) Complete Collected Poems. Three Vols.
Sidney's (Sir Philip) Complete Poetical Works. Three Vols.

Edgcumbe (Sir E. R. Pearce).—Zephyrus: A Holiday in Brazil and on the River Plate. With 41 Illustrations. Crown 8vo, cloth extra, 5s.

Edison, The Life and Inventions of Thomas A. By W. K. L. and ANTONIA DICKSON. With 200 Illustrations by R. F. OUTCALT, &c. Demy 4to, cloth gilt, 18s.

Edwardes (Mrs. Annie), Novels by.
Post 8vo, illustrated boards, 2s. each.
Archie Lovell. | A Point of Honour.

Edwards (Eliezer).—Words, Facts, and Phrases: A Dictionary
of Curious, Quaint, and Out-of-the-Way Matters. Crown 8vo, cloth, 7s. 6d.

Edwards (M. Betham-), Novels by.
Kitty. Post 8vo, boards, 2s.; cloth, 2s. 6d. | Felicia. Post 8vo, illustrated boards, 2s.

Egerton (Rev. J. C., M.A.). — Sussex Folk and Sussex Ways.
With Introduction by Rev. Dr. H. WACE, and Four Illustrations. Crown 8vo, cloth extra, 5s.

Eggleston (Edward).—Roxy: A Novel. Post 8vo, illust. boards, 2s.

Englishman's House, The: A Practical Guide for Selecting or Build-
ing a House. By C. J. RICHARDSON. Coloured Frontispiece and 534 Illusts. Cr. 8vo, cloth, 7s. 6d.

Ewald (Alex. Charles, F.S.A.), Works by.
The Life and Times of Prince Charles Stuart, Count of Albany (THE YOUNG PRETEN-
DER). With a Portrait. Crown 8vo, cloth extra, 7s. 6d.
Stories from the State Papers. With Autotype Frontispiece. Crown 8vo, cloth, 6s.

Eyes, Our: How to Preserve Them. By JOHN BROWNING. Cr. 8vo, 1s.

Familiar Short Sayings of Great Men. By SAMUEL ARTHUR BENT,
A.M. Fifth Edition, Revised and Enlarged. Crown 8vo, cloth extra, 7s. 6d.

Faraday (Michael), Works by. Post 8vo, cloth extra, 4s. 6d. each.
The Chemical History of a Candle: Lectures delivered before a Juvenile Audience. Edited
by WILLIAM CROOKES, F.C.S. With numerous Illustrations.
On the Various Forces of Nature, and their Relations to each other. Edited by
WILLIAM CROOKES, F.C.S. With Illustrations.

Farrer (J. Anson), Works by.
Military Manners and Customs. Crown 8vo, cloth extra, 6s.
War: Three Essays, reprinted from 'Military Manners and Customs.' Crown 8vo, 1s.; cloth, 1s. 6d.

Fenn (G. Manville), Novels by.
Crown 8vo, cloth extra, 3s. 6d. each; post 8vo, illustrated boards, 2s. each.
The New Mistress. | Witness to the Deed.

Crown 8vo, cloth extra, 3s. 6d. each.
The Tiger Lily: A Tale of Two Passions. | The White Virgin.

Fin-Bec.—The Cupboard Papers: Observations on the Art of Living
and Dining. Post 8vo, cloth limp, 2s. 6d.

Fireworks, The Complete Art of Making; or, The Pyrotechnist's
Treasury. By THOMAS KENTISH. With 267 Illustrations. Crown 8vo, cloth, 5s.

First Book, My. By WALTER BESANT, JAMES PAYN, W. CLARK RUS-
SELL, GRANT ALLEN, HALL CAINE, GEORGE R. SIMS, RUDYARD KIPLING, A. CONAN DOYLE,
M. E. BRADDON, F. W. ROBINSON, H. RIDER HAGGARD, R. M. BALLANTYNE, I. ZANGWILL,
MORLEY ROBERTS, D. CHRISTIE MURRAY, MARY CORELLI, J. K. JEROME, JOHN STRANGE
WINTER, BRET HARTE, 'Q.,' ROBERT BUCHANAN, and R. L. STEVENSON. With a Prefatory Story
by JEROME K. JEROME, and 185 Illustrations. Small demy 8vo, cloth extra, 7s. 6d.

Fitzgerald (Percy), Works by.
The World Behind the Scenes. Crown 8vo, cloth extra, 3s. 6d.
Little Essays: Passages from the Letters of CHARLES LAMB. Post 8vo, cloth, 2s. 6d.
A Day's Tour: A Journey through France and Belgium. With Sketches. Crown 4to, 1s.
Fatal Zero. Crown 8vo, cloth extra, 3s. 6d.; post 8vo, illustrated boards, 2s.

Post 8vo, illustrated boards, 2s. each.
Bella Donna. | The Lady of Brantome. | The Second Mrs. Tillotson.
Polly. | Never Forgotten. | Seventy-five Brooke Street.

The Life of James Boswell (of Auchinleck). With Illusts. Two Vols., demy 8vo, cloth, 24s.
The Savoy Opera. With 60 Illustrations and Portraits. Crown 8vo, cloth, 3s. 6d.
Sir Henry Irving: Twenty Years at the Lyceum. With Portrait. Crown 8vo, 1s.; cloth, 1s. 6d.

Flammarion (Camille), Works by.
Popular Astronomy: A General Description of the Heavens. Translated by J. ELLARD GORE,
F.R.A.S. With Three Plates and 288 Illustrations. Medium 8vo, cloth, 16s.
Urania: A Romance. With 87 Illustrations. Crown 8vo, cloth extra, 5s.

Fletcher's (Giles, B.D.) Complete Poems: Christ's Victorie in
Heaven, Christ's Victorie on Earth, Christ's Triumph over Death, and Minor Poems. With Notes by
Rev. A. B. GROSART, D.D. Crown 8vo, cloth boards, 6s.

Fonblanque (Albany).—Filthy Lucre. Post 8vo, illust. boards, 2s.

Francillon (R. E.), Novels by.
Crown 8vo, cloth extra, 3s. 6d. each; post 8vo, illustrated boards, 2s. each.

One by One. | A Real Queen. | King or Knave.
Ropes of Sand. Illustrated. | | A Dog and his Shadow.

Post 8vo, illustrated boards, 2s. each.

Queen Cophetua. | Olympia. | Romances of the Law.

Jack Doyle's Daughter. Crown 8vo, cloth, 3s. 6d.
Esther's Glove. Fcap. 8vo, picture cover, 1s.

Frederic (Harold), Novels by. Post 8vo, illust. boards, 2s. each.
Seth's Brother's Wife. | The Lawton Girl.

French Literature, A History of. By HENRY VAN LAUN. Three
Vols., demy 8vo, cloth boards, 7s. 6d. each.

Friswell (Hain).—One of Two: A Novel. Post 8vo, illust. bds., 2s.

Frost (Thomas), Works by. Crown 8vo, cloth extra, 3s. 6d. each.
Circus Life and Circus Celebrities. | Lives of the Conjurers.
The Old Showman and the Old London Fairs.

Fry's (Herbert) Royal Guide to the London Charities. Edited
by JOHN LANE. Published Annually. Crown 8vo, cloth, 1s. 6d.

Gardening Books. Post 8vo, 1s. each; cloth limp. 1s. 6d. each.
A Year's Work in Garden and Greenhouse. By GEORGE GLENNY.
Household Horticulture. By TOM and JANE JERROLD. Illustrated.
The Garden that Paid the Rent. By TOM JERROLD.

My Garden Wild. By FRANCIS G. HEATH. Crown 8vo, cloth extra, 6s.

Gardner (Mrs. Alan).—Rifle and Spear with the Rajpoots: Being
the Narrative of a Winter's Travel and Sport in Northern India. With numerous Illustrations by the
Author and F. H. TOWNSEND. Demy 4to, half-bound, 21s.

Garrett (Edward).—The Capel Girls: A Novel. Crown 8vo, cloth
extra, with two Illustrations, 3s. 6d.; post 8vo, illustrated boards, 2s.

Gaulot (Paul).—The Red Shirts: A Story of the Revolution. Translated by JOHN DE VILLIERS. With a Frontispiece by STANLEY WOOD. Crown 8vo, cloth, 3s. 6d.

Gentleman's Magazine, The. 1s. Monthly. Contains Stories,
Articles upon Literature, Science, Biography, and Art, and 'Table Talk' by SYLVANUS URBAN.
%* Bound Volumes for recent years kept in stock, 8s. 6d. each. Cases for binding, 2s.

Gentleman's Annual, The. Published Annually in November. 1s.

German Popular Stories. Collected by the Brothers GRIMM and
Translated by EDGAR TAYLOR. With Introduction by JOHN RUSKIN, and 22 Steel Plates after
GEORGE CRUIKSHANK. Square 8vo, cloth, 6s. 6d.; gilt edges, 7s. 6d.

Gibbon (Charles), Novels by.
Crown 8vo, cloth extra, 3s. 6d. each; post 8vo, illustrated boards, 2s. each.

Robin Gray. Frontispiece. | The Golden Shaft. Frontispiece. | Loving a Dream.

Post 8vo, illustrated boards, 2s. each.

The Flower of the Forest. | In Love and War.
The Dead Heart. | A Heart's Problem.
For Lack of Gold. | By Mead and Stream.
What Will the World Say? | The Braes of Yarrow.
For the King. | A Hard Knot. | Fancy Free. | Of High Degree.
Queen of the Meadow. | In Honour Bound.
In Pastures Green. | Heart's Delight. | Blood-Money.

Gibney (Somerville).—Sentenced! Crown 8vo, 1s.; cloth, 1s. 6d.

Gilbert (W. S.), Original Plays by. In Three Series, 2s. 6d. each.
The FIRST SERIES contains: The Wicked World—Pygmalion and Galatea—Charity—The Princess—
The Palace of Truth—Trial by Jury.
The SECOND SERIES: Broken Hearts—Engaged—Sweethearts—Gretchen—Dan'l Druce—Tom Cobb
—H.M.S. 'Pinafore'—The Sorcerer—The Pirates of Penzance.
The THIRD SERIES: Comedy and Tragedy—Foggerty's Fairy—Rosencrantz and Guildenstern—
Patience—Princess Ida—The Mikado—Ruddigore—The Yeomen of the Guard—The Gondoliers—
The Mountebanks—Utopia.

Eight Original Comic Operas written by W. S. GILBERT. Containing: The Sorcerer—H.M.S.
'Pinafore'—The Pirates of Penzance—Iolanthe—Patience—Princess Ida—The Mikado—Trial by
Jury. Demy 8vo, cloth limp, 2s. 6d.
The Gilbert and Sullivan Birthday Book: Quotations for Every Day in the Year, selected
from Plays by W. S. GILBERT set to Music by Sir A. SULLIVAN. Compiled by ALEX. WATSON.
Royal 16mo, Japanese leather, 2s. 6d.

Gilbert (William), Novels by. Post 8vo, illustrated bds., 2s. each.
Dr. Austin's Guests. | James Duke, Costermonger.
The Wizard of the Mountain.

Glanville (Ernest), Novels by.
Crown 8vo, cloth extra, 3s. 6d. each; post 8vo, illustrated boards, 2s. each.
The Lost Heiress: A Tale of Love, Battle, and Adventure. With Two Illustrations by H. NISBET.
The Fossicker: A Romance of Mashonaland. With Two Illustrations by HUME NISBET.
A Fair Colonist. With a Frontispiece by STANLEY WOOD.

The Golden Rock. With a Frontis. by STANLEY WOOD. Crown 8vo, cloth extra, 3s. 6d.

Glenny (George).—A Year's Work in Garden and Greenhouse:
Practical Advice as to the Management of the Flower, Fruit, and Frame Garden. Post 8vo, 1s.; cl. lp., 1s. 6d.

Godwin (William).—Lives of the Necromancers. Post 8vo, cl., 2s.

Golden Treasury of Thought, The: An Encyclopædia of QUOTA-
TIONS. Edited by THEODORE TAYLOR. Crown 8vo, cloth gilt, 7s. 6d.

Gontaut, Memoirs of the Duchesse de (Gouvernante to the Chil-
dren of France), 1773-1836. With Two Photogravures. Two Vols., demy 8vo, cloth extra, 21s.

Goodman (E. J.).—The Fate of Herbert Wayne. Cr. 8vo, 3s. 6d.

Graham (Leonard).—The Professor's Wife: A Story. Fcp. 8vo, 1s.

Greeks and Romans, The Life of the, described from Antique
Monuments. By ERNST GUHL and W. KONER. Edited by Dr. F. HUEFFER. With 545 Illustrations. Large crown 8vo, cloth extra, 7s. 6d.

Greenwood (James), Works by. Crown 8vo, cloth extra, 3s. 6d. each.
The Wilds of London. | Low-Life Deeps.

Greville (Henry), Novels by.
Nikanor. Translated by ELIZA E. CHASE. Post 8vo, illustrated boards, 2s.
A Noble Woman. Crown 8vo, cloth extra, 5s.; post 8vo, illustrated boards, 2s.

Griffith (Cecil).—Corinthia Marazion: A Novel. Crown 8vo, cloth
extra, 3s. 6d.; post 8vo, illustrated boards, 2s.

Grundy (Sydney).—The Days of his Vanity: A Passage in the
Life of a Young Man. Crown 8vo, cloth extra, 3s. 6d.; post 8vo, illustrated boards, 2s.

Habberton (John, Author of 'Helen's Babies '), Novels by.
Post 8vo, illustrated boards, 2s. each: cloth limp, 2s. 6d. each.
Brueton's Bayou. | Country Luck.

Hair, The: Its Treatment in Health, Weakness, and Disease. Translated from the German of Dr. J. PINCUS. Crown 8vo, 1s.; cloth, 1s. 6d.

Hake (Dr. Thomas Gordon), Poems by. Cr. 8vo, cl. ex., 6s. each.
New Symbols. | Legends of the Morrow. | The Serpent Play.

Maiden Ecstasy. Small 4to, cloth extra, 8s.

Hall (Owen).—The Track of a Storm. Crown 8vo, cloth, 6s.

Hall (Mrs. S. C.).—Sketches of Irish Character. With numerous
Illustrations on Steel and Wood by MACLISE, GILBERT, HARVEY, and GEORGE CRUIKSHANK.
Small demy 8vo, cloth extra, 7s. 6d.

Halliday (Andrew).—Every-day Papers. Post 8vo, boards, 2s.

Handwriting, The Philosophy of. With over 100 Facsimiles and
Explanatory Text. By DON FELIX DE SALAMANCA. Post 8vo, cloth limp, 2s. 6d.

Hanky-Panky: Easy and Difficult Tricks, White Magic, Sleight of
Hand, &c. Edited by W. H. CREMER. With 200 Illustrations. Crown 8vo, cloth extra, 4s. 6d.

Hardy (Lady Duffus).—Paul Wynter's Sacrifice. Post 8vo, bds., 2s.

Hardy (Thomas).—Under the Greenwood Tree. Crown 8vo, cloth
extra, with Portrait and 15 Illustrations, 3s. 6d.; post 8vo, illustrated boards, 2s. cloth limp, 2s. 6d.

Harper (Charles G.), Works by. Demy 8vo, cloth extra, 16s. each.
The Brighton Road. With Photogravure Frontispiece and 90 Illustrations.
From Paddington to Penzance: The Record of a Summer Tramp. With 105 Illustrations.

Harwood (J. Berwick).—The Tenth Earl. Post 8vo, boards, 2s.

Harte's (Bret) Collected Works.   Revised by the Author.   LIBRARY
EDITION, in Eight Volumes, crown 8vo, cloth extra, 6s. each.
Vol.   I. COMPLETE POETICAL AND DRAMATIC WORKS. With Steel-plate Portrait.
"   II. THE LUCK OF ROARING CAMP—BOHEMIAN PAPERS—AMERICAN LEGENDS.
"   III. TALES OF THE ARGONAUTS—EASTERN SKETCHES.
"   IV. GABRIEL CONROY. | Vol. V. STORIES—CONDENSED NOVELS, &c.
"   VI. TALES OF THE PACIFIC SLOPE.
"   VII. TALES OF THE PACIFIC SLOPE—II. With Portrait by JOHN PETTIE, R.A.
"   VIII. TALES OF THE PINE AND THE CYPRESS.

The Select Works of Bret Harte, in Prose and Poetry. With Introductory Essay by J. M.
BELLEW, Portrait of the Author, and 50 Illustrations. Crown 8vo, cloth extra, 7s. 6d.
Bret Harte's Poetical Works. Printed on hand-made paper. Crown 8vo, buckram, 4s. 6d.
The Queen of the Pirate Isle. With 28 Original Drawings by KATE GREENAWAY, reproduced
in Colours by EDMUND EVANS. Small 4to, cloth, 5s.

Crown 8vo, cloth extra, 3s. 6d. each ; post 8vo, picture boards, 2s. each.
A Waif of the Plains. With 60 Illustrations by STANLEY L. WOOD.
A Ward of the Golden Gate. With 59 Illustrations by STANLEY L. WOOD.

Crown 8vo, cloth extra, 3s. 6d. each.
A Sappho of Green Springs, &c. With Two Illustrations by HUME NISBET.
Colonel Starbottle's Client, and Some Other People. With a Frontispiece.
Susy: A Novel. With Frontispiece and Vignette by J. A. CHRISTIE.
Sally Dows, &c. With 47 Illustrations by W. D. ALMOND and others.
A Protegee of Jack Hamlin's. With 26 Illustrations by W. SMALL and others.
The Bell-Ringer of Angel's, &c. With 39 Illustrations by DUDLEY HARDY and others.
Clarence: A Story of the American War. With Eight Illustrations by A. JULE GOODMAN.

Post 8vo, illustrated boards, 2s. each.

Gabriel Conroy.	**The Luck of Roaring Camp,** &c.
An Heiress of Red Dog, &c.	**Californian Stories.**

Post 8vo, illustrated boards, 2s. each ; cloth, 2s. 6d. each.

Flip.	**Maruja.**	**A Phyllis of the Sierras.**

Fcap. 8vo, picture cover, 1s. each.

Snow-Bound at Eagle's.	**Jeff Briggs's Love Story.**

Haweis (Mrs. H. R.), Works by.
The Art of Beauty. With Coloured Frontispiece and 91 Illustrations. Square 8vo, cloth bds., 6s.
The Art of Decoration. With Coloured Frontispiece and 74 Illustrations. Sq. 8vo, cloth bds., 6s.
The Art of Dress. With 32 Illustrations. Post 8vo, 1s. ; cloth, 1s. 6d.
Chaucer for Schools. Demy 8vo, cloth limp, 2s. 6d.
Chaucer for Children. With 38 Illustrations (8 Coloured). Crown 4to, cloth extra, 3s. 6d.

Haweis (Rev. H. R., M.A.).—American Humorists: WASHINGTON
IRVING, OLIVER WENDELL HOLMES, JAMES RUSSELL LOWELL, ARTEMUS WARD, MARK
TWAIN, and BRET HARTE. Third Edition. Crown 8vo, cloth extra, 6s.

Hawthorne (Julian), Novels by.
Crown 8vo, cloth extra, 3s. 6d. each   post 8vo, illustrated boards, 2s. each.

Garth.	**Ellice Quentin.**	**Beatrix Randolph.** With Four Illusts.
Sebastian Strome.		**David Poindexter's Disappearance.**
Fortune's Fool.	**Dust.** Four Illusts.	**The Spectre of the Camera.**

Post 8vo, illustrated boards, 2s. each.

Miss Cadogna.	**Love—or a Name.**

Mrs. Gainsborough's Diamonds. Fcap. 8vo, illustrated cover, 1s.

Hawthorne (Nathaniel).—Our Old Home.   Annotated with Pas-
sages from the Author's Note-books, and Illustrated with 31 Photogravures. Two Vols., cr. 8vo, 15s.

**Heath (Francis George).—My Garden Wild, and What I Grew
There.** Crown 8vo, cloth extra, gilt edges, 6s.

Helps (Sir Arthur), Works by.   Post 8vo, cloth limp, 2s. 6d. each.
Animals and their Masters. | **Social Pressure.**

Ivan de Biron: A Novel. Crown 8vo, cloth extra, 3s. 6d. ; post 8vo, illustrated boards, 2s.

Henderson (Isaac).— Agatha Page: A Novel.   Cr. 8vo, cl., 3s. 6d.

Henty (G. A.), Novels by.   Crown 8vo, cloth extra, 3s. 6d. each.
Rujub the Juggler. With Eight Illustrations by STANLEY L. WOOD.
Dorothy's Double.

Herman (Henry).—A Leading Lady.   Post 8vo, bds., 2s. ; cl., 2s. 6d.

**Herrick's (Robert) Hesperides, Noble Numbers, and Complete
Collected Poems.** With Memorial-Introduction and Notes by the Rev. A. B. GROSART, D.D.,
Steel Portrait, &c. Three Vols., crown 8vo, cloth boards, 18s.

Hertzka (Dr. Theodor).—Freeland: A Social Anticipation. Translated by ARTHUR RANSOM. Crown 8vo, cloth extra, 6s.

Hesse-Wartegg (Chevalier Ernst von).— Tunis: The Land and the People. With 22 Illustrations. Crown 8vo, cloth extra, 3s. 6d.

Hill (Headon).—Zambra the Detective. Post 8vo, bds., 2s.; cl., 2s. 6d.

Hill (John), Works by.
Treason-Felony. Post 8vo, boards, 2s. | The Common Ancestor. Cr. 8vo, cloth, 3s. 6d.

Hindley (Charles), Works by.
Tavern Anecdotes and Sayings: Including Reminiscences connected with Coffee Houses, Clubs, &c. With Illustrations. Crown 8vo, cloth extra, 3s. 6d.
The Life and Adventures of a Cheap Jack. Crown 8vo, cloth extra, 3s. 6d.

Hodges (Sydney).—When Leaves were Green. 3 vols., 15s. net. [Shortly.

Hoey (Mrs. Cashel).—The Lover's Creed. Post 8vo, boards, 2s.

Hollingshead (John).—Niagara Spray. Crown 8vo, 1s.

Holmes (Gordon, M.D.)—The Science of Voice Production and Voice Preservation. Crown 8vo, 1s.; cloth, 1s. 6d.

Holmes (Oliver Wendell), Works by.
The Autocrat of the Breakfast-Table. Illustrated by J. GORDON THOMSON. Post 8vo, cloth limp, 2s. 6d.—Another Edition, post 8vo, cloth, 2s.
The Autocrat of the Breakfast-Table and The Professor at the Breakfast-Table. In One Vol. Post 8vo, half-bound, 2s.

Hood's (Thomas) Choice Works in Prose and Verse. With Life of the Author, Portrait, and 200 Illustrations. Crown 8vo, cloth extra, 7s. 6d.
Hood's Whims and Oddities. With 85 Illustrations. Post 8vo, half-bound, 2s.

Hood (Tom).—From Nowhere to the North Pole: A Noah's Arkæological Narrative. With 25 Illustrations by W. BRUNTON and E. C. BARNES. Cr. 8vo, cloth, 6s.

Hook's (Theodore) Choice Humorous Works; including his Ludicrous Adventures, Bons Mots, Puns, and Hoaxes. With Life of the Author, Portraits, Facsimiles, and Illustrations. Crown 8vo, cloth extra, 7s. 6d.

Hooper (Mrs. Geo.).—The House of Raby. Post 8vo, boards, 2s.

Hopkins (Tighe).—''Twixt Love and Duty.' Post 8vo, boards, 2s.

Horne (R. Hengist). — Orion: An Epic Poem. With Photograph Portrait by SUMMERS. Tenth Edition. Crown 8vo, cloth extra, 7s.

Hungerford (Mrs., Author of ' Molly Bawn '), Novels by.
Post 8vo, illustrated boards, 2s. each; cloth limp, 2s. 6d. each.
A Maiden All Forlorn. | In Durance Vile. | A Mental Struggle.
Marvel. | A Modern Circe. |
Crown 8vo, cloth extra, 3s. 6d. each.
The Red-House Mystery. | The Three Graces. With 6 Illusts. [Shortly.
Lady Verner's Flight. Crown 8vo, cloth, 3s. 6d.; post 8vo, illustrated boards, 2s.
The Professor's Experiment. Three Vols., crown 8vo, 15s. net.

Hunt's (Leigh) Essays: A Tale for a Chimney Corner, &c. Edited by EDMUND OLLIER. Post 8vo, half-bound, 2s.

Hunt (Mrs. Alfred), Novels by.
Crown 8vo, cloth extra, 3s. 6d. each; post 8vo, illustrated boards, 2s. each.
The Leaden Casket. | Self-Condemned. | That Other Person.
Thornicroft's Model. Post 8vo, boards, 2s. | Mrs. Juliet. Crown 8vo, cloth extra, 3s. 6d.

Hutchison (W. M.).—Hints on Colt-breaking. With 25 Illustrations. Crown 8vo, cloth extra, 3s. 6d.

Hydrophobia: An Account of M. PASTEUR'S System ; The Technique of his Method, and Statistics. By RENAUD SUZOR, M.B. Crown 8vo, cloth extra, 6s.

Hyne (C. J. Cutcliffe).— Honour of Thieves. Cr. 8vo, cloth, 3s. 6d.

Idler (The): An Illustrated Magazine. Edited by J. K. JEROME. 6d. Monthly. The First SEVEN VOLS. are now ready, cloth extra, 5s. each; Cases for Binding, 1s. 6d. each.

Impressions (The) of Aureole.   Crown 8vo, printed on blush-rose
paper and handsomely bound, 6s.

Indoor Paupers. By ONE OF THEM. Crown 8vo, 1s. ; cloth, 1s. 6d.

Ingelow (Jean).—Fated to be Free. Post 8vo, illustrated bds., 2s.

Innkeeper's Handbook (The) and Licensed Victualler's Manual.
By J. TREVOR-DAVIES. Crown 8vo, 1s. ; cloth, 1s. 6d.

Irish Wit and Humour, Songs of.   Collected and Edited by A.
PERCEVAL GRAVES. Post 8vo, cloth limp, 2s. 6d.

Irving (Sir Henry) : A Record of over Twenty Years at the Lyceum.
By PERCY FITZGERALD. With Portrait. Crown 8vo, 1s. ; cloth, 1s. 6d.

James (C. T. C.). — A Romance of the Queen's Hounds.   Post
8vo, picture cover, 1s. ; cloth limp, 1s. 6d.

Jameson (William).—My Dead Self. Post 8vo, bds., 2s. ; cl., 2s. 6d.

Japp (Alex. H., LL.D.).—Dramatic Pictures, &c. Cr. 8vo, cloth, 5s.

Jay (Harriett), Novels by. Post 8vo, illustrated boards, 2s. each.
The Dark Colleen. | The Queen of Connaught.

Jefferies (Richard), Works by. Post 8vo, cloth limp, 2s. 6d. each.
Nature near London. | The Life of the Fields. | The Open Air.
• Also the HAND-MADE PAPER EDITION, crown 8vo, buckram, gilt top, 6s. each.

The Eulogy of Richard Jefferies. By Sir WALTER BESANT. With a Photograph Portrait,
Crown 8vo, cloth extra, 6s.

Jennings (Henry J.), Works by.
Curiosities of Criticism. Post 8vo, cloth limp, 2s. 6d.
Lord Tennyson : A Biographical Sketch. With Portrait. Post 8vo, 1s. ; cloth, 1s. 6d.

Jerome (Jerome K.), Books by.
Stageland. With 64 Illustrations by J. BERNARD PARTRIDGE. Fcap. 4to, picture cover, 1s.
John Ingerfield, &c. With 9 Illusts. by A. S. BOYD and JOHN GULICH. Fcap. 8vo, pic. cov. 1s. 6d.
The Prude's Progress : A Comedy by J. K. JEROME and EDEN PHILLPOTTS. Cr. 8vo, 1s. 6d.

Jerrold (Douglas).—The Barber's Chair ; and **The Hedgehog**
Letters. Post 8vo, printed on laid paper and half-bound, 2s.

Jerrold (Tom), Works by. Post 8vo, 1s. ea. ; cloth limp, 1s. 6d. ea.
The Garden that Paid the Rent.
Household Horticulture : A Gossip about Flowers. Illustrated.

Jesse (Edward).—Scenes and Occupations of a Country Life.
Post 8vo, cloth limp, 2s.

Jones (William, F.S.A.), Works by. Cr. 8vo, cl. extra, 7s. 6d. ea.
Finger-Ring Lore : Historical, Legendary, and Anecdotal. With nearly 300 Illustrations. Second
Edition, Revised and Enlarged.
Credulities, Past and Present. Including the Sea and Seamen, Miners, Talismans, Word and
Letter Divination, Exorcising and Blessing of Animals, Birds, Eggs, Luck, &c. With Frontispiece.
Crowns and Coronations : A History of Regalia. With 100 Illustrations.

Jonson's (Ben) Works.   With Notes Critical and Explanatory, and
a Biographical Memoir by WILLIAM GIFFORD. Edited by Colonel CUNNINGHAM. Three Vols.,
crown 8vo, cloth extra, 6s. each.

Josephus, The Complete Works of. Translated by WHISTON. Con-
taining 'The Antiquities of the Jews' and 'The Wars of the Jews.' With 52 Illustrations and Maps.
Two Vols., demy 8vo, half-bound, 12s. 6d.

Kempt (Robert).—Pencil and Palette : Chapters on Art and Artists.
Post 8vo, cloth limp, 2s. 6d.

Kershaw (Mark). — Colonial Facts and Fictions : Humorous
Sketches. Post 8vo, illustrated boards, 2s. ; cloth, 2s. 6d.

Keyser (Arthur).—Cut by the Mess. Crown 8vo, 1s. ; cloth, 1s. 6d.

King (R. Ashe), Novels by. Cr. 8vo, cl., 3s. 6d. ea.; post 8vo, bds., 2s. ea.
A Drawn Game. | 'The Wearing of the Green.'

Post 8vo, illustrated boards, 2s. each.
Passion's Slave. | Bell Barry.

Knight (William, M.R.C.S., and Edward, L.R.C.P.). — The Patient's Vade Mecum: How to Get Most Benefit from Medical Advice. Cr. 8vo, 1s.; cl., 1s. 6d.

Knights (The) of the Lion: A Romance of the Thirteenth Century. Edited, with an Introduction, by the MARQUESS OF LORNE, K.T. Crown 8vo, cloth extra, 6s.

Lamb's (Charles) Complete Works in Prose and Verse, including 'Poetry for Children' and 'Prince Dorus.' Edited, with Notes and Introduction, by R. H. SHEP-HERD. With Two Portraits and Facsimile of the 'Essay on Roast Pig.' Crown 8vo, half-bd., 7s. 6d.
The Essays of Elia. Post 8vo, printed on laid paper and half-bound, 2s.
Little Essays: Sketches and Characters by CHARLES LAMB, selected from his Letters by PERCY FITZGERALD. Post 8vo, cloth limp, 2s. 6d.
The Dramatic Essays of Charles Lamb. With Introduction and Notes by BRANDER MAT-THEWS, and Steel-plate Portrait. Fcap. 8vo, half-bound, 2s. 6d.

Landor (Walter Savage).—Citation and Examination of William Shakspeare, &c., before Sir Thomas Lucy, touching Deer-stealing, 19th September, 1582. To which is added, **A Conference of Master Edmund Spenser** with the Earl of Essex, touching the State of Ireland, 1595. Fcap. 8vo, half-Roxburghe, 2s. 6d.

Lane (Edward William).—The Thousand and One Nights, commonly called in England **The Arabian Nights' Entertainments.** Translated from the Arabic, with Notes. Illustrated with many hundred Engravings from Designs by HARVEY. Edited by EDWARD STANLEY POOLE. With Preface by STANLEY LANE-POOLE. Three Vols., demy 8vo, cloth, 7s. 6d. ea.

Larwood (Jacob), Works by.
The Story of the London Parks. With Illustrations. Crown 8vo, cloth extra, 3s. 6d.
Anecdotes of the Clergy. Post 8vo, laid paper, half-bound, 2s.
Post 8vo, cloth limp, 2s. 6d. each.
Forensic Anecdotes. | **Theatrical Anecdotes.**

Lehmann (R. C.), Works by. Post 8vo, 1s. each; cloth, 1s. 6d. each.
Harry Fludyer at Cambridge.
Conversational Hints for Young Shooters: A Guide to Polite Talk.

Leigh (Henry S.), Works by.
Carols of Cockayne. Printed on hand-made paper, bound in buckram, 5s.
Jeux d'Esprit. Edited by HENRY S. LEIGH. Post 8vo, cloth limp, 2s. 6d.

Lepelletier (Edmond). — Madame Sans-Gêne. Translated from the French by JOHN DE VILLIERS. Crown 8vo, cloth extra, 3s. 6d.

Leys (John).—The Lindsays: A Romance. Post 8vo, illust. bds., 2s.

Lindsay (Harry).—Rhoda Roberts: A Welsh Mining Story. Crown 8vo, cloth, 3s. 6d.

Linton (E. Lynn), Works by. Post 8vo, cloth limp, 2s. 6d. each.
Witch Stories. | **Ourselves:** Essays on Women.
Crown 8vo, cloth extra, 3s. 6d. each; post 8vo, illustrated boards, 2s. each.
Patricia Kemball. | **Ione.** | **Under which Lord?** With 12 Illustrations.
The Atonement of Leam Dundas. | **'My Love!'** | **Sowing the Wind.**
The World Well Lost. With 12 Illusts. | **Paston Carew,** Millionaire and Miser.
Post 8vo, illustrated boards, 2s each.
The Rebel of the Family. | **With a Silken Thread.**
The One Too Many. Crown 8vo, cloth extra, 3s. 6d.
Dulcie Everton. Two Vols., crown 8vo, 10s. net. [Shortly.
Freeshooting: Extracts from the Works of Mrs. LYNN LINTON. Post 8vo, cloth, 2s. 6d.

Lucy (Henry W.).—Gideon Fleyce: A Novel. Crown 8vo, cloth extra, 3s. 6d.; post 8vo, illustrated boards, 2s.

Macalpine (Avery), Novels by.
Teresa Itasca. Crown 8vo, cloth extra, 1s.
Broken Wings. With Six Illustrations by W. J. HENNESSY. Crown 8vo, cloth extra, 6s.

MacColl (Hugh), Novels by.
Mr. Stranger's Sealed Packet. Post 8vo, illustrated boards, 2s.
Ednor Whitlock. Crown 8vo, cloth extra, 6s.

Macdonell (Agnes).—Quaker Cousins. Post 8vo, boards, 2s.

MacGregor (Robert).—Pastimes and Players: Notes on Popular Games. Post 8vo, cloth limp, 2s. 6d.

Mackay (Charles, LL.D.). — Interludes and Undertones; or, Music at Twilight. Crown 8vo, cloth extra, 6s.

McCarthy (Justin, M.P.), Works by.

A History of Our Own Times, from the Accession of Queen Victoria to the General Election of 1880. Four Vols., demy 8vo, cloth extra, 12s. each.—Also a POPULAR EDITION, in Four Vols., crown 8vo, cloth extra, 6s. each.—And the JUBILEE EDITION, with an Appendix of Events to the end of 1886, in Two Vols., large crown 8vo, cloth extra, 7s. 6d. each.

A Short History of Our Own Times. One Vol., crown 8vo, cloth extra, 6s.—Also a CHEAP POPULAR EDITION, post 8vo, cloth limp, 2s. 6d.

A History of the Four Georges. Four Vols., demy 8vo, cl. ex., 12s. each. [Vols. I. & II. *ready.*

Crown 8vo, cloth extra, 3s. 6d. each; post 8vo, illustrated boards, 2s. each; cloth limp, 2s. 6d. each.

The Waterdale Neighbours.	**Donna Quixote.** With 12 Illustrations.
My Enemy's Daughter.	**The Comet of a Season.**
A Fair Saxon.	**Maid of Athens.** With 12 Illustrations.
Linley Rochford.	**Camiola:** A Girl with a Fortune.
Dear Lady Disdain.	**The Dictator.**
Miss Misanthrope. With 12 Illustrations.	**Red Diamonds.**

'**The Right Honourable.**' By JUSTIN McCARTHY, M.P., and Mrs. CAMPBELL PRAED. Crown 8vo, cloth extra, 6s.

McCarthy (Justin Huntly), Works by.

The French Revolution. (Constituent Assembly, 1789-91). Four Vols., demy 8vo, cloth extra, 12s. each. Vols. I. & II. *ready*; Vols. III. & IV. *in the press.*

An Outline of the History of Ireland. Crown 8vo, 1s.; cloth, 1s. 6d.

Ireland Since the Union: Sketches of Irish History, 1798-1886. Crown 8vo, cloth, 6s.

Hafiz in London: Poems. Small 8vo, gold cloth, 3s. 6d.

Our Sensation Novel. Crown 8vo, picture cover, 1s.; cloth limp, 1s. 6d.

Doom: An Atlantic Episode. Crown 8vo, picture cover, 1s.

Dolly: A Sketch. Crown 8vo, picture cover, 1s.; cloth limp, 1s. 6d.

Lily Lass: A Romance. Crown 8vo, picture cover, 1s.; cloth limp, 1s. 6d.

The Thousand and One Days. With Two Photogravures. Two Vols., crown 8vo, half-bd., 12s.

A London Legend. Crown 8vo, cloth, 3s. 6d. [*Shortly.*

MacDonald (George, LL.D.), Books by.

Works of Fancy and Imagination. Ten Vols., 16mo, cloth, gilt edges, in cloth case, 21s.; or the Volumes may be had separately, in Grolier cloth, at 2s. 6d. each.

Vol. I. WITHIN AND WITHOUT.—THE HIDDEN LIFE.
  " II. THE DISCIPLE.—THE GOSPEL WOMEN.—BOOK OF SONNETS.—ORGAN SONGS.
  " III. VIOLIN SONGS.—SONGS OF THE DAYS AND NIGHTS.—A BOOK OF DREAMS.—ROADSIDE POEMS.—POEMS FOR CHILDREN.
  " IV. PARABLES.—BALLADS.—SCOTCH SONGS.
  " V. & VI. PHANTASTES: A Faerie Romance. | Vol. VII. THE PORTENT.
  " VIII. THE LIGHT PRINCESS.—THE GIANT'S HEART.—SHADOWS.
  " IX. CROSS PURPOSES.—THE GOLDEN KEY.—THE CARASOYN.—LITTLE DAYLIGHT.
  "   X. THE CRUEL PAINTER.—THE WOW O' RIVVEN.—THE CASTLE.—THE BROKEN SWORDS. —THE GRAY WOLF.—UNCLE CORNELIUS.

Poetical Works of George MacDonald. Collected and Arranged by the Author. Two Vols. crown 8vo, buckram, 12s.

A Threefold Cord. Edited by GEORGE MACDONALD. Post 8vo, cloth, 5s.

Phantastes: A Faerie Romance. With 25 Illustrations by J. BELL. Crown 8vo, cloth extra, 3s. 6d.

Heather and Snow: A Novel. Crown 8vo, cloth extra, 3s. 6d.

Lilith: A Romance. Crown 8vo, cloth extra, 6s.

Maclise Portrait Gallery (The) of Illustrious Literary Characters: 85 Portraits by DANIEL MACLISE; with Memoirs—Biographical, Critical, Bibliographical, and Anecdotal—illustrative of the Literature of the former half of the Present Century, by WILLIAM BATES, B.A. Crown 8vo, cloth extra, 7s. 6d.

Macquoid (Mrs.), Works by. Square 8vo, cloth extra, 6s. each.

In the Ardennes. With 50 Illustrations by THOMAS R. MACQUOID.

Pictures and Legends from Normandy and Brittany. 34 Illusts. by T. R. MACQUOID.

Through Normandy. With 92 Illustrations by T. R. MACQUOID, and a Map.

Through Brittany. With 35 Illustrations by T. R. MACQUOID, and a Map.

About Yorkshire. With 67 Illustrations by T. R. MACQUOID.

Post 8vo, illustrated boards, 2s. each.

The Evil Eye, and other Stories. | **Lost Rose,** and other Stories.

Magician's Own Book, The: Performances with Eggs, Hats, &c.
Edited by W. H. CREMER. With 200 Illustrations. Crown 8vo, cloth extra, 4s. 6d.

Magic Lantern, The, and its Management: Including full Practical Directions. By T. C. HEPWORTH. With 10 Illustrations. Crown 8vo, 1s.; cloth, 1s. 6d.

Magna Charta: An Exact Facsimile of the Original in the British Museum, 3 feet by 2 feet, with Arms and Seals emblazoned in Gold and Colours, 5s.

Mallory (Sir Thomas). — Mort d'Arthur: The Stories of King Arthur and of the Knights of the Round Table. (A Selection.) Edited by B. MONTGOMERIE RANKING. Post 8vo, cloth limp, 2s.

Mallock (W. H.), Works by.
The New Republic. Post 8vo, picture cover, 2s.; cloth limp, 2s. 6d.
The New Paul & Virginia: Positivism on an Island. Post 8vo, cloth, 2s. 6d.
A Romance of the Nineteenth Century. Crown 8vo, cloth 6s.; post 8vo, illust. boards, 2s.

Poems. Small 4to, parchment, 8s.
Is Life Worth Living? Crown 8vo, cloth extra, 6s.

Mark Twain, Books by. Crown 8vo, cloth extra, 7s. 6d. each.
The Choice Works of Mark Twain. Revised and Corrected throughout by the Author. With Life, Portrait, and numerous Illustrations.
Roughing It; and The Innocents at Home. With 200 Illustrations by F. A. FRASER.
Mark Twain's Library of Humour. With 197 Illustrations.

Crown 8vo, cloth extra (illustrated), 7s. 6d. each; post 8vo, illustrated boards, 2s. each.
The Innocents Abroad; or, The New Pilgrim's Progress. With 234 Illustrations. (The Two Shilling Edition is entitled Mark Twain's Pleasure Trip.)
The Gilded Age. By MARK TWAIN and C. D. WARNER. With 212 Illustrations.
The Adventures of Tom Sawyer. With 111 Illustrations.
A Tramp Abroad. With 314 Illustrations.
The Prince and the Pauper. With 190 Illustrations.
Life on the Mississippi. With 300 Illustrations.
The Adventures of Huckleberry Finn. With 174 Illustrations by E. W. KEMBLE.
A Yankee at the Court of King Arthur. With 220 Illustrations by DAN BEARD.

Crown 8vo, cloth extra, 3s. 6d. each.
The American Claimant. With 81 Illustrations by HAL HURST and others.
Tom Sawyer Abroad. With 26 Illustrations by DAN. BEARD.
Pudd'nhead Wilson. With Portrait and Six Illustrations by LOUIS LOEB.
Tom Sawyer, Detective, &c. With numerous Illustrations.   [Shortly.

The £1,000,000 Bank-Note. Crown 8vo, cloth, 3s. 6d.; post 8vo, picture boards 2s.

Post 8vo, illustrated boards, 2s. each.
The Stolen White Elephant. | Mark Twain's Sketches.

Marks (H. S., R.A.), Pen and Pencil Sketches by. With Four Photogravures and 126 Illustrations. Two Vols. demy 8vo, cloth, 32s.

Marlowe's Works. Including his Translations. Edited, with Notes and Introductions, by Colonel CUNNINGHAM. Crown 8vo, cloth extra, 6s.

Marryat (Florence), Novels by. Post 8vo, illust. boards, 2s. each.
A Harvest of Wild Oats. | Fighting the Air.
Open! Sesame! | Written in Fire.

Massinger's Plays. From the Text of WILLIAM GIFFORD. Edited by Col. CUNNINGHAM. Crown 8vo, cloth extra, 6s.

Masterman (J.).—Half-a-Dozen Daughters. Post 8vo, boards, 2s.

Matthews (Brander).—A Secret of the Sea, &c. Post 8vo, illustrated boards, 2s.; cloth limp, 2s. 6d.

Mayhew (Henry).—London Characters, and the Humorous Side of London Life. With numerous Illustrations. Crown 8vo, cloth, 3s. 6d.

Meade (L. T.), Novels by. Crown 8vo, cloth, 3s. 6d. each.
A Soldier of Fortune. | In an Iron Grip.
The Voice of the Charmer. Three Vols., 15s. net.

Merrick (Leonard).—The Man who was Good. Post 8vo, illustrated boards, 2s.

Mexican Mustang (On a), through Texas to the Rio Grande. By A. E. SWEET and J. ARMOY KNOX. With 265 Illustrations. Crown 8vo, cloth extra, 7s. 6d.

Middlemass (Jean), Novels by. Post 8vo, illust. boards, 2s. each.
Touch and Go. | Mr. Dorillion.

Miller (Mrs. F. Fenwick).—Physiology for the Young; or, The House of Life. With numerous Illustrations. Post 8vo, cloth limp, 2s. 6d.

Milton (J. L.), Works by. Post 8vo, 1s. each; cloth, 1s. 6d. each.
The Hygiene of the Skin. With Directions for Diet, Soaps, Baths, Wines, &c.
The Bath in Diseases of the Skin.
The Laws of Life, and their Relation to Diseases of the Skin.

Minto (Wm.).—Was She Good or Bad? Cr. 8vo, 1s.; cloth, 1s. 6d.

Mitford (Bertram), Novels by. Crown 8vo, cloth extra, 3s. 6d. each.
The Gun-Runner: A Romance of Zululand. With a Frontispiece by STANLEY L. WOOD.
The Luck of Gerard Ridgeley. With a Frontispiece by STANLEY L. WOOD.
The King's Assegai. With Six full-page Illustrations by STANLEY L. WOOD.
Renshaw Fanning's Quest. With a Frontispiece by STANLEY L. WOOD.

Molesworth (Mrs.), Novels by.
Hathercourt Rectory. Post 8vo, illustrated boards, 2s.
That Girl in Black. Crown 8vo, cloth, 1s. 6d.

Moncrieff (W. D. Scott-).—The Abdication: An Historical Drama.
With Seven Etchings by JOHN PETTIE, W. Q. ORCHARDSON, J. MACWHIRTER, COLIN HUNTER,
R. MACBETH and TOM GRAHAM. Imperial 4to, buckram, 21s.

Moore (Thomas), Works by.
The Epicurean; and Alciphron. Post 8vo, half-bound, 2s.
Prose and Verse; including Suppressed Passages from the MEMOIRS OF LORD BYRON. Edited
by R. H. SHEPHERD. With Portrait. Crown 8vo, cloth extra, 7s. 6d.

Muddock (J. E.) Stories by.
Stories Weird and Wonderful. Post 8vo, illustrated boards, 2s.; cloth, 2s. 6d.
The Dead Man's Secret. Frontispiece by F. BARNARD. Cr. 8vo, cloth, 5s.; post 8vo, boards, 2s.
From the Bosom of the Deep. Post 8vo. Illustrated boards, 2s.
Maid Marian and Robin Hood. With 12 Illusts. by STANLEY WOOD. Cr. 8vo, cloth extra, 3s. 6d.
Basile the Jester. Crown 8vo, cloth, 3s. 6d. [Shortly.

Murray (D. Christie), Novels by.
Crown 8vo, cloth extra, 3s. 6d. each; post 8vo, illustrated boards, 2s. each.

A Life's Atonement.	The Way of the World.	A Bit of Human Nature.
Joseph's Coat. 12 Illusts.	A Model Father.	First Person Singular.
Coals of Fire. 3 Illusts.	Old Blazer's Hero.	Bob Martin's Little Girl.
Val Strange.	Cynic Fortune. Frontisp.	Time's Revenges.
Hearts.	By the Gate of the Sea.	A Wasted Crime.

Crown 8vo, cloth extra, 3s. 6d. each.
In Direst Peril. | Mount Despair, &c. Frontispiece by GRENVILLE MANTON.

The Making of a Novelist: An Experiment in Autobiography. With a Collotype Portrait and
Vignette. Crown 8vo, art linen, 6s.

Murray (D. Christie) and Henry Herman, Novels by.
Crown 8vo, cloth extra, 3s. 6d. each; post 8vo, illustrated boards, 2s. each.
One Traveller Returns. | The Bishops' Bible.
Paul Jones's Alias, &c. With Illustrations by A. FORESTIER and G. NICOLET.

Murray (Henry), Novels by.
Post 8vo, illustrated boards, 2s. each; cloth, 2s. 6d. each.
A Game of Bluff. | A Song of Sixpence.

Newbolt (Henry).—Taken from the Enemy. Fcp. 8vo, cloth, 1s. 6d.

Nisbet (Hume), Books by.
'Bail Up.' Crown 8vo, cloth extra, 3s. 6d.; post 8vo, illustrated boards, 2s.
Dr. Bernard St. Vincent. Post 8vo, illustrated boards, 2s.

Lessons in Art. With 21 Illustrations. Crown 8vo, cloth extra, 2s. 6d.
Where Art Begins. With 27 Illustrations. Square 8vo, cloth extra, 3s. 6d.

Norris (W. E.), Novels by. Crown 8vo, cloth, 3s. 6d. each.
Saint Ann's. | Billy Bellew. With Frontispiece. [Shortly.

O'Hanlon (Alice), Novels by. Post 8vo, illustrated boards, 2s. each.
The Unforeseen. | Chance? or Fate?

Ouida, Novels by. Cr. 8vo, cl., 3s. 6d. ea.; post 8vo, illust. bds., 2s. ea.

Held in Bondage.	Folle-Farine.	Moths.	Pipistrello.
Tricotrin.	A Dog of Flanders.	A Village Commune.
Strathmore.	Pascarel.	Signa.	In Maremma.	Wanda.
Chandos.	Two Wooden Shoes.	Bimbi.	Syrlin.
Cecil Castlemaine's Gage	In a Winter City.	Frescoes.	Othmar.
Under Two Flags.	Ariadne.	Princess Napraxine.
Puck.	Idalia.	Friendship.	Guilderoy.	Ruffino.

Square 8vo, cloth extra, 5s. each.
Bimbi. With Nine Illustrations by EDMUND H. GARRETT.
A Dog of Flanders, &c. With Six Illustrations by EDMUND H. GARRETT.

Santa Barbara, &c. Square 8vo, cloth, 6s.; crown 8vo, cloth, 3s. 6d.; post 8vo, illustrated boards, 2s.
Two Offenders. Square 8vo, cloth extra, 6s.; crown 8vo, cloth extra, 3s. 6d.

Wisdom, Wit, and Pathos, selected from the Works of OUIDA by F. SYDNEY MORRIS. Post
8vo, cloth extra, 5s.—CHEAP EDITION, illustrated boards, 2s.

Ohnet (Georges), Novels by. Post 8vo, illustrated boards, 2s. each.
Doctor Rameau. | A Last Love.
A Weird Gift. Crown 8vo, cloth, 3s. 6d.; post 8vo, picture boards, 2s.

Oliphant (Mrs.), Novels by. Post 8vo, illustrated boards, 2s. each.
The Primrose Path. | Whiteladies.
The Greatest Heiress in England.

O'Reilly (Mrs.).—Phœbe's Fortunes. Post 8vo, illust. boards, 2s.

Page (H. A.), Works by.
Thoreau: His Life and Aims. With Portrait. Post 8vo, cloth limp, 2s. 6d.
Animal Anecdotes. Arranged on a New Principle. Crown 8vo, cloth extra, 5s.

Pandurang Hari; or, Memoirs of a Hindoo. With Preface by Sir
BARTLE FRERE. Crown 8vo, cloth, 3s. 6d.; post 8vo, illustrated boards, 2s.

Pascal's Provincial Letters. A New Translation, with Historical
Introduction and Notes by T. M'CRIE, D.D. Post 8vo, cloth limp, 2s.

Paul (Margaret A.).—Gentle and Simple. Crown 8vo, cloth, with
Frontispiece by HELEN PATERSON, 3s. 6d.; post 8vo, illustrated boards, 2s.

Payn (James), Novels by.

Crown 8vo, cloth extra, 3s. 6d. each; post 8vo, illustrated boards, 2s. each.

Lost Sir Massingberd.	Holiday Tasks.
Walter's Word.	The Canon's Ward. With Portrait.
Less Black than We're Painted.	The Talk of the Town. With 12 Illusts.
By Proxy. | For Cash Only.	Glow-Worm Tales.
High Spirits.	The Mystery of Mirbridge.
Under One Roof.	The Word and the Will.
A Confidential Agent. With 12 Illusts.	The Burnt Million.
A Grape from a Thorn. With 12 Illusts.	Sunny Stories. | A Trying Patient.

Post 8vo, illustrated boards, 2s. each.

Humorous Stories. | From Exile.	Found Dead.
The Foster Brothers.	Gwendoline's Harvest.
The Family Scapegrace.	A Marine Residence.
Married Beneath Him.	Mirk Abbey.
Bentinck's Tutor.	Some Private Views.
A Perfect Treasure.	Not Wooed, But Won.
A County Family.	Two Hundred Pounds Reward.
Like Father, Like Son.	The Best of Husbands.
A Woman's Vengeance.	Halves.
Carlyon's Year. | Cecil's Tryst.	Fallen Fortunes.
Murphy's Master.	What He Cost Her.
At Her Mercy.	Kit: A Memory.
The Clyffards of Clyffe.	A Prince of the Blood.

In Peril and Privation. With 17 Illustrations. Crown 8vo, cloth, 3s. 6d.
Notes from the 'News.' Crown 8vo, portrait cover, 1s.; cloth, 1s. 6d.

Pennell (H. Cholmondeley), Works by. Post 8vo, cloth, 2s. 6d. ea.
Puck on Pegasus. With Illustrations.
Pegasus Re-Saddled. With Ten full-page Illustrations by G. DU MAURIER.
The Muses of Mayfair: Vers de Société. Selected by H. C. PENNELL.

Phelps (E. Stuart), Works by. Post 8vo, 1s. ea.; cloth, 1s. 6d. ea.
Beyond the Gates. | An Old Maid's Paradise. | Burglars in Paradise.
Jack the Fisherman. Illustrated by C. W. REED. Crown 8vo, 1s.; cloth, 1s. 6d.

Phil May's Sketch-Book. Containing 50 full-page Drawings. Imp.
4to, art canvas, gilt top, 10s. 6d.

Pirkis (C. L.), Novels by.
Trooping with Crows. Fcap. 8vo, picture cover, 1s.
Lady Lovelace. Post 8vo, illustrated boards, 2s.

Planche (J. R.), Works by.
The Pursuivant of Arms. With Six Plates and 209 Illustrations. Crown 8vo, cloth, 7s. 6d.
Songs and Poems, 1819-1879. With Introduction by Mrs. MACKARNESS. Crown 8vo, cloth, 6s.

Plutarch's Lives of Illustrious Men. With Notes and a Life of
Plutarch by JOHN and WM. LANGHORNE, and Portraits. Two Vols., demy 8vo, half-bound 10s. 6d.

Poe's (Edgar Allan) Choice Works in Prose and Poetry. With Int
duction by CHARLES BAUDELAIRE. Portrait and Facsimiles. Crown 8vo, cloth, 7s. 6d.
The Mystery of Marie Roget, &c. Post 8vo, illustrated boards, 2s.

Pope's Poetical Works.   Post 8vo, cloth limp, 2s.

Praed (Mrs. Campbell), Novels by.   Post 8vo, illust. bds., 2s. each.
The Romance of a Station. | The Soul of Countess Adrian.

Outlaw and Lawmaker.   Crown 8vo, cloth, 3s. 6d.; post 8vo, boards, 2s.
Christina Chard.   With Frontispiece by W. PAGET.   Crown 8vo, cloth, 3s. 6d.

Price (E. C.), Novels by.
Crown 8vo, cloth extra, 3s. 6d. each; post 8vo, illustrated boards, 2s. each.
Valentina. | The Foreigners. | Mrs. Lancaster's Rival.

Gerald.   Post 8vo, illustrated boards, 2s.

Princess Olga.—Radna: A Novel.   Crown 8vo, cloth extra, 6s.

Proctor (Richard A., B.A.), Works by.
Flowers of the Sky.   With 55 Illustrations.   Small crown 8vo, cloth extra, 3s. 6d.
Easy Star Lessons.   With Star Maps for every Night in the Year.   Crown 8vo, cloth, 6s.
Familiar Science Studies.   Crown 8vo, cloth extra, 6s.
Saturn and its System.   With 13 Steel Plates.   Demy 8vo, cloth extra, 10s. 6d.
Mysteries of Time and Space.   With numerous Illustrations.   Crown 8vo, cloth extra, 6s.
The Universe of Suns, &c.   With numerous Illustrations.   Crown 8vo, cloth extra, 6s.
Wages and Wants of Science Workers.   Crown 8vo, 1s. 6d.

Pryce (Richard).—Miss Maxwell's Affections.   Crown 8vo, cloth,
with Frontispiece by HAL LUDLOW, 3s. 6d.; post 8vo, illustrated boards, 2s.

Rambosson (J.).—Popular Astronomy.   Translated by C. B. PIT-
MAN.   With Coloured Frontispiece and numerous Illustrations.   Crown 8vo, cloth extra, 7s. 6d.

Randolph (Lieut.-Col. George, U.S.A.).—Aunt Abigail Dykes:
A Novel.   Crown 8vo, cloth extra, 7s. 6d.

Reade's (Charles) Novels.
Crown 8vo, cloth extra, mostly Illustrated, 3s. 6d. each; post 8vo, Illustrated boards, 2s. each.
Peg Woffington. | Christie Johnstone.   Hard Cash. | Griffith Gaunt.
'It is Never Too Late to Mend.'   Foul Play. | Put Yourself in His Place.
The Course of True Love Never Did Run   A Terrible Temptation.
Smooth.   A Simpleton. | The Wandering Heir.
The Autobiography of a Thief; Jack of   A Woman-Hater.
all Trades; and James Lambert.   Singleheart and Doubleface.
Love Me Little, Love Me Long.   Good Stories of Men and other Animals.
The Double Marriage.   The Jilt, and other Stories.
The Cloister and the Hearth.   A Perilous Secret. | Readiana.

A New Collected LIBRARY EDITION, complete in Seventeen Volumes, set in new long primer type,
printed on laid paper, and elegantly bound in cloth, price 3s. 6d. each, is now in course of publication. The
volumes will appear in the following order:—

1. Peg Woffington; and Christie John-   7. Love Me Little, Love me Long. [Mar.
   stone.   8. The Double Marriage.   [April.
2. Hard Cash.   9. Griffith Gaunt.   [May.
3. The Cloister and the Hearth.   With a   10. Foul Play.   [June.
   Preface by Sir WALTER BESANT.   11. Put Yourself in His Place.   [July.
4. 'It is Never too Late to Mend.'   [Dec.   12. A Terrible Temptation.   [August.
5. The Course of True Love Never Did   13. A Simpleton.   [Sept.
   Run Smooth; and Singleheart and   14. A Woman-Hater.   [Oct.
   Doubleface.   [Jan. 1896.   15. The Jilt, and other Stories; and Good
6. The Autobiography of a Thief; Jack   Stories of Men & other Animals.[Nov.
   of all Trades; A Hero and a Mar-   16. A Perilous Secret.   [Dec.
   tyr; and The Wandering Heir.   [Feb.   17. Readiana; & Bible Characters.[Jan.'97

POPULAR EDITIONS, medium 8vo, 6d. each : cloth, 1s. each.
'It is Never Too Late to Mend.' | The Cloister and the Hearth.
Peg Woffington; and Christie Johnstone.

Christie Johnstone.   With Frontispiece.   Choicely printed in Elzevir style.   Fcap. 8vo, half-Roxb.2s.6d.
Peg Woffington.   Choicely printed in Elzevir style.   Fcap. 8vo, half-Roxburghe, 2s. 6d.
The Cloister and the Hearth.   In Four Vols., post 8vo, with an Introduction by Sir WALTER BE-
SANT, and a Frontispiece to each Vol., 14s. the set; and the ILLUSTRATED LIBRARY EDITION,
with Illustrations on every page, Two Vols., crown 8vo, cloth gilt, 42s. net.
Bible Characters.   Fcap. 8vo, leatherette, 1s.

Selections from the Works of Charles Reade.   With an Introduction by Mrs. ALEX. IRE-
LAND.   Crown 8vo, buckram, with Portrait, 6s.; CHEAP EDITION, post 8vo, cloth limp, 2s. 6d.

Riddell (Mrs. J. H.), Novels by.
Weird Stories.   Crown 8vo, cloth extra, 3s. 6d.; post 8vo, illustrated boards, 2s.

Post 8vo, illustrated boards, 2s. each.
The Uninhabited House.   Fairy Water.
The Prince of Wales's Garden Party.   Her Mother's Darling.
The Mystery in Palace Gardens.   The Nun's Curse. | Idle Tales.

Rimmer (Alfred), Works by. Square 8vo, cloth gilt, 7s. 6d. each.
Our Old Country Towns. With 55 Illustrations by the Author.
Rambles Round Eton and Harrow. With 50 Illustrations by the Author.
About England with Dickens. With 58 Illustrations by C. A. VANDERHOOF and A. RIMMER.

Rives (Amelie).—Barbara Dering. Crown 8vo, cloth extra, 3s. 6d. ;
post 8vo, illustrated boards, 2s.

Robinson Crusoe. By DANIEL DEFOE. (MAJOR'S EDITION.) With
37 Illustrations by GEORGE CRUIKSHANK. Post 8vo, half-bound, 2s.

Robinson (F. W.), Novels by.
Women are Strange. Post 8vo, illustrated boards, 2s.
The Hands of Justice. Crown 8vo, cloth extra, 3s. 6d. ; post 8vo, illustrated boards, 2s.

The Woman in the Dark. Two Vols., 10s. net.

Robinson (Phil), Works by. Crown 8vo, cloth extra, 6s. each.
The Poets' Birds. | The Poets' Beasts.
The Poets and Nature: Reptiles, Fishes, and Insects.

Rochefoucauld's Maxims and Moral Reflections. With Notes
and an Introductory Essay by SAINTE-BEUVE. Post 8vo, cloth limp, 2s.

Roll of Battle Abbey, The: A List of the Principal Warriors who
came from Normandy with William the Conqueror, 1066. Printed in Gold and Colours, 5s.

Rosengarten (A.).—A Handbook of Architectural Styles. Translated by W. COLLETT-SANDARS. With 639 Illustrations. Crown 8vo, cloth extra, 7s. 6d.

Rowley (Hon. Hugh), Works by. Post 8vo, cloth, 2s. 6d. each.
Puniana: Riddles and Jokes. With numerous Illustrations.
More Puniana. Profusely Illustrated.

Runciman (James), Stories by. Post 8vo, bds., 2s. ea.; cl., 2s. 6d. ea.
Skippers and Shellbacks. | Grace Balmaign's Sweetheart.
Schools and Scholars.

Russell (Dora), Novels by. Crown 8vo, cloth, 3s. 6d. each.
A Country Sweetheart. | The Drift of Fate.   [Shortly.

Russell (W. Clark), Books and Novels by.
Crown 8vo, cloth extra, 6s. each ; post 8vo, illustrated boards, 2s. each ; cloth limp, 2s. 6d. each.
Round the Galley-Fire. | A Book for the Hammock.
In the Middle Watch. | The Mystery of the 'Ocean Star.'
A Voyage to the Cape. | The Romance of Jenny Harlowe.

Crown 8vo, cloth extra, 3s. 6d. each ; post 8vo, illustrated boards, 2s. each ; cloth limp, 2s. 6d. each.
An Ocean Tragedy. | My Shipmate Louisa. | Alone on a Wide Wide Sea.

Crown 8vo, cloth, 3s. 6d. each.
Is He the Man? | The Phantom Death, &c. With Frontispiece.
The Good Ship 'Mohock.' | The Convict Ship.   [Shortly.

On the Fo'k'sle Head. Post 8vo, illustrated boards, 2s. ; cloth limp, 2s. 6d.
Heart of Oak. Three Vols., crown 8vo, 15s. net.
The Tale of the Ten. Three Vols., crown 8vo, 15s. net.   [Shortly.

Saint Aubyn (Alan), Novels by.
Crown 8vo, cloth extra, 3s. 6d. each ; post 8vo, illustrated boards, 2s. each.
A Fellow of Trinity. With a Note by OLIVER WENDELL HOLMES and a Frontispiece.
The Junior Dean. | The Master of St. Benedict's. | To His Own Master.

Fcap. 8vo, cloth boards, 1s. 6d. each.
The Old Maid's Sweetheart. | Modest Little Sara.

Crown 8vo, cloth extra, 3s. 6d. each.
Orchard Damerel. | In the Face of the World. | The Tremlett Diamonds. [Shortly

Sala (George A.).—Gaslight and Daylight. Post 8vo, boards, 2s.

Sanson. — Seven Generations of Executioners: Memoirs of the
Sanson Family (1688 to 1847). Crown 8vo, cloth extra, 3s. 6d.

Saunders (John), Novels by.
Crown 8vo, cloth extra, 3s. 6d. each ; post 8vo, illustrated boards, 2s. each.
Guy Waterman. | The Lion in the Path. | The Two Dreamers.
Bound to the Wheel. Crown 8vo, cloth extra, 3s. 6d.

Saunders (Katharine), Novels by.
Crown 8vo, cloth extra, 3s. 6d. each ; post 8vo, illustrated boards, 2s. each.

Margaret and Elizabeth. | Heart Salvage.
The High Mills. | Sebastian.

Joan Merryweather. Post 8vo, illustrated boards, 2s.
Gideon's Rock. Crown 8vo, cloth extra, 3s. 6d.

Scotland Yard, Past and Present: Experiences of Thirty-seven Years.
By Ex-Chief-Inspector CAVANAGH. Post 8vo, illustrated boards, 2s. ; cloth, 2s. 6d.

Secret Out, The: One Thousand Tricks with Cards; with Entertaining Experiments in Drawing-room or 'White' Magic. By W. H. CREMER. With 300 Illustrations. Crown 8vo, cloth extra, 4s. 6d.

Seguin (L. G.), Works by.
The Country of the Passion Play (Oberammergau) and the Highlands of Bavaria. With Map and 37 Illustrations. Crown 8vo, cloth extra, 3s. 6d.
Walks in Algiers. With Two Maps and 16 Illustrations. Crown 8vo, cloth extra, 6s.

Senior (Wm.).—By Stream and Sea. Post 8vo, cloth, 2s. 6d.

Sergeant (Adeline).—Dr. Endicott's Experiment. Crown 8vo, buckram, 3s. 6d.

Shakespeare for Children: Lamb's Tales from Shakespeare.
With Illustrations, coloured and plain, by J. MOYR SMITH. Crown 4to, cloth gilt, 3s. 6d.

Sharp (William).—Children of To-morrow. Crown 8vo, cloth, 6s.

Shelley's (Percy Bysshe) Complete Works in Verse and Prose.
Edited, Prefaced, and Annotated by R. HERNE SHEPHERD. Five Vols., crown 8vo, cloth, 3s. 6d. each.
Poetical Works, in Three Vols. :
Vol. I. Introduction by the Editor ; Posthumous Fragments of Margaret Nicholson ; Shelley's Correspondence with Stockdale ; The Wandering Jew ; Queen Mab, with the Notes ; Alastor, and other Poems ; Rosalind and Helen ; Prometheus Unbound ; Adonais, &c.
„ II. Laon and Cythna : The Cenci ; Julian and Maddalo ; Swellfoot the Tyrant ; The Witch of Atlas ; Epipsychidion ; Hellas.
„ III. Posthumous Poems ; The Masque of Anarchy ; and other Pieces.
Prose Works, in Two Vols. :
Vol. I. The Two Romances of Zastrozzi and St. Irvyne : the Dublin and Marlow Pamphlets ; A Refutation of Deism ; Letters to Leigh Hunt, and some Minor Writings and Fragments.
„ II. The Essays ; Letters from Abroad ; Translations and Fragments, edited by Mrs. SHELLEY. With a Biography of Shelley, and an Index of the Prose Works.
*** Also a few copies of a LARGE-PAPER EDITION, 5 vols., cloth, £2 12s. 6d.

Sherard (R. H.).—Rogues: A Novel. Crown 8vo, 1s. ; cloth, 1s. 6d.

Sheridan (General P. H.), Personal Memoirs of. With Portraits, Maps, and Facsimiles. Two Vols., demy 8vo, cloth, 24s.

Sheridan's (Richard Brinsley) Complete Works, with Life and Anecdotes. Including his Dramatic Writings, his Works in Prose and Poetry, Translations, Speeches, and Jokes. With 10 Illustrations. Crown 8vo, half-bound, 7s. 6d.
The Rivals, The School for Scandal, and other Plays. Post 8vo, half-bound, 2s.
Sheridan's Comedies: The Rivals and The School for Scandal. Edited, with an Introduction and Notes to each Play, and a Biographical Sketch, by BRANDER MATTHEWS. With Illustrations. Demy 8vo, half-parchment, 12s. 6d.

Sidney's (Sir Philip) Complete Poetical Works, including all those in 'Arcadia.' With Portrait, Memorial-Introduction, Notes, &c., by the Rev. A. B. GROSART D.D. Three Vols., crown 8vo, cloth boards, 18s.

Sims (George R.), Works by.
Post 8vo, illustrated boards, 2s. each ; cloth limp, 2s. 6d. each.

Rogues and Vagabonds. | Tales of To-day.
The Ring o' Bells. | Dramas of Life. With 60 Illustrations.
Mary Jane's Memoirs. | Memoirs of a Landlady.
Mary Jane Married. | My Two Wives.
Tinkletop's Crime. | Scenes from the Show.
Zeph: A Circus Story, &c. | The Ten Commandments: Stories. [Shortly.

Crown 8vo, picture cover, 1s. each ; cloth, 1s. 6d. each.
How the Poor Live; and Horrible London.
The Dagonet Reciter and Reader: Being Readings and Recitations in Prose and Verse, selected from his own Works by GEORGE R. SIMS.
The Case of George Candlemas. | Dagonet Ditties. (From The Referee.)

Dagonet Abroad. Crown 8vo, cloth, 3s. 6d.

Signboards: Their History, including Anecdotes of Famous Taverns and Remarkable Characters. By JACOB LARWOOD and JOHN CAMDEN HOTTEN. With Coloured Frontispiece and 94 Illustrations. Crown 8vo, cloth extra, 7s. 6d.

Sister Dora: A Biography. By MARGARET LONSDALE. With Four Illustrations. Demy 8vo, picture cover, 4d.; cloth, 6d.

Sketchley (Arthur).—A Match in the Dark. Post 8vo, boards, 2s

Slang Dictionary (The): Etymological, Historical, and Anecdotal. Crown 8vo, cloth extra, 6s. 6d.

Smart (Hawley).—Without Love or Licence: A Novel. Crown 8vo, cloth extra, 3s. 6d.; post 8vo, illustrated boards, 2s.

Smith (J. Moyr), Works by.
The Prince of Argolis. With 130 Illustrations. Post 8vo, cloth extra, 3s. 6d.
The Wooing of the Water Witch. With numerous Illustrations. Post 8vo, cloth, 6s.

Society in London. Crown 8vo, 1s.; cloth, 1s. 6d.

Society in Paris: The Upper Ten Thousand. A Series of Letters from Count PAUL VASILI to a Young French Diplomat. Crown 8vo, cloth, 6s.

Somerset (Lord Henry).—Songs of Adieu. Small 4to, Jap. vel., 6s.

Spalding (T. A., LL.B.).— Elizabethan Demonology: An Essay on the Belief in the Existence of Devils. Crown 8vo, cloth extra, 5s.

Speight (T. W.), Novels by.
Post 8vo, illustrated boards, 2s. each.

The Mysteries of Heron Dyke.	Back to Life.
By Devious Ways, &c.	The Loudwater Tragedy.
Hoodwinked; & Sandycroft Mystery.	Burgo's Romance.
The Golden Hoop.	Quittance in Full.

Post 8vo, cloth limp, 1s. 6d. each.

A Barren Title.	Wife or No Wife?

The Sandycroft Mystery. Crown 8vo, picture cover, 1s.

Crown 8vo, cloth extra, 3s. 6d. each.

A Secret of the Sea.	The Grey Monk. [Shortly.

Spenser for Children. By M. H. TOWRY. With Coloured Illustrations by WALTER J. MORGAN. Crown 4to, cloth extra, 3s. 6d.

Starry Heavens (The): A POETICAL BIRTHDAY BOOK. Royal 16mo, cloth extra, 2s. 6d.

Stedman (E. C.), Works by. Crown 8vo, cloth extra, 9s. each.
Victorian Poets. | The Poets of America.

Sterndale (R. Armitage).—The Afghan Knife: A Novel. Crown 8vo, cloth extra, 3s. 6d.; post 8vo, illustrated boards, 2s.

Stevenson (R. Louis), Works by. Post 8vo, cloth limp, 2s. 6d. ea.
Travels with a Donkey. With a Frontispiece by WALTER CRANE.
An Inland Voyage. With a Frontispiece by WALTER CRANE.

Crown 8vo, buckram, gilt top, 6s. each.
Familiar Studies of Men and Books.
The Silverado Squatters. With Frontispiece by J. D. STRONG.
The Merry Men. | Underwoods: Poems.
Memories and Portraits.
Virginibus Puerisque, and other Papers. | Ballads. | Prince Otto.
Across the Plains, with other Memories and Essays.

New Arabian Nights. Crown 8vo, buckram, gilt top, 6s.; post 8vo, illustrated boards, 2s.
The Suicide Club; and The Rajah's Diamond. (From NEW ARABIAN NIGHTS.) With Eight Illustrations by W. J. HENNESSY. Crown 8vo, cloth, 5s.
Father Damien: An Open Letter to the Rev. Dr. Hyde. Cr. 8vo, hand-made and brown paper, 1s.
The Edinburgh Edition of the Works of Robert Louis Stevenson. Twenty Vols. demy 8vo. This Edition (which is limited to 1,000 copies) is sold only in Sets, the price of which may be learned from the Booksellers. The Vols are appearing at the rate of one a month, beginning Nov. 1894.

Weir of Hermiston: (R. L. STEVENSON'S LAST WORK.) Large crown 8vo, 6s. [Shortly.

Stoddard (C. Warren).—Summer Cruising in the South Seas. Illustrated by WALLIS MACKAY. Crown 8vo, cloth extra, 3s. 6d.

Stories from Foreign Novelists. With Notices by HELEN and ALICE ZIMMERN. Crown 8vo, cloth extra, 3s. 6d.; post 8vo, illustrated boards, 2s.

Strange Manuscript (A) Found in a Copper Cylinder. Crown 8vo, cloth extra, with 19 Illustrations by GILBERT GAUL, 5s.; post 8vo, illustrated boards, 2s.

Strange Secrets. Told by PERCY FITZGERALD, CONAN DOYLE, FLORENCE MARRYAT, &c. Post 8vo, illustrated boards, 2s.

Strutt (Joseph).—The Sports and Pastimes of the People of England; including the Rural and Domestic Recreations, May Games, Mummeries, Shows, &c., from the Earliest Period to the Present Time. Edited by WILLIAM HONE. With 140 Illustrations. Crown 8vo, cloth extra, 7s. 6d.

Swift's (Dean) Choice Works, in Prose and Verse. With Memoir, Portrait, and Facsimiles of the Maps in 'Gulliver's Travels.' Crown 8vo, cloth, 7s. 6d.
Gulliver's Travels, and A Tale of a Tub. Post 8vo, half-bound, 2s.
Jonathan Swift: A Study. By J. CHURTON COLLINS. Crown 8vo, cloth extra, 8s.

Swinburne (Algernon C.), Works by.

Selections from the Poetical Works of A. C. Swinburne. Fcap. 8vo, 6s.
Atalanta in Calydon. Crown 8vo, 6s.
Chastelard: A Tragedy. Crown 8vo, 7s.
Poems and Ballads. FIRST SERIES. Crown 8vo, or fcap. 8vo, 9s.
Poems and Ballads. SECOND SERIES. Crown 8vo, 9s.
Poems & Ballads. THIRD SERIES. Cr. 8vo, 7s.
Songs before Sunrise. Crown 8vo, 10s. 6d.
Bothwell: A Tragedy. Crown 8vo, 12s. 6d.
Songs of Two Nations. Crown 8vo, 6s.
George Chapman. (See Vol. II. of G. CHAPMAN'S Works.) Crown 8vo, 6s.
Essays and Studies. Crown 8vo, 12s.
Erechtheus: A Tragedy. Crown 8vo, 6s.

A Note on Charlotte Bronte. Cr. 8vo, 6s.
A Study of Shakespeare. Crown 8vo, 8s.
Songs of the Springtides. Crown 8vo, 6s.
Studies in Song. Crown 8vo, 7s.
Mary Stuart: A Tragedy. Crown 8vo, 8s.
Tristram of Lyonesse. Crown 8vo, 9s.
A Century of Roundels. Small 4to, 8s.
A Midsummer Holiday. Crown 8vo, 7s.
Marino Faliero: A Tragedy. Crown 8vo, 6s.
A Study of Victor Hugo. Crown 8vo, 6s.
Miscellanies. Crown 8vo, 12s.
Locrine: A Tragedy. Crown 8vo, 6s.
A Study of Ben Jonson. Crown 8vo, 7s.
The Sisters: A Tragedy. Crown 8vo, 6s.
Astrophel, &c. Crown 8vo, 7s.
Studies in Prose and Poetry. Cr. 8vo, 9s.

Syntax's (Dr.) Three Tours: In Search of the Picturesque, in Search of Consolation, and in Search of a Wife. With ROWLANDSON'S Coloured Illustrations, and Life of the Author by J. C. HOTTEN. Crown 8vo, cloth extra, 7s. 6d.

Taine's History of English Literature. Translated by HENRY VAN LAUN. Four Vols., small demy 8vo, cloth boards, 30s.—POPULAR EDITION, Two Vols., large crown 8vo, cloth extra, 15s.

Taylor (Bayard).—Diversions of the Echo Club: Burlesques of Modern Writers. Post 8vo, cloth limp, 2s.

Taylor (Dr. J. E., F.L.S.), Works by. Crown 8vo, cloth, 5s. each.
The Sagacity and Morality of Plants: A Sketch of the Life and Conduct of the Vegetable Kingdom. With a Coloured Frontispiece and 100 Illustrations.
Our Common British Fossils, and Where to Find Them. With 331 Illustrations.
The Playtime Naturalist. With 366 Illustrations.

Taylor (Tom).—Historical Dramas. Containing 'Clancarty,' 'Jeanne Darc,' 'Twixt Axe and Crown,' 'The Fool's Revenge,' 'Arkwright's Wife,' 'Anne Boleyn,' 'Plot and Passion.' Crown 8vo, cloth extra, 7s. 6d.
*** The Plays may also be had separately, at 1s. each.

Tennyson (Lord): A Biographical Sketch. By H. J. JENNINGS. Post 8vo, portrait cover, 1s.; cloth, 1s. 6d.

Thackerayana: Notes and Anecdotes. With Coloured Frontispiece and Hundreds of Sketches by WILLIAM MAKEPEACE THACKERAY. Crown 8vo, cloth extra, 7s. 6d.

Thames, A New Pictorial History of the. By A. S. KRAUSSE. With 340 Illustrations. Post 8vo, 1s.; cloth, 1s. 6d.

Thiers (Adolphe).—History of the Consulate and Empire of France under Napoleon. Translated by D. FORBES CAMPBELL and JOHN STEBBING. With 36 Steel Plates. 12 Vols., demy 8vo, cloth extra, 12s. each.

Thomas (Bertha), Novels by. Cr. 8vo, cl., 3s. 6d. ea.; post 8vo, 2s. ea.
The Violin-Player. | Proud Maisie.

Cressida. Post 8vo, illustrated boards, 2s.

Thomson's Seasons, and The Castle of Indolence. With Introduction by ALLAN CUNNINGHAM, and 48 Illustrations. Post 8vo, half-bound, 2s.

Thornbury (Walter), Books by.
The Life and Correspondence of J. M. W. Turner. With Illustrations in Colours. Crown 8vo, cloth extra, 7s. 6d.

Post 8vo, illustrated boards, 2s. each.
Old Stories Re-told. | Tales for the Marines.

Timbs (John), Works by. Crown 8vo, cloth extra, 7s. 6d. each.
The History of Clubs and Club Life in London: Anecdotes of its Famous Coffee-houses, Hostelries, and Taverns. With 42 Illustrations.
English Eccentrics and Eccentricities: Stories of Delusions, Impostures, Sporting Scenes, Eccentric Artists, Theatrical Folk, &c. With 48 Illustrations.

Trollope (Anthony), Novels by.
Crown 8vo, cloth extra, 3s. 6d. each; post 8vo, illustrated boards, 2s. each.
The Way We Live Now. | Mr. Scarborough's Family.
Frau Frohmann. | The Land-Leaguers.

Post 8vo, illustrated boards, 2s. each.
Kept in the Dark. | The American Senator.
The Golden Lion of Granpere. | John Caldigate. | Marion Fay.

Trollope (Frances E.), Novels by.
Crown 8vo, cloth extra, 3s. 6d. each; post 8vo, illustrated boards, 2s. each.
Like Ships Upon the Sea. | Mabel's Progress. | Anne Furness.

Trollope (T. A.).—Diamond Cut Diamond. Post 8vo, illust. bds., 2s.

Trowbridge (J. T.).—Farnell's Folly. Post 8vo, illust. boards, 2s.

Tytler (C. C. Fraser-).—Mistress Judith: A Novel. Crown 8vo, cloth extra, 3s. 6d.; post 8vo, illustrated boards, 2s.

Tytler (Sarah), Novels by.
Crown 8vo, cloth extra, 3s. 6d. each; post 8vo, illustrated boards, 2s. each.
Lady Bell. | Buried Diamonds. | The Blackhall Ghosts.

Post 8vo, illustrated boards, 2s. each.
What She Came Through. | The Huguenot Family.
Citoyenne Jacqueline. | Noblesse Oblige.
The Bride's Pass. | Beauty and the Beast.
Saint Mungo's City. | Disappeared.

The Macdonald Lass. With Frontispiece. Crown 8vo, cloth, 3s. 6d.

Upward (Allen), Novels by.
The Queen Against Owen. Crown 8vo, cloth, with Frontispiece, 3s. 6d.; post 8vo, boards, 2s.
The Prince of Balkistan. Crown 8vo, cloth extra, 3s. 6d.

Vashti and Esther. By the Writer of ' Belle's ' Letters in The World. Crown 8vo, cloth extra, 3s. 6d.

Villari (Linda).—A Double Bond: A Story. Fcap. 8vo, 1s.

Vizetelly (Ernest A.).—The Scorpion: A Romance of Spain. With a Frontispiece. Crown 8vo, cloth extra, 3s. 6d.

Walton and Cotton's Complete Angler; or, The Contemplative Man's Recreation, by IZAAK WALTON; and Instructions How to Angle, for a Trout or Grayling in a clear Stream, by CHARLES COTTON. With Memoirs and Notes by Sir HARRIS NICHOLAS, and 61 Illustrations. Crown 8vo, cloth antique, 7s. 6d.

Walt Whitman, Poems by. Edited, with Introduction, by WILLIAM M. ROSSETTI. With Portrait. Crown 8vo, hand-made paper and buckram, 6s.

Ward (Herbert), Books by.
Five Years with the Congo Cannibals. With 92 Illustrations. Royal 8vo, cloth, 14s.
My Life with Stanley's Rear Guard. With Map. Post 8vo, 1s.; cloth, 1s. 6d.

Walford (Edward, M.A.), Works by.
Walford's County Families of the United Kingdom (1896). Containing the Descent, Birth, Marriage, Education, &c., of 12,000 Heads of Families, their Heirs, Offices, Addresses, Clubs, &c. Royal 8vo, cloth gilt, 50s.
Walford's Shilling Peerage (1896). Containing a List of the House of Lords, Scotch and Irish Peers, &c. 32mo, cloth, 1s.
Walford's Shilling Baronetage (1896). Containing a List of the Baronets of the United Kingdom, Biographical Notices, Addresses, &c. 32mo, cloth, 1s.
Walford's Shilling Knightage (1896). Containing a List of the Knights of the United Kingdom, Biographical Notices, Addresses, &c. 32mo, cloth, 1s.
Walford's Shilling House of Commons (1896). Containing a List of all the Members of the New Parliament, their Addresses, Clubs, &c. 32mo, cloth, 1s.
Walford's Complete Peerage, Baronetage, Knightage, and House of Commons (1896). Royal 32mo, cloth, gilt edges, 5s. *[Preparing.*

Tales of our Great Families. Crown 8vo, cloth extra, 3s. 6d.

Warner (Charles Dudley).—A Roundabout Journey. Crown 8vo, cloth extra, 6s.

Warrant to Execute Charles I. A Facsimile, with the 59 Signatures and Seals. Printed on paper 22 in. by 14 in. 2s.
Warrant to Execute Mary Queen of Scots. A Facsimile, including Queen Elizabeth's Signature and the Great Seal. 2s.

Washington's (George) Rules of Civility Traced to their Sources and Restored by MONCURE D. CONWAY. Fcap. 8vo, Japanese vellum, 2s. 6d.

Wassermann (Lillias), Novels by.
The Daffodils. Crown 8vo, 1s. ; cloth, 1s. 6d.

The Marquis of Carabas. By AARON WATSON and LILLIAS WASSERMANN. Post 8vo, illustrated boards, 2s.

Weather, How to Foretell the, with the Pocket Spectroscope.
By F. W. CORY. With Ten Illustrations. Crown 8vo, 1s. ; cloth, 1s. 6d.

Webber (Byron).—Fun, Frolic, and Fancy. With 43 Illustrations by PHIL MAY and CHARLES MAY. Fcap. 4to, cloth, 5s.

Westall (William), Novels by.
Trust-Money. Post 8vo, illustrated boards, 2s. ; cloth, 2s. 6d.
Sons of Belial. Two Vols., crown 8vo, 10s. net.

Whist, How to Play Solo. By ABRAHAM S. WILKS and CHARLES F. PARDON. Post 8vo, cloth limp, 2s.

White (Gilbert).—The Natural History of Selborne. Post 8vo, printed on laid paper and half-bound, 2s.

Williams (W. Mattieu, F.R.A.S.), Works by.
Science in Short Chapters. Crown 8vo, cloth extra, 7s. 6d.
A Simple Treatise on Heat. With Illustrations. Crown 8vo, cloth, 2s. 6d.
The Chemistry of Cookery. Crown 8vo, cloth extra, 6s.
The Chemistry of Iron and Steel Making. Crown 8vo, cloth extra, 9s.
A Vindication of Phrenology. With Portrait and 43 Illusts. Demy 8vo, cloth extra, 12s. 6d.

Williamson (Mrs. F. H.).—A Child Widow. Post 8vo, bds., 2s.

Wilson (Dr. Andrew, F.R.S.E.), Works by.
Chapters on Evolution. With 259 Illustrations. Crown 8vo, cloth extra, 7s. 6d.
Leaves from a Naturalist's Note-Book. Post 8vo, cloth limp, 2s. 6d.
Leisure-Time Studies. With Illustrations. Crown 8vo, cloth extra, 6s.
Studies in Life and Sense. With numerous Illustrations. Crown 8vo, cloth extra, 6s.
Common Accidents: How to Treat Them. With Illustrations. Crown 8vo, 1s. ; cloth, 1s. 6d.
Glimpses of Nature. With 35 Illustrations. Crown 8vo, cloth extra, 3s. 6d.

Winter (J. S.), Stories by. Post 8vo, illustrated boards, 2s. each ; cloth limp, 2s. 6d. each.
Cavalry Life. | **Regimental Legends.**

A Soldier's Children. With 34 Illustrations by E. G. THOMSON and E. STUART HARDY. Crown 8vo, cloth extra, 3s. 6d.

Wissmann (Hermann von). — My Second Journey through
Equatorial Africa. With 92 Illustrations. Demy 8vo, cloth, 16s.

Wood (H. F.), Detective Stories by. Post 8vo, boards, 2s. each.
The Passenger from Scotland Yard. | The Englishman of the Rue Cain.

Wood (Lady).—Sabina: A Novel.   Post 8vo, illustrated boards, 2s.

Woolley (Celia Parker).—Rachel Armstrong; or, Love and Theology. Post 8vo, illustrated boards, 2s.; cloth, 2s. 6d.

Wright (Thomas), Works by. Crown 8vo, cloth extra, 7s. 6d. each.
The Caricature History of the Georges. With 400 Caricatures, Squibs, &c.
History of Caricature and of the Grotesque in Art, Literature, Sculpture, and Painting. Illustrated by F. W. FAIRHOLT, F.S.A.

Wynman (Margaret).—My Flirtations. With 13 Illustrations by J. BERNARD PARTRIDGE. Post 8vo, cloth, 3s. 6d.

Yates (Edmund), Novels by. Post 8vo, illustrated boards, 2s. each.
Land at Last. | The Forlorn Hope. | Castaway.

Zangwill (I.). — Ghetto Tragedies. With Three Illustrations by A. S. BOYD. Fcap. 8vo, picture cover, 1s. net.

Zola (Emile), Novels by. Crown 8vo, cloth extra, 3s. 6d. each.
The Fat and the Thin. Translated by ERNEST A. VIZETELLY.
Money. Translated by ERNEST A. VIZETELLY.
The Downfall. Translated by E. A. VIZETELLY.
The Dream. Translated by ELIZA CHASE. With Eight Illustrations by JEANNIOT.
Doctor Pascal. Translated by E. A. VIZETELLY. With Portrait of the Author.
Lourdes. Translated by ERNEST A. VIZETELLY.
Rome. Translated by ERNEST A. VIZETELLY.   [Shortly.

SOME BOOKS CLASSIFIED IN SERIES.

. For fuller cataloguing, see alphabetical arrangement, pp. 1-26.

The Mayfair Library.   Post 8vo, cloth limp, 2s. 6d. per Volume.

A Journey Round My Room. By X. OR MAISTRE. Translated by Sir HENRY ATTWELL.
Quips and Quiddities. By W. D. ADAMS.
The Agony Column of 'The Times.'
Melancholy Anatomised: Abridgment of BURTON.
Poetical Ingenuities. By W. T. DOBSON.
The Cupboard Papers. By FIN-BEC.
W. S. Gilbert's Plays. Three Series.
Songs of Irish Wit and Humour.
Animals and their Masters. By Sir A. HELPS.
Social Pressure. By Sir A. HELPS.
Curiosities of Criticism. By H. J. JENNINGS.
The Autocrat of the Breakfast-Table. By OLIVER WENDELL HOLMES.
Pencil and Palette. By R. KEMPT.
Little Essays: from LAMB'S LETTERS.
Forensic Anecdotes. By JACOB LARWOOD.

Theatrical Anecdotes. By JACOB LARWOOD.
Jeux d'Esprit. Edited by HENRY S. LEIGH.
Witch Stories. By E. LYNN LINTON.
Ourselves. By E. LYNN LINTON.
Pastimes and Players. By R. MACGREGOR.
New Paul and Virginia. By W. H. MALLOCK.
The New Republic. By W. H. MALLOCK.
Puck on Pegasus. By H. C. PENNELL.
Pegasus Re-saddled. By H. C. PENNELL.
Muses of Mayfair. Edited by H. C. PENNELL.
Thoreau: His Life and Aims. By H. A. PAGE.
Puniana. By Hon. HUGH ROWLEY.
More Puniana. By Hon. HUGH ROWLEY.
The Philosophy of Handwriting.
By Stream and Sea. By WILLIAM SENIOR.
Leaves from a Naturalist's Note-Book. By Dr. ANDREW WILSON.

The Golden Library.   Post 8vo, cloth limp, 2s. per Volume.

Diversions of the Echo Club. BAYARD TAYLOR.
Songs for Sailors. By W. C. BENNETT.
Lives of the Necromancers. By W. GODWIN.
The Poetical Works of Alexander Pope.
Scenes of Country Life. By EDWARD JESSE.
Tale for a Chimney Corner. By LEIGH HUNT.

The Autocrat of the Breakfast Table. By OLIVER WENDELL HOLMES.
La Mort d'Arthur: Selections from MALLORY.
Provincial Letters of Blaise Pascal.
Maxims and Reflections of Rochefoucauld.

The Wanderer's Library.   Crown 8vo, cloth extra, 3s. 6d. each.

Wanderings in Patagonia. By JULIUS BEERBOHM. Illustrated.
Merrie England in the Olden Time. By G. DANIEL. Illustrated by ROBERT CRUIKSHANK.
Circus Life. By THOMAS FROST.
Lives of the Conjurers. By THOMAS FROST.
The Old Showmen and the Old London Fairs. By THOMAS FROST.
Low-Life Deeps. By JAMES GREENWOOD.
The Wilds of London. By JAMES GREENWOOD.

Tunis. By Chev. HESSE-WARTEGG. 22 Illusts.
Life and Adventures of a Cheap Jack.
World Behind the Scenes. By P. FITZGERALD.
Tavern Anecdotes and Sayings.
The Genial Showman. By E. P. HINGSTON.
Story of London Parks. By JACOB LARWOOD.
London Characters. By HENRY MAYHEW.
Seven Generations of Executioners.
Summer Cruising in the South Seas. By C. WARREN STODDARD. Illustrated.

THE PICCADILLY (3/6) NOVELS—*continued.*

By J. LEITH DERWENT.
Our Lady of Tears. | Circe's Lovers.

By DICK DONOVAN.
Tracked to Doom. | Man from Manchester.

By A. CONAN DOYLE.
The Firm of Girdlestone.

By S. JEANNETTE DUNCAN.
A Daughter of To-day. | Vernon's Aunt.

By G. MANVILLE FENN.
The New Mistress. | The Tiger Lily.
Witness to the Deed. | The White Virgin.

By PERCY FITZGERALD.
Fatal Zero.

By R. E. FRANCILLON.
One by One. | King or Knave?
A Dog and his Shadow. | Ropes of Sand.
A Real Queen. | Jack Doyle's Daughter.

Prefaced by Sir BARTLE FRERE.
Pandurang Hari.

By EDWARD GARRETT.
The Capel Girls.

By PAUL GAULOT.
The Red Shirts.

By CHARLES GIBBON.
Robin Gray. | The Golden Shaft.
Loving a Dream. |

By E. GLANVILLE.
The Lost Heiress. | The Fossicker.
A Fair Colonist. |

By E. J. GOODMAN.
The Fate of Herbert Wayne.

By CECIL GRIFFITH.
Corinthia Marazion.

By SYDNEY GRUNDY.
The Days of his Vanity.

By THOMAS HARDY.
Under the Greenwood Tree.

By BRET HARTE.
A Waif of the Plains. | Susy.
A Ward of the Golden | Sally Dows.
  Gate. | A Protégée of Jack
A Sappho of Green | Hamlin's.
  Springs. | Bell-Ringer of Angel's.
Col. Starbottle's Client. | Clarence.

By JULIAN HAWTHORNE.
Garth. | Beatrix Randolph.
Ellice Quentin. | David Poindexter's Dis-
Sebastian Strome. | appearance.
Dust. | The Spectre of the
Fortune's Fool. | Camera.

By Sir A. HELPS.
Ivan de Biron.

By I. HENDERSON.
Agatha Page.

By G. A. HENTY.
Rujub the Juggler. | Dorothy's Double.

By JOHN HILL.
The Common Ancestor.

By Mrs. HUNGERFORD.
Lady Verner's Flight. | The Red-House Mystery.
The Three Graces. |

By Mrs. ALFRED HUNT.
The Leaden Casket. | Self-Condemned.
That Other Person. | Mrs. Juliet.

By C. J. CUTCLIFFE HYNE.
Honour of Thieves.

By R. ASHE KING.
A Drawn Game.
'The Wearing of the Green.'

By EDMOND LEPELLETIER.
Madame Sans-Gêne.

By HARRY LINDSAY.
Rhoda Roberts.

By E. LYNN LINTON.
Patricia Kemball. | Sowing the Wind.
Under which Lord? | The Atonement of Leam
'My Love!' | Dundas.
Ione. | The World Well Lost.
Paston Carew. | The One Too Many.

By H. W. LUCY.
Gideon Fleyce.

By JUSTIN McCARTHY.
A Fair Saxon. | Miss Misanthrope.
Linley Rochford. | Donna Quixote.
Dear Lady Disdain. | Red Diamonds.
Camiola. | Maid of Athens.
Waterdale Neighbours. | The Dictator.
My Enemy's Daughter. | The Comet of a Season.

By JUSTIN H. McCARTHY.
A London Legend.

By GEORGE MACDONALD.
Heather and Snow. | Phantastes.

By L. T. MEADE.
A Soldier of Fortune. | In an Iron Grip.

By BERTRAM MITFORD.
The Gun-Runner. | The King's Assegai.
The Luck of Gerard | Renshaw Fanning's
  Ridgeley. | Quest.

By J. E. MUDDOCK.
Maid Marian and Robin Hood.
Basile the Jester.

By D. CHRISTIE MURRAY.
A Life's Atonement. | First Person Singular.
Joseph's Coat. | Cynic Fortune.
Coals of Fire. | The Way of the World.
Old Blazer's Hero. | Bob Martin's Little Girl.
Val Strange. | Hearts. | Time's Revenges.
A Model Father. | A Wasted Crime.
By the Gate of the Sea. | In Direst Peril.
A Bit of Human Nature. | Mount Despair.

By MURRAY and HERMAN.
The Bishops' Bible. | Paul Jones's Alias.
One Traveller Returns. |

By HUME NISBET.
'Bail Up!'

By W. E. NORRIS.
Saint Ann's. | Billy Bellew.

By G. OHNET.
A Weird Gift.

By OUIDA.
Held in Bondage. | Two Little Wooden
Strathmore. | Shoes.
Chandos. | In a Winter City.
Under Two Flags. | Friendship.
Idalia. | Moths.
Cecil Castlemaine's | Ruffino.
  Gage. | Pipistrello.
Tricotrin. | A Village Commune.
Puck. | Bimbi.
Folle Farine. | Wanda.
A Dog of Flanders. | Frescoes. | Othmar.
Pascarel. | In Maremma.
Signa. | Syrlin. | Guilderoy.
Princess Napraxine. | Santa Barbara.
Ariadne. | Two Offenders.

By MARGARET A. PAUL.
Gentle and Simple.

By JAMES PAYN.
Lost Sir Massingberd. | High Spirits.
Less Black than We're | Under One Roof.
  Painted. | Glow-worm Tales.
A Confidential Agent. | The Talk of the Town.
A Grape from a Thorn. | Holiday Tasks.
In Peril and Privation. | For Cash Only.
The Mystery of Mir- | The Burnt Million.
By Proxy. [bridge. | The Word and the Will.
The Canon's Ward. | Sunny Stories.
Walter's Word. | A Trying Patient.

THE PICCADILLY (3/6) NOVELS—*continued*.

By Mrs. CAMPBELL PRAED.
Outlaw and Lawmaker. | Christina Chard.

By E. C. PRICE.
Valentina. | Mrs. Lancaster's Rival.
The Foreigners. |

By RICHARD PRYCE.
Miss Maxwell's Affections.

By CHARLES READE.
It is Never Too Late to | Singleheart and Double-
Mend. | face.
The Double Marriage. | Good Stories of Men
Love Me Little, Love | and other Animals.
Me Long. | Hard Cash.
The Cloister and the | Peg Woffington.
Hearth. | Christie Johnstone.
The Course of True | Griffith Gaunt.
Love. | Foul Play.
The Autobiography of | The Wandering Heir.
a Thief. | A Woman-Hater.
Put Yourself in His | A Simpleton.
Place. | A Perilous Secret.
A Terrible Temptation. | Readiana.
The Jilt. |

By Mrs. J. H. RIDDELL.
Weird Stories.

By AMELIE RIVES.
Barbara Dering.

By F. W. ROBINSON.
The Hands of Justice.

By DORA RUSSELL.
A Country Sweetheart. | The Drift of Fate.

By W. CLARK RUSSELL.
Ocean Tragedy. | Is He the Man?
My Shipmate Louise. | The Good Ship 'Mo-
Alone on Wide Wide Sea | hock.'
The Phantom Death. | The Convict Ship.

By JOHN SAUNDERS.
Guy Waterman. | The Two Dreamers.
Bound to the Wheel. | The Lion in the Path.

By KATHARINE SAUNDERS.
Margaret and Elizabeth | Heart Salvage.
Gideon's Rock. | Sebastian.
The High Mills. |

By ADELINE SERGEANT.
Dr. Endicott's Experiment.

By HAWLEY SMART.
Without Love or Licence.

By T. W. SPEIGHT.
A Secret of the Sea. | The Grey Monk.

By ALAN ST. AUBYN.
A Fellow of Trinity. | In Face of the World.
The Junior Dean. | Orchard Damerel.
Master of St. Benedict's. | The Tremlett Diamonds.
To his Own Master. |

By R. A. STERNDALE.
The Afghan Knife.

By BERTHA THOMAS.
Proud Maisie. | The Violin-Player.

By ANTHONY TROLLOPE.
The Way we Live Now. | Scarborough's Family.
Frau Frohmann. | The Land-Leaguers.

By FRANCES E. TROLLOPE.
Like Ships upon the | Anne Furness.
Sea. | Mabel's Progress.

By IVAN TURGENIEFF, &c.
Stories from Foreign Novelists.

By MARK TWAIN.
The American Claimant. | Pudd'nhead Wilson.
The £1,000,000 Bank-note. | Tom Sawyer, Detective.
Tom Sawyer Abroad. |

By C. C. FRASER-TYTLER.
Mistress Judith.

By SARAH TYTLER.
Lady Bell. | The Blackhall Ghosts.
Buried Diamonds. | The Macdonald Lass.

By ALLEN UPWARD.
The Queen against Owen.
The Prince of Balkistan.

By E. A. VIZETELLY.
The Scorpion : A Romance of Spain.

By J. S. WINTER.
A Soldier's Children.

By MARGARET WYNMAN.
My Flirtations.

By E. ZOLA.
The Downfall. | Money. | Lourdes.
The Dream. | The Fat and the Thin.
Dr. Pascal. | Rome.

CHEAP EDITIONS OF POPULAR NOVELS.
Post 8vo, illustrated boards, 2s. each.

By ARTEMUS WARD.
Artemus Ward Complete.

By EDMOND ABOUT.
The Fellah.

By HAMILTON AÏDÉ.
Carr of Carrlyon. | Confidences.

By MARY ALBERT.
Brooke Finchley's Daughter.

By Mrs. ALEXANDER.
Maid, Wife or Widow? | Valerie's Fate.

By GRANT ALLEN.
Philistia. | The Great Taboo.
Strange Stories. | Dumaresq's Daughter.
Babylon | Duchess of Powysland.
For Maimie's Sake. | Blood Royal.
In all Shades. | Ivan Greet's Master-
The Beckoning Hand. | piece.
The Devil's Die. | The Scallywag.
The Tents of Shem. | This Mortal Coil.

By E. LESTER ARNOLD.
Phra the Phœnician.

By Rev. S. BARING-GOULD.
Spider. | Eve.

BY FRANK BARRETT.
Fettered for Life. | Honest Davie.
Little Lady Lifton. | A Prodigal's Progress.
Between Life & Death. | Found Guilty.
The Sin of Olga Zassou- | A Recoiling Vengeance.
lich. | For Love and Honour.
Folly Morrison. | John Ford; and His
Lieut. Barnabas. | Helpmate.

By SHELSLEY BEAUCHAMP.
Grantley Grange.

By Sir W. BESANT and J. RICE.
Ready-Money Mortiboy | By Celia's Arbour.
My Little Girl. | Chaplain of the Fleet.
With Harp and Crown. | The Seamy Side.
This Son of Vulcan. | The Case of Mr. Lucraft.
The Golden Butterfly. | In Trafalgar's Bay.
The Monks of Thelema. | The Ten Years' Tenant.

By Sir WALTER BESANT.
All Sorts and Condi- | For Faith and Freedom.
tions of Men. | To Call Her Mine.
The Captains' Room. | The Bell of St. Paul's.
All in a Garden Fair. | The Holy Rose.
Dorothy Forster. | Armorel of Lyonesse.
Uncle Jack. | S. Katherine's by Tower.
The World Went Very | Verbena Camellia Ste-
Well Then. | phanotis.
Children of Gibeon. | The Ivory Gate.
Herr Paulus. | The Rebel Queen.

Two-Shilling Novels—*continued.*

By AMBROSE BIERCE.
In the Midst of Life.

By FREDERICK BOYLE.
Camp Notes. | Chronicles of No-man's
Savage Life. | Land.

BY BRET HARTE.
Californian Stories. | Flip. | Maruja.
Gabriel Conroy. | A Phyllis of the Sierras.
The Luck of Roaring | A Waif of the Plains.
Camp. | A Ward of the Golden
An Heiress of Red Dog. | Gate.

By HAROLD BRYDGES.
Uncle Sam at Home.

By ROBERT BUCHANAN.
Shadow of the Sword. | The Martyrdom of Ma-
A Child of Nature. | deline.
God and the Man. | Annan Water.
Love Me for Ever. | The New Abelard.
Foxglove Manor. | Matt.
The Master of the Mine. | The Heir of Linne.

By HALL CAINE.
The Shadow of a Crime. | The Deemster.
A Son of Hagar.

By Commander CAMERON.
The Cruise of the 'Black Prince.'

By Mrs. LOVETT CAMERON.
Deceivers Ever. | Juliet's Guardian.

By HAYDEN CARRUTH.
The Adventures of Jones.

By AUSTIN CLARE.
For the Love of a Lass.

By Mrs. ARCHER CLIVE.
Paul Ferroll.
Why Paul Ferroll Killed his Wife.

By MACLAREN COBBAN.
The Cure of Souls. | The Red Sultan.

By C. ALLSTON COLLINS.
The Bar Sinister.

By MORT. & FRANCES COLLINS.
Sweet Anne Page. | Sweet and Twenty.
Transmigration. | The Village Comedy.
From Midnight to Mid- | You Play me False.
night. | Blacksmith and Scholar
A Fight with Fortune. | Frances.

By WILKIE COLLINS.
Armadale. | My Miscellanies.
After Dark. | The Woman in White.
No Name. | The Moonstone.
Antonina. | Man and Wife.
Basil. | Poor Miss Finch.
Hide and Seek. | The Fallen Leaves.
The Dead Secret. | Jezebel's Daughter.
Queen of Hearts. | The Black Robe.
Miss or Mrs.? | Heart and Science.
The New Magdalen. | 'I Say No!'
The Frozen Deep. | The Evil Genius.
The Law and the Lady. | Little Novels.
The Two Destinies. | Legacy of Cain.
The Haunted Hotel. | Blind Love.
A Rogue's Life.

By M. J. COLQUHOUN.
Every Inch a Soldier.

By DUTTON COOK.
Leo. | Paul Foster's Daughter.

By C. EGBERT CRADDOCK.
The Prophet of the Great Smoky Mountains.

By MATT CRIM.
The Adventures of a Fair Rebel.

By B. M. CROKER.
Pretty Miss Neville. | A Bird of Passage.
Diana Barrington. | Proper Pride.
'To Let.' | A Family Likeness.

By W. CYPLES.
Hearts of Gold.

By ALPHONSE DAUDET.
The Evangelist; or, Port Salvation.

By ERASMUS DAWSON.
The Fountain of Youth.

By JAMES DE MILLE.
A Castle in Spain.

By J. LEITH DERWENT.
Our Lady of Tears. | Circe's Lovers.

By CHARLES DICKENS.
Sketches by Boz. | Nicholas Nickleby.
Oliver Twist.

By DICK DONOVAN.
The Man-Hunter. | From Information Re-
Tracked and Taken. | ceived.
Caught at Last! | Tracked to Doom.
Wanted! | Link by Link
Who Poisoned Hetty | Suspicion Aroused.
Duncan? | Dark Deeds.
Man from Manchester. | The Long Arm of the
A Detective's Triumphs | Law.
In the Grip of the Law. |

By Mrs. ANNIE EDWARDES.
A Point of Honour. | Archie Lovell.

By M. BETHAM-EDWARDS.
Felicia. | Kitty.

By EDWARD EGGLESTON.
Roxy.

By G. MANVILLE FENN.
The New Mistress. | Witness to the Deed.

By PERCY FITZGERALD.
Bella Donna. | Second Mrs. Tillotson.
Never Forgotten. | Seventy - five Brooke
Polly. | Street.
Fatal Zero. | The Lady of Brantome.

By P. FITZGERALD and others.
Strange Secrets.

By ALBANY DE FONBLANQUE.
Filthy Lucre.

By R. E. FRANCILLON.
Olympia. | King or Knave?
One by One. | Romances of the Law.
A Real Queen. | Ropes of Sand.
Queen Cophetua. | A Dog and his Shadow.

By HAROLD FREDERIC.
Seth's Brother's Wife. | The Lawton Girl.

Prefaced by Sir BARTLE FRERE.
Pandurang Hari.

By HAIN FRISWELL.
One of Two.

By EDWARD GARRETT.
The Capel Girls.

By GILBERT GAUL.
A Strange Manuscript.

By CHARLES GIBBON.
Robin Gray. | In Honour Bound.
Fancy Free. | Flower of the Forest.
For Lack of Gold. | The Braes of Yarrow.
What will the World | The Golden Shaft.
Say? | Of High Degree.
In Love and War. | By Mead and Stream.
For the King. | Loving a Dream.
In Pastures Green. | A Hard Knot.
Queen of the Meadow. | Heart's Delight.
A Heart's Problem. | Blood-Money.
The Dead Heart.

By WILLIAM GILBERT.
Dr. Austin's Guests. | The Wizard of the
James Duke. | Mountain.

By ERNEST GLANVILLE.
The Lost Heiress. | The Fossicker.
A Fair Colonist.

By HENRY GREVILLE.
A Noble Woman. | Nikanor.

By CECIL GRIFFITH.
Corinthia Marazion.

By SYDNEY GRUNDY.
The Days of his Vanity.

By JOHN HABBERTON.
Brueton's Bayou. | Country Luck.

By ANDREW HALLIDAY.
Every-day Papers.

By Lady DUFFUS HARDY.
Paul Wynter's Sacrifice.

Two-Shilling Novels—continued.

By THOMAS HARDY.
Under the Greenwood Tree.

By J. BERWICK HARWOOD.
The Tenth Earl.

By JULIAN HAWTHORNE.

Garth.	Beatrix Randolph.
Ellice Quentin.	Love—or a Name.
Fortune's Fool.	David Poindexter's Dis-
Miss Cadogna.	appearance.
Sebastian Strome.	The Spectre of the
Dust.	Camera.

By Sir ARTHUR HELPS.
Ivan de Biron.

By HENRY HERMAN.
A Leading Lady.

By HEADON HILL.
Zambra the Detective.

By JOHN HILL.
Treason Felony.

By Mrs. CASHEL HOEY.
The Lover's Creed.

By Mrs. GEORGE HOOPER.
The House of Raby.

By TIGHE HOPKINS.
Twixt Love and Duty.

By Mrs. HUNGERFORD.

A Maiden all Forlorn.	A Mental Struggle.
In Durance Vile.	A Modern Circe.
Marvel.	Lady Verner's Flight.

By Mrs. ALFRED HUNT.

Thornicroft's Model.	Self-Condemned.
That Other Person.	The Leaden Casket.

By JEAN INGELOW.
Fated to be Free.

By WM. JAMESON.
My Dead Self.

By HARRIETT JAY.
The Dark Colleen. | Queen of Connaught.

By MARK KERSHAW.
Colonial Facts and Fictions.

By R. ASHE KING.

A Drawn Game.	Passion's Slave.
'The Wearing of the	Bell Barry.
Green.'	

By JOHN LEYS.
The Lindsays.

By E. LYNN LINTON.

Patricia Kemball.	The Atonement of Leam
The World Well Lost.	Dundas.
Under which Lord?	With a Silken Thread.
Paston Carew.	The Rebel of the
'My Love!'	Family.
Ione.	Sowing the Wind.

By HENRY W. LUCY.
Gideon Fleyce.

By JUSTIN McCARTHY.

Dear Lady Disdain.	Camiola.
Waterdale Neighbours.	Donna Quixote.
My Enemy's Daughter.	Maid of Athens.
A Fair Saxon.	The Comet of a Season.
Linley Rochford.	The Dictator.
Miss Misanthrope.	Red Diamonds.

By HUGH MACCOLL.
Mr. Stranger's Sealed Packet.

By AGNES MACDONELL.
Quaker Cousins.

By KATHARINE S. MACQUOID.
The Evil Eye. | Lost Rose.

By W. H. MALLOCK.
Romance of the Nine- | The New Republic.
teenth Century. |

By FLORENCE MARRYAT.

Open! Sesame!	A Harvest of Wild Oats.
Fighting the Air.	Written in Fire.

By J. MASTERMAN.
Half-a-dozen Daughters.

By BRANDER MATTHEWS.
A Secret of the Sea.

By LEONARD MERRICK.
The Man who was Good.

By JEAN MIDDLEMASS.
Touch and Go. | Mr. Dorillion.

By Mrs. MOLESWORTH.
Hathercourt Rectory.

By J. E. MUDDOCK.

Stories Weird and Won-	From the Bosom of the
derful.	Deep.
The Dead Man's Secret.	

By D. CHRISTIE MURRAY.

A Model Father.	A Life's Atonement.
Joseph's Coat.	By the Gate of the Sea.
Coals of Fire.	A Bit of Human Nature.
Val Strange.	First Person Singular.
Old Blazer's Hero.	Bob Martin's Little
Hearts.	Girl.
The Way of the World	Time's Revenges.
Cynic Fortune.	A Wasted Crime.

By MURRAY and HERMAN.
One Traveller Returns. | The Bishops' Bible.
Paul Jones's Alias. |

By HENRY MURRAY.
A Game of Bluff. | A Song of Sixpence.

By HUME NISBET.
'Bail Up!' | Dr. Bernard St. Vincent.

By ALICE O'HANLON.
The Unforeseen. | Chance? or Fate?

By GEORGES OHNET.
Dr. Rameau. | A Weird Gift.
A Last Love. |

By Mrs. OLIPHANT.

Whiteladies.	The Greatest Heiress in
The Primrose Path.	England.

By Mrs. ROBERT O'REILLY.
Phœbe's Fortunes.

By OUIDA.

Held in Bondage.	Two Little Wooden
Strathmore.	Shoes.
Chandos.	Moths.
Idalia.	Bimbi.
Under Two Flags.	Pipistrello.
Cecil Castlemaine's Gage	A Village Commune.
Tricotrin.	Wanda.
Puck.	Othmar.
Folle Farine.	Frescoes.
A Dog of Flanders.	In Maremma.
Pascarel.	Guilderoy.
Signa.	Ruffino.
Princess Napraxine.	Syrlin.
In a Winter City.	Santa Barbara.
Ariadne.	Ouida's Wisdom, Wit,
Friendship.	and Pathos.

By MARGARET AGNES PAUL.
Gentle and Simple.

By C. L. PIRKIS.
Lady Lovelace.

By EDGAR A. POE.
The Mystery of Marie Roget.

By Mrs. CAMPBELL PRAED.
The Romance of a Station.
The Soul of Countess Adrian.
Outlaw and Lawmaker.

By E. C. PRICE.

Valentina.	Mrs. Lancaster's Rival.
The Foreigners.	Gerald.

By RICHARD PRYCE.
Miss Maxwell's Affections.

Two-Shilling Novels—*continued.*

By JAMES PAYN.

Bentinck's Tutor.	The Talk of the Town.
Murphy's Master.	Holiday Tasks.
A County Family.	A Perfect Treasure.
At Her Mercy.	What He Cost Her.
Cecil's Tryst.	A Confidential Agent.
The Clyffards of Clyffe.	Glow worm Tales.
The Foster Brothers.	The Burnt Million.
Found Dead	Sunny Stories.
The Best of Husbands.	Lost Sir Massingberd.
Walter's Word.	A Woman's Vengeance.
Halves.	The Family Scapegrace.
Fallen Fortunes.	Gwendoline's Harvest.
Humorous Stories.	Like Father, Like Son.
£200 Reward.	Married Beneath Him.
A Marine Residence.	Not Wooed, but Won.
Mirk Abbey.	Less Black than We're
By Proxy.	Painted.
Under One Roof.	Some Private Views.
High Spirits.	A Grape from a Thorn.
Carlyon's Year.	The Mystery of Mir-
From Exile.	bridge.
For Cash Only.	The Word and the Will.
Kit.	A Prince of the Blood.
The Canon's Ward.	A Trying Patient.

By CHARLES READE.

It is Never Too Late to	A Terrible Temptation.
Mend.	Foul Play.
Christie Johnstone.	The Wandering Heir.
The Double Marriage.	Hard Cash.
Put Yourself in His	Singleheart and Double-
Place	face.
Love Me Little, Love	Good Stories of Men and
Me Long.	other Animals.
The Cloister and the	Peg Woffington.
Hearth.	Griffith Gaunt.
The Course of True	A Perilous Secret.
Love.	A Simpleton.
The Jilt.	Readiana.
The Autobiography of	A Woman-Hater.
a Thief.	

By Mrs. J. H. RIDDELL.

Weird Stories.	The Uninhabited House.
Fairy Water.	The Mystery in Palace.
Her Mother's Darling.	Gardens.
The Prince of Wales's	The Nun's Curse.
Garden Party.	Idle Tales.

By AMELIE RIVES.

Barbara Dering.

By F. W. ROBINSON.

Women are Strange. | The Hands of Justice.

By JAMES RUNCIMAN.

Skippers and Shellbacks.
Grace Balmaign's Sweetheart.
Schools and Scholars.

By W. CLARK RUSSELL.

Round the Galley Fire.	The Romance of Jenny
On the Fo'k'sle Head.	Harlowe.
In the Middle Watch.	An Ocean Tragedy.
A Voyage to the Cape.	My Shipmate Louise.
A Book for the Ham-	Alone on a Wide Wide
mock.	Sea.
The Mystery of the	
'Ocean Star.'	

By GEORGE AUGUSTUS SALA.

Gaslight and Daylight.

By JOHN SAUNDERS.

Guy Waterman. | The Lion in the Path.
The Two Dreamers. |

By KATHARINE SAUNDERS.

Joan Merryweather.	Sebastian.
The High Mills.	Margaret and Eliza-
Heart Salvage.	beth.

By GEORGE R. SIMS.

Rogues and Vagabonds.	Tinkletop's Crime.
The Ring o' Bells.	Zeph.
Mary Jane's Memoirs.	My Two Wives.
Mary Jane Married.	Memoirs of a Landlady.
Tales of To-day.	Scenes from the Show.
Dramas of Life.	Ten Commandments.

By ARTHUR SKETCHLEY.

A Match in the Dark.

By HAWLEY SMART.

Without Love or Licence.

By T. W. SPEIGHT.

The Mysteries of Heron	Back to Life.
Dyke.	The Loudwater Tragedy
The Golden Hoop.	Burgo's Romance.
Hoodwinked.	Quittance in Full.
By Devious Ways.	

By ALAN ST. AUBYN.

A Fellow of Trinity. | Master of St. Benedict's
The Junior Dean. | To His Own Master.

By R. A. STERNDALE.

The Afghan Knife.

By R. LOUIS STEVENSON.

New Arabian Nights. | Prince Otto.

By BERTHA THOMAS.

Cressida. | The Violin-Player.
Proud Maisie. |

By WALTER THORNBURY.

Tales for the Marines. | Old Stories Retold.

By T. ADOLPHUS TROLLOPE.

Diamond Cut Diamond.

By F. ELEANOR TROLLOPE.

Like Ships upon the | Anne Furness.
Sea. | Mabel's Progress.

By ANTHONY TROLLOPE.

Frau Frohmann.	The American Senator.
Marion Fay.	Mr. Scarborough's
Kept in the Dark.	Family.
John Caldigate.	The Golden Lion of
The Way We Live Now.	Granpere.
The Land-Leaguers.	

By J. T. TROWBRIDGE.

Farnell's Folly.

By IVAN TURGENIEFF, &c.

Stories from Foreign Novelists.

By MARK TWAIN.

A Pleasure Trip on the	Life on the Mississippi.
Continent.	The Prince and the
The Gilded Age.	Pauper.
Huckleberry Finn.	A Yankee at the Court
Mark Twain's Sketches.	of King Arthur.
Tom Sawyer.	The £1,000,000 Bank-
A Tramp Abroad.	Note.
Stolen White Elephant.	

By C. C. FRASER-TYTLER.

Mistress Judith.

By SARAH TYTLER.

The Bride's Pass.	The Huguenot Family.
Buried Diamonds.	The Blackhall Ghosts.
St. Mungo's City.	What She Came Through
Lady Bell.	Beauty and the Beast.
Noblesse Oblige.	Citoyenne Jaqueline.
Disappeared.	

By ALLEN UPWARD.

The Queen against Owen.

By AARON WATSON and LILLIAS WASSERMANN.

The Marquis of Carabas.

By WILLIAM WESTALL.

Trust-Money.

By Mrs. F. H. WILLIAMSON.

A Child Widow.

By J. S. WINTER.

Cavalry Life. | Regimental Legends.

By H. F. WOOD.

The Passenger from Scotland Yard.
The Englishman of the Rue Cain.

By Lady WOOD.

Sabina.

By CELIA PARKER WOOLLEY.

Rachel Armstrong; or, Love and Theology.

By EDMUND YATES.

The Forlorn Hope. | Castaway.
Land at Last. |

OGDEN, SMALE AND CO., LIMITED, PRINTERS, GREAT SAFFRON HILL, E.C.